ISBN 978-1-331-68151-9
PIBN 10220708

1 MONTH OF
FREE
READING

at

www.ForgottenBooks.com

By purchasing this book you are
eligible for one month membership to
ForgottenBooks.com, giving you
unlimited access to our entire
collection of over 1,000,000 titles via
our web site and mobile apps.

To claim your free month visit:

www.forgottenbooks.com/free220708

English
Français
Deutsche
Italiano
Español
Português

www.forgottenbooks.com

Mythology Photography **Fiction**
Fishing Christianity **Art** Cooking
Essays Buddhism Freemasonry
Medicine **Biology** Music **Ancient
Egypt** Evolution Carpentry Physics
Dance Geology **Mathematics** Fitness
Shakespeare **Folklore** Yoga Marketing
Confidence Immortality Biographies
Poetry **Psychology** Witchcraft
Electronics Chemistry History **Law**
Accounting **Philosophy** Anthropology
Alchemy Drama Quantum Mechanics
Atheism Sexual Health **Ancient History**
Entrepreneurship Languages Sport
Paleontology Needlework Islam
Metaphysics Investment Archaeology
Parenting Statistics Criminology
Motivational

THE

NORFOLK GARLAND:

A COLLECTION OF THE

SUPERSTITIOUS BELIEFS AND PRACTICES, PROVERBS,

CURIOUS CUSTOMS, BALLADS AND SONGS,

OF

THE PEOPLE OF NORFOLK,

AS WELL AS

ANECDOTES

ILLUSTRATIVE OF THE GENIUS OR PECULIARITIES OF NORFOLK CELEBRITIES.

COMPILED AND EDITED BY

JOHN GLYDE, Jun.,

AUTHOR OF "SUFFOLK IN THE NINETEENTH CENTURY,"
"THE NEW SUFFOLK GARLAND."

LONDON:

JARROLD AND SONS, 3, PATERNOSTER BUILDINGS.

AND LONDON STREET, NORWICH.

AND OF THE AUTHOR, ST. MATTHEW'S, IPSWICH.

CONTENTS.

PREFACE.

Norfolk is rich in legendary lore, and it has often been mentioned with regret that no general attempt has been made to note down those legends, beliefs, and practices that have been transmitted to us from remote antiquity, and which are fast disappearing. I have endeavoured in this volume to present in a collected form a mass of those traditions that have from time immemorial been floating among the peasantry of this county. This "folk lore," as it has been aptly termed, will often be found to exhibit beautiful touches of a loving nature as well as fine poetic feeling, and will go far to illustrate the habits and manners of our forefathers.

Besides the "Folk Lore," I have from various out-of-the-way sources collected much curious information illustrating customs and local usages now obsolete; songs and ballads belonging to the county that reflect the superstitions of the people, or are remarkable for their historic or heroic character; and anecdotes which photograph, as it were, the habits and the dispositions of many of those of whom Norfolk men and women have reason to be proud; the whole forming a volume of miscellanies that I trust will be welcome to all lovers of East Anglian literature.

I intended when I mapped out the work to include extracts from the writings of living poets among the selections which I proposed to give, but I found as I proceeded that the poets and rhymers were too numerous for me to embrace them in this volume.

My thanks are especially due to Mr. William Henderson, author of *Notes on the Folk Lore of the Northern Counties of England,* to the proprietors of *Notes and Queries* and *Chambers' Book of Days* for their kind permission to use from their volumes whatever would help to make the collection more perfect, and I am under obligations to many gentlemen who have kindly noted for me morsels of folk lore known in their districts. My thanks also are especially due to those gentlemen who sent me orders for the volume before publication, thereby to a great extent shielding me from any risk of loss by its publication. It is gratifying to me to see that this list includes so many of the working members of the Norfolk and Norwich Archæological Society —the men that are best able to judge of the extent and value of my labours.

November, 1872.

Folk Lore, Curious Customs, &c.

Folk Lore.

LIFE AND DEATH OF MAN.

Mr. Henderson, in his opening chapter on the *Folk Lore of the Northern Counties*, has remarked that throughout the Borders, and in the six northern counties of England, peculiar rites and customs are bound up with every stage of human life. To begin at the beginning—the nursery has *there* a folk lore of its own. We have no doubt that in every district in England, careful enquiry would show that peculiar " rites and customs are bound up with every stage of human life," and that the stray beliefs of the peasantry in the North and in the East, though differing in degree, are the same in kind, and have had, in the majority of cases, a common tradition for their origin. The three great events of human life—Birth, Marriage, and Death, with their Church rites of Baptism, Wedding, and Burial—have naturally drawn around them some of the most curious and most deeply-rooted customs and beliefs. To these I shall first solicit attention.

BIRTH AND BAPTISM.

In our rural villages it is thought particularly disgraceful to cross the highway after childbirth and before being " churched," and some people say that a mother must not go into a neighbour's house till after she has been churched. The principle of this is a good one, but in practice it some-times degenerates in this district into mere superstition. Mr. Henderson says : " I am informed that old custom enjoins Irish women to stay at home till after their churching as rigidly as their English sisters. They have, however, their own way of evading it. They will pull a little thatch from their roof, or take a splinter of slate or tile off it, fasten this at the top of their bonnet, and go where they please, stoutly averring afterwards to the priest, or any one else, that they have not gone from under their own roof."

In the North of England it is believed that children born during the hour after midnight have the power through life of seeing the spirits of the departed. In the Eastern dis-trict, however, this faculty of seeing much that is hidden from others is given to children born at the " chime hours," i.e., the hours of three, six, nine, or twelve. In addition, it is said that such children cannot be bewitched. The gift of " seeing," however, is not without its inconveniences at times, as many stories, fearful or grotesque, testify; for those so gifted never see a hearse nor pass a churchyard at night without some such vision.

Many people hold that it is unlucky to weigh new-born children. If weighed, they will probably die, or, at any rate, will not thrive. An East Anglian, writing in *Chambers' Book of Days*, says, " I have caused great concern in the mind of a worthy old monthly nurse by insisting on weighing mine. They have, however, all done very well, with the exception of one, the weighing of whom was accidentally forgotten. The nurses always protested against the weighing, though in a timorous sort of way, saying that no doubt it was all non-sense, but still it had better not be done."

One nursery practice common here exists also in the North and in the extreme West of England—that of not cutting a baby's nails until it is a year old. They are generally bitten off by the mother or the nurse. The reason assigned is that if they are cut, the child will become a thief. After the first twelve months of the child's life have passed over, it is even then, according to Folk Lore, very important on what day baby's nails are given up to the scissors. Friday is a day to be specially avoided, and Sunday is a still worse day for nail trimming. In Durham they say :

> Better a child had ne'er been born,
> Than cut his nails on a Sunday morn !

But in Norfolk the old rhyme is :

> Cut them on Monday, cut them for health ;
> Cut them on Tuesday, cut them for wealth ;
> Cut them on Wednesday, cut them for news ;
> Cut them on Thursday, for a new pair of shoes ;
> Cut them on Friday, cut them for sorrow ;
> Cut them on Saturday, see your true love to-morrow ;
> Cut them on Sunday, and the devil will be with you all the week.

Small white specks on the nails is a sure indication of good coming to the fortunate possessor. The proverb runs :

> A gift on the thumb is sure to come;
> A gift on the finger is sure to linger.

Some sagacious elderly dames shrewdly explain the meaning of the speck by the finger upon which it happens to be They commence with the thumb, and say, " Gift—Friend— Foe—Sweetheart—Journey to go."

The belief, I find, is still existing that it is very important that a child should go up in the world before it goes down. When children first leave their mother's room, they ought, it is said, to be carried *upstairs* before they go *downstairs*, or they will never rise to riches and distinction in their after life; and accordingly when, as is often the case, the mother's room is the highest in the house, and there is no upstairs for the nurse to climb, she will get over the difficulty by placing a chair near the door, and then step upon that with the babe in her arms as she leaves the room. This has been done in Suffolk. An Essex clergyman informs me that he has known the practice adopted in his neighbourhood; and Mr. Rayson, of Pulham St. Mary, says: "In the last century Mr. Robert Self, who was then the owner and occupier of the Pulham Market Hall estate, used to have his new-born children carried to the uppermost room in the house in compliance with this superstition."

To rock an empty cradle is considered very unlucky, it being an omen of the child's death. The belief thus expressed holds its ground also in the southern counties of Scotland, particularly in Selkirkshire. It crops out, too, in Holland, where it is affirmed to be injurious to the infant and a prognostic of its death; and in Sweden, where they say that it makes the child noisy and given to crying. It is also deprecated on another ground, that it is ominous of another claimant for that place of rest. The writer on East Anglian superstitions in *Chambers' Book of Days* says: "It is quite curious to see the face of alarm with which a poor woman, with her tenth baby in her arms, will dash across a room to prevent the baby but one from engaging in such a dangerous amusement as rocking the empty cradle." This idea is prevalent in the counties of Durham and Yorkshire.

Some folks hold that it is not good for children to sleep upon bones, that is, upon the lap; while others aver that if the mother gives away *all* the baby's clothes she has, or the cradle, she will be sure to have another baby. On baby's first visit to another house it is expected that an offering will be made to it, and an egg is frequently given on these occasions.

It is affirmed that cats suck the breath of infants, and so kill them. This extremely unphilosophical notion of cats preferring exhausted to pure air is frequently a cause of great annoyance to poor pussy, when after having established herself close to baby in a snug warm cradle, she finds herself ignominiously hustled out under suspicion of compassing the death of her quiet new acquaintance, who is not yet big enough to pull her tail. Another superstition connected with infants in which poor pussy is the victim is thus illustrated by a Norfolk author in *Rambles in an Old City*—"Not long since, a woman holding quite a respectable rank among the working classes, and in her way a perfect character, avowed herself determined to *drownd* the cat as soon as ever her baby, which was lying ill, should die; for which determination the only explanation she could offer was that the cat jumped upon the nurse's lap as the baby lay there soon after it was born, from which time it ailed, and ever since that time the cat had regularly gone under its bed once a day and coughed twice. These mysterious actions of poor 'Tabby' were assigned as the cause of the baby wasting, and its fate was to be sealed as soon as that of the poor infant was decided. That the baby happened to be the twenty-fourth child of his mother, who had succeeded in rearing four only of the two dozen, was a fact that seemed to possess no weight whatever in her estimation."

These notions are just about as authoritative as that respecting children born with a caul (holy or fortunate hood) around their heads. It is deemed that such are lucky, and that they can never be drowned. Seaman used to purchase cauls to save them from the dangers of the seas. Sir Thomas Browne noticed the belief " that children are sometimes born with this natural cap, which midwives were wont to sell to credulous lawyers who held an opinion that it contributed to their promotion " or endued them with eloquence. Brand says, twenty guineas were asked for one in 1779, twelve pounds in 1813, six guineas in 1848. In this last case the caul was of some antiquity, and fifteen pounds had originally been given for it by a seaman, who had carried it about with him for thirty years. The belief as to the fortunate character of a caul is also prevalent in Holland.

Baptism is believed to affect the child physically. The

Rev. Robert Forby tells us in the Appendix to his *Vocabu-lary*, that it is generally believed by Norfolk nurses that a child never thrives well till it is named, and this is one cause of the earnest desire frequently expressed to have children privately baptised. If the child is sick, baptism is even supposed to promote the cure, and this virtue is also believed to be inherent in the rite of confirmation. From two clergymen long resident in Border parishes I have received corroborative testimony. They inform me, also, that it is considered lucky for the child to cry at its baptism. The fact of its not crying when sprinkled with baptismal water is held to be a sure sign that the child will not live—that it is too good for this wicked world.

A clergyman informs me that it is in his district considered unlucky to receive the rite of confirmation from the Bishop's *left* hand, though he has not heard the reason why. In the North of England, according to Henderson's *Folk Lore of the Northern Counties*, the evil is very pointedly defined :— " The unfortunate recipients of the left hand are doomed on the spot to a life of single blessedness."

The Rev. Robert Forby mentions that at one of the con-firmations of the venerable Bishop Bathurst, an old woman was observed eagerly pressing forward to the church. A stander-by, struck with the contrast between her and the youthful candidates around her, enquired if she was going to be confirmed, and being answered in the affirmative, ex-pressed his surprise that she should have deferred it to such an advanced age. The old woman replied, with some degree of asperity, " that it was not so ; that she had already been bishopped seven times, and intended to be again ; *it was so good for her rheumatism !* "

COURTSHIP AND MARRIAGE.

Passing from the Folk Lore of Birth and Infancy to that of Courtship and Marriage, I find much that is very curious, and much that manifests a depth of superstition that seems incredible. The charms, omens, and portents connected with an event naturally looked upon as the happiest of human life, are numerous, and the list I am enabled to give will show that in the Eastern Counties, as well as in the Northern Counties, of England, charms and spells are not all spent upon the sick and wounded.

COURTSHIP.

The omen-instructed damsel is ever on the watch for some sign by which she can arrive at a knowledge of her lot in life ; and an endeavor to raise the veil of futurity, and thus get a peep at the figure of the husband that is in store for her, seems to be among the natural longings of many village maidens.

The Rev. Robert Forby says in his *Appendix* that young women keep vigil on St. Mark's Eve for the purpose of ascertaining who their future husbands will be. Precisely at midnight the husband-seeker must go alone into the garden, taking with her some hemp seed, which she is to sow, repeating at the same time the following lines :

> Hemp seed I sow,
> Hemp seed, grow ;
> He that is my true love
> Come after me and mow.

It is believed that if this be done with full faith in the efficacy of the charm, the figure of the future husband will appear with a scythe, and in the act of mowing.

Love divination by means of dumb cake is known to have been practised in this district on St. Mark's Eve. *Dumb Cake*, so called from the rigid silence which attends its manufacture, is a species of dreaming bread prepared by

unmarried females with ingredients traditionally suggested
in witches' doggerel thus :

> An egg-shell full of salt,
> An egg-shell full of wheatmeal,
> An egg-shell full of barleymeal.

It must be baked before the fire a little before twelve o'clock
at night.   The maker of the cake must be quite alone, must
be fasting, and not a word must be spoken.   By some
girls it is believed that exactly at twelve o'clock the sweetheart will come in and turn the cake.   But the more general
formula is to cut the mystic viand, when baked, into three
divisions, a part of each to be eaten and the remainder to
be put under the pillow.   When the clock strikes twelve,
the damsels must go upstairs backwards and jump into bed,
keeping a profound silence whatever may happen.   Those
who are to be married, or are full of hope, fancy they see
visions of their future husbands hurrying after them ; while
those who are to live and die old maids see nothing at all.

I have heard of the use of the following spell by the
country maidens in Norfolk :

> A clover, a clover of two, put it in your right shoe,
> The first young man you meet in field, street, or lane,
> You'll have him or one of his name.

The " clover of two " means a piece of clover with only two
leaves upon it.

It is considered that if a young woman fill an egg with
salt, and eat it before going to bed, her future husband will
bring her drink during the night, while another superstition asserts that the sweetheart or future husband is dreamed
of if wedding cake drawn through the ring be laid under
the pillow and slept upon.

The following charm has been furnished by a gentleman
residing on the borders of Norfolk:

> To-night, to-night, is Friday night,
> Lay me down in dirty white,
> Dream who my husband is to be,
> And lay my children by my side,
> If I'm to live to be his bride.

These lines are repeated three Friday nights successively, and on the last the young woman dreams of her future husband.

Other modes of matrimonial divination are adopted in this county. A common flat cake of flour, water, currants, &c., is made, and a wedding-ring and a sixpence are put therein. When the company are about to retire on the wedding day, the cake is broken and distributed amongst the unmarried females. She who gets the ring in her portion of the cake will shortly be married, and she who gets the sixpence will die an old maid. At marriage festivals a wedding-ring is put into the posset, and after serving it out, the unmarried person whose cup contains the ring will be the first of the company to be married. This and the previous formula for divination at marriages are well known in Lancashire. If while shelling green peas, a maiden finds one having *nine* peas, she should lay it on the lintel of the kitchen door, and the first male who enters it will be her husband or sweetheart. At the first full moon of the New Year, young women take a pail of water into the garden and look into it. The number of years they have to wait before marriage is made known to them by the number of moons they see pass on the face of the water. Over-anxious maidens sometimes try to *summon* their future husbands thus : A blade-bone of mutton is laid in a secret place, and taken out on three successive Friday evenings and a slit cut in it and replaced, after which it is affirmed the future husband will cut his finger, and come to have it bound up.

It is interesting to compare the spells made use of in different districts. A young woman at Wakefield, in Yorkshire, not long ago, thus practised a variation of this mutton bone spell. She obtained the bladebone of a shoulder of mutton, and into its thinnest part drove a new penknife; then she went secretly into the garden and buried knife and bone together, firmly believing that so long as they were in the ground, her betrothed would be in a state of uneasiness, which would gradually increase till he would be compelled to visit her.

I know an instance of a cook in a gentleman's family—a Norfolk woman rather above the average in intelligence—who, on one occasion, in order to force her lover to an interview, used the following spell. She thrust a penknife into the post at the foot of the bed, reciting as she did it the following doggerel rhyme :

> It's not this post alone I stick,
> But Will Marshall's heart I mean to prick,
> Whether he be asleep or awake,
> I'd have him come to me and speak.

This spell is differently used in Buckinghamshire. There the damsel desirous of seeing her lover sticks two pins across through the candle she is burning, taking care that the pins pass through the wick, using the same rhyme adapted to the candle. By the time the candle burn down to the pins and go out the lover, it is believed, is certain to present himself. In the North of England a similar use of candles and pins prevails. A servant in the city of Durham peeped, out of curiosity, into the box of her fellow-servant and was astonished to find there the end of a tallow candle stuck through and through with pins. "What's that, Molly," said Bessie, "that I see'd i' thy box?" "Oh," said Molly, "it's to bring my sweetheart. Thou see'st sometimes he's slow a coming, and if I stick a candle full o' pins it always fetches him." *

---

* In the neighbourhood of the Hartz Mountains the girls try to obtain a glimpse of their future husbands in the following manner :—At nightfall the maiden shut herself in her sleeping-room, takes off all her clothes and

At midnight on New Year's Eve, *four* girls prepare supper for *five*, the fifth plate being for the future husband of one of the party. They watch in silence, one at each of the four corners of the room, and as the clock strikes twelve, the gentleman will come in to supper. In some places the following method is tried by anxious young women. Four young men are selected, whose names are written on separate slips of paper, and on a fifth slip is written the word "Death." They draw lots, and if "Death" is drawn they select four more names, and try again till they succeed in drawing a young man. My informant assures me that he knows of two instances in which the lottery proved correct. The following variation of this spell has been made known to me by a clergyman of this district. The maiden who desires to try divination in this form writes several Christian names of men, as well as her own Christian name, upon separate slips of paper. Each name is rolled up in a ball of clay, and the whole put into a pail of water, and as the clay dissolves they are gradually liberated. The first man's name that floats to the top of the water is that of the girl's future husband; but should it be her own name, she is doomed to die an old maid.

On Christmas Eve, and also on New Year's Eve, maidens in this district have been known to wash their chemises, leaving them in front of the fire to dry, and sit watching until midnight for the purpose of discovering their future husbands.

places upon a table covered with a white cloth two beakers, the one filled with wine, the other with pure water. She then repeats the following words :

My dear St. Andrew,
Let now appear before me
My heart's beloved ;
If he shall be rich,
He will pour a cup of wine ;
If he shall be poor,
Let him pour a cup of water.

This done the form of the future husband will appear, and drink from one of the cups. If poor he will sip the water, if rich the wine.

Exactly as the clock strikes twelve they expect their sweethearts to come in and turn the linen. A word must not be spoken during the time of watching.

To discover the trade of the future husband, the following plan is adopted :—On St. Mark's Eve, just prior to retiring to bed, two maidens wash the hearth-stone perfectly clean. They then take two pewter pots and place one on each side of the hearthstone, bottom upwards, retiring from the room backwards, and going upstairs in the same manner. In addition to this, they have to undress with their back to the bed, and get into bed backwards. If a word is spoken during this operation, the spell is broken. As soon as they awake in the morning, they rush down to see what is under each of the pewter pots. If it is a small quantity of earth, then the husband is to be a laborer; if a piece of wood or shaving, then he will be a carpenter, &c., &c.

The first egg laid by a pullet is sought for by young men, who present it to their sweethearts with the idea that it is the luckiest gift that can be bestowed. Girls, however, use eggs for more mystical purposes. The first egg which a hen has laid is made use of by some over-curious maidens to gain a knowledge of the occupation of their future husbands. The egg (it must be a maiden one) is broken into a tumbler of water about noon, when the sun is out on Midsummer day. It is allowed to stand for some time in the sun, and the shape which the white assumes denotes the trade of the future husband. That is, should it bear a fanciful resemblance to a ship, the girl will be sure to marry a sailor; if it resemble a pair of scissors, her husband will be a tailor; if a sugar-loaf, a grocer; if a shoe, a shoemaker, &c., &c. I have heard of young women breaking the egg when they go to bed, and examining the glass in the morning.

I have been informed of the following observances :—
Girls make a hole in the road, at a four cross ways, and, it is said, apply their ears to it with the hope of learning what

trade their future husband is to be. It is also said that in travelling along the road, to see three crows not flying but sitting in the road denotes a wedding.

This branch of our subject does not lack a considerable list of omens. The dandelion *(Leontodon taraxacum)* is used as a plant of omen by young men and maidens. When its seeds are ripened, they stand above the head of the plant in a globular form, with a feathery tuft at the end of each seed, and then are easily detached. The flower stalk must be plucked carefully, so as not to injure the globe of seeds, and you are then to blow off the seeds with your breath. So many puffs as are required to blow every seed clean off, so many years it will be before you are married. Another plant of omen is the yarrow *(Schillœa millefolium)*, called by us yarroway. The mode of divination is this :—You must take one of the serrated leaves of the plant, and with it tickle the inside of the nostrils, repeating at the same time the following lines :

> Yarroway, yarroway, bear a white blow ;
> If my love love me, my nose will bleed now.

If the blood follows this charm, success in courtship is held to be certain. If a brake is cut across, the veins are supposed to show the initials of the name of the future husband.

MARRIAGE.

I am not aware of any particular day in the week that is looked upon as more auspicious than the others for the celebration of the marriage ceremony. Friday is looked upon as an unlucky day for the commencement of any new undertaking, and but few marriages occur on that day. Good Friday, however, is made use of by the working classes for the celebration ; and Christmas Day, a noted day for weddings, if it falls on a Friday is not less popular.

To marry during the harvest time is very unlucky. The proverb runs :

> They that wive
> Between sickle and scythe
> Shall never thrive.

The following old rhyme is also known here :

> If you marry in Lent,
> You will live to repent.

Many of the clergy have endeavored to discourage marriage during this period.

The notion that it is unlucky to marry in May is still unexploded in some circles, though practically I do not see that it has much influence. A young lady who intended to be married in May (1867) told me that the widow of a medical gentleman had tried to dissuade her from doing so in that unlucky month; and Sir Walter Scott so far respected the prejudice that he hurried away from London in order that his daughter Sophia's wedding might take place before that inauspicious month commenced. An old couplet says :

> From the marriages in May
> All the bairns die and decay.

The superstition is as old as the days of Ovid, and has descended to Christianity from Pagan observances.

There is a saying of Hesiod's *(Works and Days, 1–700)* to the effect that it is better to marry a woman from the neighbourhood than one from a distance. A writer in *Chambers' Book of Days* says : " I am not aware of the existence of any proverb to this effect in East Anglia, but the usual practice of the working classes is in strict accordance with it. Whole parishes have intermarried to such an extent that almost everybody is related to, or connected with, everybody else. One curious result of this is that no one is counted as a 'relation' beyond first cousins, for if relationship went further than that, it might almost as well include the whole parish."

A curious marriage custom is known to have been practised in this district of England—that of the elder sister dancing in a hog's trough in consequence of the younger sister marrying before her. Upon one occasion, a brother went through the ceremony also; and the dancers performed their part so well, that the trough itself was danced to pieces. In the West of England it is a fixed rule that the lady should dance in *green stockings*, but I have not heard of such a peculiarity being adopted here.

It is considered unlucky for a woman to marry a man whose surname begins with the same letter as her own, and the proverb is common in the district :

> To change the name, and not the letter,
> Is a change for the worse, and not for the better.

The East Anglian whom I have previously quoted says : "The attendance at the weddings of agricultural labourers is naturally very small, but it is very remarkable that neither father nor mother of bride or bridegroom come with them to church. I can hardly recollect more than one instance of any of the parents being present at the ceremony." The experience of a Registrar of Marriages, who has officially attended at several hundred weddings, does not correspond with this statement. He says : " At labourers' weddings the father is frequently an attendant, the mother very seldom ; yet I have known two or three cases in which the mother has been present and signed the register. The bridesmaid and groomsman are frequently an engaged couple, who purpose in a short time going to the altar, or the communion rails, on a similar errand upon their own account. I have known the ceremony to be completed without any ring being used, and I have known the ring to be borrowed for the occasion.

Sometimes the bridegroom makes a jocular remark, that he considers the job a very dear one." A clergyman says: "Once a man took the trouble to pay my fee entirely in threepenny and fourpenny pieces, which was, I suppose, a very good joke; not so much so, however, as when a friend of mine had his fee paid in coppers."

It is customary at the marriage of a young lady of social rank and influence for the pathway from the church to the carriage to be strewed with flowers by young girls. This is an old English custom. Shakspeare says:

> Our bridal flowers serve for a buried corpse.

And another poet says:

> Come straw apace; Lord, shall I ever live
> To walk to church on flowers? O 'tis fine
> To see a bride trip it to church so lightly,
> As if her new choppines would scorn to bruze
> A silly flower.

As an illustration of the peculiarities of certain districts, I may mention that in some parts of Kent it was formerly the fashion to strew a wedding couple's pathway, not with flowers, but with emblems of the bridegroom's trade; thus a carpenter walked on shavings, a butcher on sheepskin, a shoemaker on leather parings, a paper-hanger on slips of paper, and a blacksmith on pieces of old iron. Mr. Nall, in his interesting chapters on *East Anglia*, gives an illustration of the mode adopted by the friends of the bride and bridegroom to manifest their joyfulness on the occasion. He was visiting Bradwell, near Yarmouth, when his note-taking was interrupted by a rural wedding. As the wedding party came out at the south porch, the girls of the village lined the pathway, strewing the gravel walk with fern leaves. They had mustered all the handbells of the neighbourhood to greet the happy couple with a wedding peal. In the lane the young men had prepared a rougher salute of guns and pistols; and the clergyman, who joined Mr. Nall after the service, assured him that as the evening drew on a continual discharge of firearms would be kept up. This custom, which is peculiar in this district to the villages on the Norfolk coast, and in the hundreds of Flegg, Walsham, and Blofield, is quite tame when compared with the wildness of the wedding customs in the dales of Yorkshire. There the friends of the bride and bridegroom career round the bridal party like Arabs of the desert, galloping over ground on which, in cooler moments, they would hesitate even to walk a horse—shouting all the time, and firing volleys from the guns they carry with them. In rural parts, too, of the County of Durham, the bridal party is escorted to church by men armed with guns, which they fire again and again close to the ears of the bride and bridegroom.

At marriages among the labouring classes I have frequently seen the man who attended to give the bride away, hurriedly show his right to kiss the bride first, in consequence of his position as "daddy." In this we have the remnant of an old custom. The Romans confirmed their nuptials by a kiss. The early Christians adopted the same affectionate salute at their betrothals, and the modern Greeks gave a ceremonious kiss at their marriages. The nuptial kiss in church is enjoined by the York Missal. Shakespeare refers to the custom in his " Taming of the Shrew."

> He took the bride about the neck
> And kist her lips with such a clamorous smack,
> That, at the parting, all the church did echo.

At the marriage of Mary Queen of Scots to Lord Darnley the latter kissed the former. I have been present at weddings among the middle classes, where the bridegroom has rather ostentatiously saluted the bride by a nuptial kiss, not merely before leaving the altar rails, but the moment the marriage ceremony was concluded. But I have never seen, what I find in former times was not an unusual circumstance, *i.e.*, that the clergyman who performed the ceremony claimed the first kiss as his peculiar privilege.

A gentleman who has had long experience among the clergy, tells me that though he cannot refer me to an actual case, yet the idea that it is the clergyman's privilege is of such universal acceptance, that he has no doubt that in years gone by the privilege was exercised. Another tells me that he has known it done in the Woodland district, and a friend informs me that she recollects the privilege, in her young time, being used by a clergyman residing in a town on the borders of Norfolk. On one occasion, a gentleman from Norwich was to marry at Bungay a lady residing at that town. He was aware of the predilection of the clergyman, and feeling much annoyed at the probability of the privilege being exercised at his wedding, determined to prevent it if possible. He therefore anxiously watched every movement after the Prayer Book was closed, and as soon as the service was fairly over, he hurried away his beloved, and exulted when he arrived at her home at his having succeeded in depriving the parson of his accustomed first kiss of the bride.*

---

*In the North of England the custom was common. Mr. Henderson says: "A clergyman, a stranger, after performing a marriage in a country village in Yorkshire, was surprised to see the party keep together, as if expecting something more. 'What are you waiting for?' he asked at last. 'Please, sir,' was the bridegroom's answer, 'ye've no kissed Molly.' And my old friend, the late Dr. Raine, used to relate how the Rev. T. E. Sacrist of the Cathedral and Vicar of Merrington, invariably kept up the custom when he performed the marriage ceremony, and this plainly as a matter of obligation, for he was one of the most shy and retiring of men. Nay, I can testify that within the last ten years, a fair lady from the county of Durham, who was married in the South of England, so undoubtedly reckoned upon the clerical salute, that after waiting for it in vain, she boldly took the initiative, and bestowed a kiss upon the much-amazed south-country vicar."—*Folk Lore of the Northern Counties*, p. 24.

DEATH AND BURIAL.

It is to the last stage of human life that we must look for the most numerous class of omens and portents. Death is predicated by such a variety of things in a peasant's Folk Lore, that they are difficult to classify.

The croaking of a raven flying over the house is an omen of a death in it, and the howling of a dog at night under the window of a room in which a sick person is lying, is looked upon as a warning of death being near. This omen of the howling of a dog is known, not only in nearly all parts of England, but also in France, in Germany, and even in Constantinople. But Mrs. Lubbock, a great authority on the superstitions of East Norfolk, had a remedy for it. She said, when asked about the howling dog, " Pull off your left foot shoe and turn it, and it will quiet him. I always used to do so when I was at service. A dog won't howl three times after."

If the body does not, very soon after death, become stiff and rigid, it is generally believed to indicate that another death in the family will take place in a short time. " Some years ago," says Mr. Rayson, "after the death of a relative, the nurse informed me that she was glad the body was quite stiff and rigid, and on my enquiring the reason of her satisfaction, she told me that if the corpse had been supple and pliable, there would have been another death in the family within the year." The Rev. Augustus Sutton, Rector of West Tofts, Brandon, having had three deaths in his parish in a very short period, was gravely informed at the last funeral that it was not to be wondered at, as the first two corpses were quite limp till the time of their burial. It is said that there is no superstition more prevalent, or more deeply rooted in the minds of the people of Norfolk, than the "limp corpse." In the City of Norwich it is as firmly believed as in the lone village. Another clergyman, writing of East

Anglia,* says : "In the case of a child of my own, every joint of the corpse was as flexible as in life. I was perplexed at this, thinking that perhaps the little fellow might after all be in a trance. While I was considering the matter, I observed a bystander looking very grave, and evidently having something on her mind. On asking her what she wished to say, I received for answer that though she did not put any faith in it herself, yet people *did* say that such a thing was the sign of another death in the family within the twelve-month."

The following are among the omens that are thoroughly believed in this district :—If a swarm of bees light on a dead tree, or the dead bough of a living tree, there will be a death in the family. The flying of a bird into a room and out again, or its tapping against the window pane several times, is held to presage death. If an apple tree or pear tree bloom twice in the year, it denotes a death in the family. If green broom be picked when in bloom, father or mother will die before the year. If you see four crows sitting in the road, you will soon lose a relative ; so also if a snake enter the house. Again, if hawthorn blossom, popularly called May blossom, be picked, the head of the family will die during the year. A gentleman from Essex says : "I well remember being at a house in Norfolk when a young lady (suffering from consumption) died rather unexpectedly in the night. The evening before there were three large winding sheets in the candle, a black retriever howled, and one of the bells rung without having been pulled. These forebodings were talked much of in the family afterwards, and very seriously too." If a grave is open on Sunday, there will be another dug in the course of the week. This saying is well known in some of the rural parishes. A woman coming from church in an East Norfolk village, and observing an open

---

* For many of my East Anglian authorities, I am indebted to *Chambers'*
Book of Days, and I desire in this way, once for all, to express my obligation to its pages.

grave, remarked, " Ah ! there will be somebody else wanting a grave before the week is out ! " Strangely enough (the population of the place was then under a thousand), her words came true, and the grave was dug for *her*. A winding sheet in a candle is also another omen of death. A winding sheet is produced from a candle, if after it has guttered, the strip which has run down, instead of being absorbed into the general tallow, remains unmelted ; if under these circumstances it curls over away from the flame, it is a presage of death to the person in whose direction it points.

In some parts of the county it is held that if any one hears the cuckoo's first note when in bed, there is sure to be illness or death to the hearer or one of his family. If any one be about to die suddenly, or lose a relation, the cuckoo will light upon a piece of touchwood, or rotten bough, and *cuckoo*.

A writer having remarked in *Notes and Queries* that in Norfolk agricultural labourers generally believe that if in drilling corn they miss putting the seed in one row, it is a certain sign that some one will die on the farm before many months have elapsed, the late Rev. E. T. Taylor of Martham wrote to the Editor stating that a friend had informed him that, before drills were invented, the labourers in Norfolk considered it unlucky to miss a "bout" in corn or seed sowing, which sometimes happened when broad-cast was the only method. The ill luck did not relate alone to a death in the family of the farmer or his dependants, but also to losses of cattle or accidents.

Mr. Rayson says : " I called one evening on an old friend more than eighty years of age, who had lost her husband about six months before. Whilst sitting with her I heard the clock strike the hour in an adjoining room, and counted it *seven*, and being surprised that it was no later, I involuntarily took out my watch and found that it was in reality *eight* o'clock. The old lady noticing this, remarked, " Ah ! the clock *lost a stroke against my poor husband's death*, and I have not altered it since."

A lighted candle left in an unoccupied room, the doors being shut, is believed to presage the death of one of the family. It is also believed if you overturn a loaf of bread in the oven, you will have a death in the house. If yew is brought into the house at Christmas amongst the evergreens used to dress it, it is held that a death will occur in the family before the end of the year. Mr. Rayson says : " An octogenarian inhabitant of another village has recently told me that in his younger days, a flight of ravens settling and croaking on the village church, which adjoins the parsonage, was considered by the villagers to be an omen of the death of the clergyman, which occurred soon after."

It is even believed, according to Mr. Forby, that a failure of the crop of ash-keys portends a death in the Royal family. With what obscure traditionary or legendary tale this foolish notion may be connected it seems impossible to discover. Probably, however, the superstition is connected with some legend. Be this as it may, the notion is still current. The failure in question is certainly in some seasons very remarkable, and many an old woman believes that if she were the fortunate finder of a bunch, and could get introduced to the king, he would give her a great deal of money for it. Mrs. Lubbock, the Rev. John Gunn's authority for the Folk Lore of his parish (Irstead), said " that when the ash-keys failed there would be a change of Government and great disturbances."

Persons curious about the death of their fellow parishioners have been known in Norfolk to watch the church porch on St. Mark's Eve, to ascertain who will be taken from this world in the coming year. The belief on this subject is that the apparitions of those who will die, or have any dangerous sickness, in the course of the following year, walk into the parish church at midnight on the 25th of April. Infants and young children not yet able to walk, are said to roll in on the pavement. Those who are to die remain there, but those who are to recover return after a longer or shorter time, according to the continuance of their future sickness. Those who wish to witness these appearances are to watch in the church porch on the night in question one hour on each side of midnight. If the watcher fall asleep during the vigil, he will die himself during the year. The Rev. Robert Forby says, writing in 1823 or 1824, that the belief in this vigil is. thought to be quite extinct in Norfolk; but the Rev. John Gunn, Rector of Irstead, communicated in 1847 to the Norfolk and Norwich Archæological Society some facts which proved the prevalence of the belief in more recent years. According to the testimony of Mrs. Lubbock, of Irstead, Robert Staff, who formerly kept the Maid's Head Inn at Stalham, opposite the church, said that he and two other men had been able to tell who were going to die or to be married in the course of the year. They watched the church porch opposite to the house on St. Mark's Eve. Those who were to die went into the church singly and stayed there, and those who were to be married went in in couples and came out again; and this Staff had seen. He often mentioned his power to see these apparitions to Mrs. Lubbock, but he would never tell anybody who were to die or to be married, "for he did not watch with that intent."

This practice is, I find from Mr. Henderson, known in Yorkshire. He says: " I have heard of one case in which intimation of death was given by the sight of the watcher's own form and features. It is that of an old woman at Scarborough, who kept St. Mark's vigil in the porch of St. Mary's in that town, about eighty years ago. Figure after figure glided into the church, turning round to her as they went in, so that she recognised their familiar faces. At last a figure turned and gazed at her, she knew herself, screamed, and fell senseless to the ground. Her neighbors found her there in the morning, and carried her home, but she did not long survive the shock. An old man who recently died at Fishlake, in the West Riding of Yorkshire, was in the habit of keeping these vigils, and was in consequence an object of some dread to his neighbors. The old sexton at —— did so too, in order, it was said, to count the gains of the coming year.

The author of *David Copperfield* has remarked the belief among the labouring population of fishing ports and villages on the Norfolk coast, that deaths mostly occur during the falling of the tide. When the true-hearted Mr. Peggotty sat and watched life's flickerings by the bedside of poor Barkis, he said to David Copperfield, "People can't die along the coast, except when the tide's pretty nigh out. They can't be born unless it's pretty nigh in—not properly born till flood. He's agoing out with the tide—he's agoing out with the tide. It's ebb at half arter three, slack water half an hour. If he lives till it turns, he'll hold his own till past the flood, and go out with the next tide." And after many hours watching, "it being low water, he went out with the tide."

It is customary in rural parishes, on the death of the master of the house in particular, to prevent the bees from deserting the hives, to make them acquainted with the event. This is done generally by giving three taps with the house key at the hive, and informing the bees that the master is dead; a piece of crape is likewise attached to each hive, and in some villages a piece of the funeral cake is placed for the bees to regale themselves upon. The before-quoted East Anglian says: "A neighbour of mine had bought a hive of bees at an auction of the goods of a farmer who had recently died. The bees seemed very sickly and not likely to thrive, when my neighbour's servant bethought him they had never been put in mourning for their late master. On this he got a piece of crape and tied to a stick, which he fastened to the hive. After this the bees recovered, and when I saw them they were in a very flourishing state—a result which was unhesitatingly attributed to their having been put into mourning."

It is believed, moreover, that bees will not tolerate being put into mourning except for their owner or one of his or her relatives, as the following instance will prove. A school-master residing on the border-ground of Norfolk says: "Putting bees into mourning in case of a death in the family, is a universal practice in this district. Last year (1866) a neighbour of mine, Mrs. John B——, had to leave her cottage and go to lodgings till another house should be vacant. Not having suitable accommodation for her hive at her temporary residence, she put it with the hives belonging to her sister-in-law, Mrs. Robert B——, and they appeared to be comfortably settled there; but after a time a death occurring in Mrs. Robert's family of some one not akin to Mrs. John, Mrs. Robert put the skeps into mourning by attaching a piece of crape about four inches square to the front of the skep, and Mrs. John's with the rest, which she ought not to have done. Mrs. John's bees found it out and took flight, leaving the comb full of honey."

In some of the villages on the moors in Yorkshire, the inhabitants, not content with informing the bees of their owner's death, go a step further, and actually invite them to the funeral, naming the day and the hour, from the belief that, if this compliment be omitted, the bees will die.

It is believed that if every remnant of Christmas decoration is not cleared out of Church before Candlemas Day (the Purification, Feb. 2nd), there will be a death that year in the family occupying the pew where a leaf or berry is left. My East Anglian authority says: "An old lady (now dead) whom I knew was so persuaded of the truth of this superstition, that she would not be contented to leave the clearing of her pew to the constituted authorities, but used to send her servant on Candlemas Eve to see that her own seat, at any rate, was free from danger."

The belief that the departure of the dying is rendered painful and prolonged if pigeons or game feathers are in the bed, holds its ground in this district. Generally speaking persons will not allow game feathers to be put into a bed, and they are generally burnt as a precaution. " Of course we don't believe that can have anything to do with a hard death," an old woman said to a friend of mine near Yarmouth. He replied, " Then you, yourself, use such feathers." " Oh, no; we always burn them, unless we want them for a chair cushion," was the answer.

Another superstition is to the effect that the clothes of the dead will never wear long, and that as the body decays so will the garments and linen which belonged to the deceased. In Essex the popular expression of the common belief is "the clothes of the dead always wear full of holes." When a person dies, and his or her clothes are given away to the poor, it is frequently remarked, " Ah, they may look very well, but they won't wear; they belong to the dead." In Denmark it is forbidden to bury a corpse in the clothes of a living person, lest as the clothes rot that person should waste away and perish.

There is a strong feeling of repugnance amongst the inhabitants of rural parishes to burial without the sanctuary. This does not mean in unconsecrated ground, but on the north side of the church or in a remote part of the churchyard. Sir John Cullum speaks of the great partiality for burying on the south and east sides of the churchyard, and observing, soon after he became Rector of Hawstead, that the south side of the church was crowded with graves, he prevailed upon a few persons to bury their friends on the north side, which was entirely vacant; but the example was not followed as he hoped it would be. A clergyman of a rural parish in Norfolk said : " If I were on any occasion to urge a parishioner to inter a deceased relative on the north side of the church, he would answer me with some expression of surprise, if not of offence, at the proposal, ' No, sir, it is not in the sanctuary.' " The Rev. R. Forby says : " In many churchyards may be seen a row of graves on the extreme verge, which are occupied by the bodies of strangers buried at the parish charge, of suicides, or of those who are considered unfit to associate underground with the good people of the parish. These are said to 'be out of the sanctuary.' "

The formation of cemeteries has indirectly tended to check the drinking customs at funerals. Prior to the closing of churchyards as places of interment in towns, it was not unusual to see a very long funeral procession consisting of mourners on foot wending its way to the place of burial. The poor especially seemed to delight in inviting a large number of friends to attend a funeral. Cake and wine, or ale, were served out to each person before starting, and the bearers of the corpse were liberally regaled with cake, and either rum, gin, or brandy. This custom among the poor was simply an imitation of the practice of their richer neighbours in the previous century, when giving drink at funerals and inviting a large number of persons was largely adopted among the middle and upper classes of Norfolk and the adjoining counties. Instances are on record of a barrel of beer, two gallons of sack, and four gallons of claret being consumed at a funeral, and the cost of wine has been five times more than the cost of the coffin. I learn from Suckling's *History of Suffolk* that in the will of James Cooke, of Sporle, near Swaffham, made in 1506, it is ordered, " I will that myn executors, as sone as it may come to ther knouleg that I am dede, that they make a drynkyng for my soul to the value of vi.s. viii.d., *in the church of Sporle.*" The drinking was accordingly held in the middle aisle. In one of the parishes on the borders of Norfolk there is a tradition that when the warrior Sir Robert Atte Tye was buried, four dozens of wine were drunk, according to his last directions, over his grave, before the coffin was covered with earth.

THE CURE OF DISEASE.

In treating of this department of the Folk Lore of this county, my aim will be specially to illustrate the superstitious character of the household medicine of our rural population. The belief in witchcraft is far from being extinct, as the patronage so freely bestowed on "cunning" men and women proves; but enquiries into the domestic treatment of disease among the poor bring us in contact with a more pleasing character, namely, "the charmer." This personage is generally an elderly woman of good reputation, and is supposed to be gifted with supernatural power, which she exercises for good. By her incantations and ceremonies she stops blood, removes swellings and warts, and destroys the effect of burns, scalds, &c. In fact, the domestic treatment of disease among the poor would be found upon enquiry to consist to no inconsiderable extent of charms and ceremonies.

Mr. George Rayson, of Pulham St. Mary, has, in the second volume of *The East Anglian*, given some very interesting illustrations of the Folk Lore of his district. He tells us that charms for the prevention and cure of various kinds of diseases are still practised to a far greater extent than many persons would readily believe, not only by ignorant and illiterate people, but also by those who from their position and general intelligence might be supposed to be beyond the influence of such old-world superstitions. But little more than fifty years ago the owner of the Hall estate in Pulham was the possessor of some very potent charms for the cure of agues and other diseases, and often practised his art for the benefit of his neighbours. Even in 1865, an intelligent man told Mr. Rayson that the formula to be used in curing by charms was of little consequence, as the cure was really effected by a miracle-working faith.

THE WHOOPING COUGH.

The charm-remedies for whooping cough are, I think, more numerous than for any other of the ills that flesh is heir to, and the directions of the medical attendant are often set aside in their favour. The following are among those to which my attention has been called.

It is necessary that a live flat-fish should be procured—"a little dab" will do. Then it must be placed whilst alive on the bare chest of the patient, and kept there till it is dead. This is considered to be a certain remedy, though it must be confessed it is one somewhat difficult of accomplishment.

Then there is the spider remedy. Let the parent of the child afflicted find a dark spider in her own house, and hold it over the head of the child, repeating three times,

> Spider, as you waste away
> Whooping cough no longer stay.

The spider must then be hung up in a bag over the mantle-shelf, and when the spider has dried up the cough will be gone.

On the border ground of Norfolk and Suffolk the following charm has been tried. A hole was dug in a meadow, and into this the poor little sufferer was placed in a bent position head downwards. The flag cut in making the hole was then placed over him, and the child remained in the hole until he coughed. It is thought that if this charm be done in the evening, with only the father or the mother to witness it, the child will soon recover. In another parish a variation of this charm was tried. The child was laid face downwards on the turf of the meadow; the turf was then cut round the child in the shape of a coffin. The child was taken up and the flag turned roots upwards, and as the grass withered it was believed the cough wasted. This also must be done secretly or the charm will fail.

To eat a roasted mouse is said to be a certain cure for the disease. I have heard of a live frog, which had been held with its head within the mouth of the person affected, being hung up the chimney of the patient's house, in the belief that as it died the whooping cough would vanish. An instance is recorded of a woman who obtained a number of small snails. These were passed through the hands of the invalid and then suspended in a chimney on a string, in order that as they died the whooping might leave the children.

Among other remedies the following may be enumerated :— Let the patient drink some milk which a ferret has lapped ; or be dragged three times, then wait three days and be dragged three times again under a gooseberry bush or bramble, both ends of which are growing in the ground ; or procure hair from the cross on the back of a donkey, and having placed it in a bag hang it round the invalid's neck next the skin. If this be done secretly a speedy cure will result. The presumed efficacy in this hair is connected no doubt with the fact that the ass is the animal which was ridden by Jesus, and with the superstition that the cross was imprinted on its back as a memorial of that event. The Rev. Cuthbert Bede was informed by the agent of a large landed proprietor in Lincolnshire, that he had known numerous instances of this charm being practised, and that in every case a cure had been effected.

THE AGUE.

The ague is a disease that was, prior to improved drainage, very prevalent in certain parts of the Eastern Counties, and as there is a notion that it cannot be cured by a regular doctor, charms for its cure are numerous. Mr. Henderson, in his *Folk Lore of the Northern Counties*, says :—" Charm remedies are almost universal for the ague. It is said in Devonshire that you may give it to your neighbour by burying under his threshold a bag containing the parings of a dead man's nails, and some of the hairs of his head; your neighbour will be afflicted with ague till the bag is removed. In Somersetshire and the adjoining counties the patient shuts a large black spider into a box and leaves it to perish. In Flanders he imprisons it between the two halves of a walnut shell and wears it round his neck; in Ireland he swallows it alive. Flemish Folk Lore enjoins any one who has the ague to go early in the morning to an old willow, make three knots in one of its branches, and say, 'Good morrow, old one; I give thee the cold; good morrow, old one.'" Miss Strickland, in her *Old Friends and New Acquaintances*, mentions the following cure, well known in the Eastern district:—" Go to the four cross-ways to-night all alone, and just as the clock strikes twelve turn yourself about three times and then drive a tenpenny nail into the ground up to the head and walk away from the place backwards before the clock is done striking, and you'll miss the ague; but the next person who passes over the nail will take it in your stead."

A clergyman in Norfolk, being afflicted with a severe tertian ague, was solicited, after the usual medical treatment had failed, to take as much of the " snuff of a candle " as would lie on a sixpence, and make into an electuary with honey. He complied, and to his surprise a complete cure was effected. It is esteemed a sovereign specific by the Norfolk rustics.

Many of the charms ignorantly used by the East Anglian peasantry as cures for the ague are evidently relics of the sacrificial rites offered to the powers of darkness by the Pagan Saxons and Danes. In one district I have heard of the following superstitious practice. A man who had been labouring under an obstinate ague for several months, purchased a new red earthen pan, in which he put the parings of his finger and toe nails, together with a lock of hair, and a small piece of raw beef, which, in order to render the charm effectual, he considered it necessary to

D

steal. He then tied a piece of black silk over the pan, and buried it in the centre of a wood, in ground that had never before been broken, in the firm belief that as the meat decayed, his fever would abate and finally disappear.

In the Fen district of Lincolnshire a spider covered with dough and taken as a pill is a charm for ague in which people place great faith, and I find that to swallow a spider or its web when placed in a small piece of apple is an acknowledged cure in Suffolk. Miss Strickland heretically mentions an instance of its being tried in vain, but its failure excited great astonishment: "As true as I'm alive, he (the ague) neither minded pepper and gin taken fasting on a Friday morning, nor blackbottle spiders made into pills with fresh butter." I have heard also that the practice of catching a shrew, boring a hole in an ash tree, inserting the animal and plugging it up alive, as a cure for the ague, is followed in the Eastern Counties. The idea is that as the creature dies and decays, so the disease gradually departs.

Fright is also looked upon in this district as a cure for ague. A writer in *Chambers' Book of Days* says: "An old woman has told me that she was actually cured in this way when she was young. She had had ague for a long time, and nothing would cure it. Now it happened that she had a fat pig in the sty, and a fat pig is an important creature in a poor man's establishment. Well aware of the importance of piggy in her eyes, and determined to give her as great a shock as possible, her husband came to her with a very long face as she was tottering downstairs one day, and told her that the pig was dead. Horror at this fearful news overcame all other feelings. She forgot all about her ague, and hurried to the scene of the catastrophe, where she found, to her great relief, that the pig was alive and well. The fright, however, had done its work, and from that day to this (she must be now about eighty years old) she has never had a touch of the ague, though she has resided on the same spot."

MISCELLANEOUS DISEASES.

WARTS OR WRITS.—There are many persons who profess to cure warts, or " writs," as they are sometimes called, by passing the hand over them and muttering at the same time some mysterious word. If persons have any scruple about consulting such accredited professors of the healing art, they may get rid of their warts in other ways. Thus, let the patient steal a piece of beef (it must be stolen or it will have no efficacy), and bury it in the ground, and then as the beef decays the warts will gradually die away. Or make the sign of the cross on each wart with a pin or pebble stone, and then throw the pin or pebble away. Or go to an ash tree which has its " keys," that is, husks with seeds, upon it, and cut the initial letter both of your Christian and surname on the bark. It is then necessary to count the exact number of the warts, and, in addition to the letters, to cut a notch for each. The result will be that as the bark grows up the warts will go away. Or take the froth of new beer and apply it on three successive mornings to the warts, when no one can see you. The froth must not be wiped away, but allowed to work off of itself, and then the warts will disappear. Or gather a green sloe, rub it on your warts, throw it over your *left* shoulder, and you will soon be free from them. I have been told of a boy thirteen years old who had a large number of " writs " on his hands. He attended school, and one Friday the schoolmaster, who had frequently seen the boy's hands dirty from the number of " writs," asked him to count them accurately, and then tell him the exact number. The lad did so, and some days afterwards he was startled by the boy who sat next him at the desk exclaiming, " Why, Tom, where are your writs ? " They were all gone.

BLEEDING AT THE NOSE.—Bleeding at the nose is cured by wearing a skein of scarlet silk round the neck, tied with nine knots down the front.* If the patient is a male, the silk should be put on and the knots tied by a female, and *vice versâ*.

CRAMP.—Mr. Rayson informs me that finger rings made from the handles of coffins are deemed sure preventives against cramp. He says : " In my boyhood the old parish clerk of the village used to preserve the old coffin handles which he found in the churchyard for the purpose of making cramp rings." Some persons wear in their pockets the patella of a sheep or lamb, known here as the " cramp bone," for the cure of this painful disorder. I knew an intelligent man, a great politician and what is termed a sceptic in theology, who always carried a cramp bone in his pocket. In Lancashire the cramp is believed to be prevented by tying the garter round the *left* leg *below* the knee.

WENS AND EXCRESCENCES.—To cure wens or fleshy excrescences the revolting remedy has been tried of passing the hand of a dead body on three successive days over the part affected. But even this remedy is mild when compared with the practice in some other counties, where it ·is considered necessary to have the wen stroked by the dead hand of a *man that had been hanged*. In some cases this has been done after the criminal is dead, but still hanging. On execution days at Northampton numbers of sufferers used to congregate round the gallows in order to receive the " dead stroke," as it is termed. In 1853 the body of a suicide, who had hanged himself in a village not far from Hartlepool, was laid in an outhouse awaiting the coroner's inquest. The wife of a pitman at Castle Eden Colliery, suffering from a wen in the neck, according to advice given her by a " cunning woman," went alone and laid all night in the outhouse with the hand of the corpse on her wen.

EPILEPSY.—Mr. Henderson says that in Yorkshire the charm to cure a person afflicted with epilepsy is a ring made out " of a half-crown from the offertory collection, but thirty pence are tendered for it, collected from as many different persons. Not ten years ago the Vicar of Danby, near Whitby, was asked for a half-crown after Holy Communion by a farmer, one of his most respectable parishioners, the thirty pence being prepared in exchange." The writer of the article on East of England superstitions in *Chambers' Book of Days* says : " I recollect that when I was a boy a person came to my father (a clergyman) and asked for a ' sacramental shilling,' *i.e.*, one out of the alms collected at the Holy Communion, to be made into a ring and worn as a cure for epilepsy." But, generally speaking, in Norfolk the charm differs slightly from this. If a young woman has fits, she obtains from nine or eleven unmarried men (if the sufferer be a man his relief comes from the liberality of maidens) a small piece of silver, either a piece of a broken spoon, buckle, brooch, or a coin, and a penny. The pieces thus obtained are taken to a silversmith or other worker in metal, who forms therefrom a ring, which is to be worn by the person afflicted on the fourth finger of the left hand. If any of the silver remains after the ring is made, the workman has it as his perquisite, and the pennies also are intended as the wages for his work. The late Rev. E. S. Taylor of Martham, writing to *Notes and Queries*, said that a friend of the sufferer gives out that he is making a collection for the purpose, and calls upon the parties expected to contribute, and the pieces of silver must be given " unasked," to ensure its efficacy. A watchmaker in the village in which the rev. gentleman resided said that he had made ten or a dozen such rings within as many years, and that he had full faith in their curative properties.

FITS.—That little animal the mole is the victim of an absurd and cruel practice arising from ignorant belief, as the following rustic prescription will show :—A gentleman residing in 1865 on the border ground of Norfolk and Suffolk, was asked by an elderly dame to " catch a live moll " for her. " For what purpose ? " said the gentleman. " Why, sir, you see, my darter's little gal is got fits, and I'm told if I get a

live moll, cut the tip of his nose off, and let nine drops bleed
onter a lump of sugar, and give that to the child, 'tis a sartin
cure."

RHEUMATISM.—The right fore foot of a female hare is the
remedy for an attack of rheumatism. Mr. Rayson, writing
in 1865, says that a tradesman in a neighbouring village was
superstitious enough to try this remedy within the last two
years. There is a very strong belief that a *galvanic ring*, as
it is called, worn on the finger will cure rheumatism. A large
number of persons may be seen with a clumsy-looking silver
ring, which has a piece of copper let into the inside, and this,
though in constant contact throughout, is supposed (aided by
the moisture of the hand) to keep up a gentle but continual
galvanic current, and so to alleviate or remove rheumatism.

TOOTHACHE.—Mr. Rayson remarks that he knew a person
who continued throughout life always to dress and undress
the left leg and foot before the right one, as a means of preventing the toothache. This plan has the merit of being
less revolting than the charm cure tried in Devonshire—that
of biting a tooth out of a skull in a churchyard, and keeping
it always in your pocket.

SMALL POX.—There are some very strange notions about
the cure of small pox. Fried mice are relied on in some
parts of the county as a specific for it, and a clergyman says,
" I am afraid that it is considered necessary that they should
be fried alive."

SORE EYES.—Earrings are considered to be a cure for sore
eyes.

THE THRUSH.—The thrush is a very common complaint
among infants and persons in the last extremity of sickness.
There is a notion about this disease that a person must have
it once in his life, either at his birth or death. Norfolk nurses
like to see it in babies. They say that it is healthy and makes
them feed more freely, but if it appears in a sick adult person
he is given over as past recovery, and it is extremely rare
in such cases that the patient survives.

REMEDIES FOR A THORN IN THE FLESH.—Mr. Rayson tells us in the *East Anglian* that to prevent a swelling from a thorn having entered the flesh, the following charm is practised

> Christ was of a Virgin born,
> And crowned was with a crown of thorn
> He did neither swell nor rebel,
> And I hope this never will.

At the same time the middle finger of the right hand must be kept in motion round the thorn, and at the end of the words, three times repeated, the thorn should be touched each time with the tip of the finger. Then with God's blessing it will give no further trouble. A thorn is extracted from the flesh by the following incantation :*

> Jesus of a maid was born,
> He was pricked with nails and thorn.
> Neither blains nor boils did fetch at the bone,
> No more shall this, by Christ our Lord. Amen.
> Lord bless what I have said. Amen.
> So be it unto thee as I have said.

BLEEDING.—To stop bleeding from arteries cut or bruised, the following words are repeated three times, desiring the blessing of God :

> Stand fast, lie as Christ did,
> When he was crucified upon the cross,
> Blood remain up in the veins,
> As Christ's did in all his pains.

---

* The following conversation, which is given in *Chambers' Book of Days*, took place in a Dorsetshire village, and it will show that our superstitious notions on the cure of diseases are quite paralleled in other counties. " Well, Betty," said a lady, " how are you ? " " Pure, thank you, ma'am, but I has been rather poorlyish." " What has been the matter with you ?" " Why, ma'am, I was troubled with a rising of the lights ; but I tooked a dose of *shot*, and that has a keepit them down."

TYPHUS FEVER.—Even for so dangerous a disease as typhus fever our rural peasantry do not hesitate to try their own remedies. Some years ago a clergyman in Norfolk, whilst visiting a poor man suffering from typhus fever, found that his wife had applied the milt or spleen of a cow to the soles of his feet, having been assured that it was an efficacious remedy. As the poor man was under regular medical treatment, the visitor persuaded the wife to remove the milt, which had actually become offensive from putrefaction. In Huntingdonshire, however, the remedy has been tried with great success. A woman told the Rev. Cuthbert Bede that when her sister lay bad with typhus fever, they applied the skirt of a sheep to the soles of her feet, and kept it there for seven hours, and this drew away the fever from her head. When the doctor paid his next visit he could not imagine what it was that had brought about so speedy a change in her symptoms, but they were afraid to tell him what they had done. The young woman recovered " in consequence of the application of the skirt." The rector of a parish in East Norfolk was solicited (in vain of course) for the loan of the church plate to lay on the stomach of a child, which was much swelled from some mesenteric disease, this being held to be a sovereign remedy in such cases.

DIARRHŒA.—The Rev. Robert Forby says : " Not more than three years ago (1830) a cottager lamented to me that her poor neighbour must certainly die of diarrhœa, for she had already given her two doses of Good Friday bread without any benefit. The patient, however, recovered." This belief in the virtues of Good Friday bread as a sovereign remedy for diarrhœa is still prevalent. The bread is not eaten, but a small portion is grated into water, and partaken of as thick sop. The writer of the article on East of England superstitions in *Chambers' Book of Days* mentions the belief that hot cross buns, if properly made, will never get mouldy. To make them properly, the whole of the business must be done on the Good Friday itself. The materials should be mixed, the dough made, and the buns baked on that day, and this, I think, before a certain hour; but whether this hour is sunrise or church-time I cannot say.

HERNIA.—The ash tree enters largely into the Folk Lore of the peasantry, and as a means of curing hernia in young children the following use has been made of it :—A young ash is split, and the child is passed, naked, three times through it at sunrise, each time with the head towards the rising sun. The tree is then tied up tightly, so that it may grow together. Mr. Rayson says that two children of respectable farmers in the parish of Pulham St. Mary were some years since passed through a tree in this manner, and their parents assured him that a cure was effected. Sir John Cullum, in the Appendix to his *History of Hawstead*, mentions that he had twice seen this custom practised in that parish within a few years. He says : " For this purpose a young ash was each time selected, and split longitudinally about five feet ; the fissure was kept wide open by my gardener, while the friend of the child, having first stripped him naked, passed him thrice through it, always head foremost. As soon as the operation was performed, the wounded tree was bound up with packthread, and as the bark healed the child was to recover. The first of these young patients was to be cured of the rickets, the second of a rupture. About the former I had no opportunity of making any enquiry, but I frequently saw the father of the latter, who assured me that his child, without any other assistance, gradually mended, and at last grew perfectly well."

Other things beside charms are allowed to interfere in the physician's province. The notion of planetary influence on the human frame, or the dominion of the moon on man's body, passing under the twelve zodiacal constellations, has even now many believers, and their influence is believed to have an equal effect upon brutes. The prevalent opinion at the commencement of the present century may be best explained by examples. Forby says a prudent dairy wife never weans a calf when the " sign " is in the head, lest it should go dizzy, and the precaution is common to kill hogs in the increase of the moon, because pork killed in the waning of the moon shrinks in boiling. A wealthy yeoman enquired of a farrier when he would perform a certain operation on his colt. The leech assumed a most oracular look, and said, with a gaze of great gravity, that he would just step home and see how the sign lay, and then let him know. About the close of the last century, a medical practitioner of great eminence sent a purge to a patient, and desired him to take it immediately. On the following day he called at his house, and enquired how it had operated. The patient (a substantial farmer) said he had not taken it, and upon the doctor remonstrating against this disobedience, the sick man gravely answered " that he looked into his almanack, and seeing the sign lay in ' bowels,' he thought that and the physic together would be too much for him."

SIGNS AND OMENS.

AMONG the mass of the people there is an intense desire to know future events, and "wise men" and "cunning women," gipsy fortune-tellers and astrologers, have in consequence reaped many a golden harvest from the credulity of the people. Besides this intense desire, there is among a large portion of the uneducated a habit of predicting particular events from the most trivial occurrences of daily life, and a large class of small circumstances are regarded as indicative of good or evil fortune to the person experiencing their influence.

A flake of soot on the bars of the grate is said to indicate the approach of a stranger. A hollow cinder thrown out of the fire by a jet of gas from burning coals is looked upon as a coffin if it be long, and as a money-box if it be round. It is unlucky to begin any piece of work on a Friday, and, as I have already mentioned, even to cut the finger nails on that day is to "cut them for sorrow." This day is said to be regarded as evil because it was the day on which our Saviour's blood was shed. The spilling of salt, or the crossing of knives, is thought to be a sure forerunner of a quarrel. To turn back after you have once started on a journey, or to be recalled and told of something previously forgotten, is considered very unlucky. To watch any one till he is out of sight is regarded as unlucky. If the foot itches, it is a sign that you will soon tread on strange ground. If the right hand itches, it indicates that you will receive money; if the left hand, that you will pay money. If you shiver, some one, it is said, is walking over your future grave. If you set the broom in a corner, you will be sure to have strangers come to the house. If a girl goes to her place by daylight, she will not stop long in it. If you make your bed at bedtime, you will look fair in the morning. If you

stumble upstairs you will be married the same year. If you
set a hen on an *even* number of eggs, you will have no
chickens. It is customary also to put a mark like a
cross on each egg. If a goose begins to sit on her
eggs when the wind is in the east, she will sit five
weeks before she hatches. A horse is believed to have
the power of seeing ghosts. This is probably derived
from the account of Balaam's ass discerning the angel.
Mushrooms will not grow after they have been seen. If you
eat the marrow of pork, you will go mad. You should always
burn a tooth when it is drawn, because if a dog should find
it and eat it, you would have a dog's tooth come in its place.
It is dangerous to let blood in the dog days. Two sticks lying
across in one's path denotes ill luck. A hare crossing the
path when going on a journey is considered unlucky. If soon
after starting a person meets a weasel or an old woman, he
had better turn back, or the journey will be unfortunate. To
find old iron or any metal is a sign of good luck. Some old
dames will not pass even a pin or a horse shoe without picking it up. If you make a present of a knife or a pair of
scissors, or any sharp instrument, the person receiving it
must give you a trifle for it, otherwise all love or friendship
between you would be cut off. If when you see a shooting
star you form a wish before it disappears, it will be sure to
be fulfilled. The spilling of salt is very ominous, and the
proverb is well known:

> Help me to salt,
> Help me to sorrow.

A man in one of the villages in East Norfolk bordering on
the sea coast, was observed for a long time to drive a horse
round whose neck something was tied, which he said would
act as a preservative against every mishap, stumbling in-
cluded. This, when stolen by a mischievous urchin at the
instigation of some village wags, was found to be the thumb

of an old leather glove, containing a transcript of the Lord's
Prayer.

There are many signs and portents connected with the
clothing. It is held to be lucky to put on any article of
dress, particularly stockings, inside out; but if you wish the
omen to hold good, you must continue to wear the reversed
portion of your attire in that condition till the regular time
comes for putting it off—that is, either till bedtime or clean-
ing time. If you set it right, you will "change the luck."
Of course it will be of no use to put on anything with the
wrong side out on purpose. If a girl's petticoat is longer
than her frock, that is a sign that her father loves her better
than her mother does. Forby says that every person must
have at least some part of his dress new on Easter Sunday,
or he will have no good fortune that year. This was more
regarded forty years ago than it is now, for though Easter
is considered to have a right to the honour, a glance round a
Church or Sunday School in Norfolk on Whit-Sunday shows
very plainly that it is the one chosen for beginning to wear
new things.

Among the host of small superstitions are some charms
and omens connected with money. If a small black spider—
a money spider it is called—descend upon you, it prognosti-
cates good luck—some persons say you will soon receive a
legacy. If when you first hear the cuckoo you turn a
penny over in your pocket, you will not be without
money all the year. It is considered lucky to turn over
a piece of money at first sight of the new moon, but
to catch the first sight of it over the left shoulder is
said to be unlucky. A gentleman who resides ten miles
from Thetford writes: "Last winter I had a set of rough
country lads in a night school. They happened to catch
sight of the new moon through the window, and all, I
think, that had any money in their pockets turned it for
luck. As may be supposed, it was done in a joking sort of
way, but still it was done. The boys could not agree what

was the right form of words to use on the occasion, but it
seemed to be understood that there was a proper formula for
it." It is also considered lucky to carry a bent sixpence in
your pocket, or one with a hole in it.

In travelling along the road, to see one crow is bad luck;
two crows, good luck; three crows, a wedding; four crows,
a burying; five crows, speed; six crows, very good luck
indeed. It is to be understood that the crows are not flying
but sitting in the road. Rooks building near a house are a
sign of prosperity, and it is said that the presence of crickets
betokens good luck to the house they inhabit, but their
sudden departure from a hearth which has long echoed with
their cry, betokens approaching misfortune. It is a popular
belief that vipers, snakes, &c., will not die till the sun is
down, no matter into how many pieces they may be cut.

Some superstitions respecting bees are firmly believed by
many of the country people in Norfolk. Bees, they say,
must not be bought, they must be obtained by barter. To
be guilty of selling bees is a grievous omen, but you may
easily obtain a hive in lieu of a small pig or some other
equivalent. There may seem little difference in the eyes of
enlightened persons between selling and bartering, but the
superstitious beekeeper sees a grand distinction, and it is not
his fault if you don't see it too. Bees will not thrive if you
quarrel about them. A clergyman was congratulating a
parishioner on her bees looking so well, and at the same time
expressing his surprise that her next door neighbour's hives,
which had formerly been so prosperous, now seemed quite
deserted, "Ah," she answered, "them bees couldn't du."
"How was that?" he asked. "Why," she said, "there was
words about them; and bees 'll never du if there's words
about them."

Many of our rustics firmly believe that if you break two
things you will break a third. A neighbour, says a clergyman,
saw one of her servants take up a coarse earthenware basin
and deliberately throw it down upon the brick floor. "What

did you do that for?" asked the mistress. "Because, ma'am, I'd broke tew things," answered the servant, "so I thout the third 'd better be this here," pointing to the remains of the least valuable piece of pottery in the establishment, which had been sacrificed to glut the vengeance of the offended ceramic deities.

Mr. Rayson, in his notes in the *East Anglian*, says: "I have just been told by a lady who has resided for some months with a Norfolk family at Kentish Town, that when the new moon first appears, all the family (including the servants) are accustomed to hasten out of the house, in order that they may not seé the new moon through glass, which is believed to be very unlucky. A respectable tradesman's wife in my own village gravely assured a lady who visited her in her illness, that she knew she should have nothing but trouble for a month to come, as she had unfortunately seen the new moon through a glass window. She added that she always dreaded such warnings, as her husband then was sure to spend most of his time at the public-house."

There are several omens connected with flowers and plants. To pluck the first primrose that appears in the garden in spring and take into the house, is believed to be an unlucky omen for the family. Into farmhouses the carrying of a single flower or a few is sometimes very strongly resented. It is said if the first primroses brought into a farm house be less than thirteen, so many eggs only will each hen or goose hatch during the season. A clergyman in East Norfolk was called upon not many years since to decide a quarrel between two old women, arising from one of them having given a single primrose to her neighbour's child, for the purpose of making her hens hatch but one chicken from each set of eggs that season. Forby says it is considered unlucky to burn elder wood, but he does not tell us why. The writer in *Chambers' Book of Days* says that in the Eastern Counties the belief exists that the cross was made of elder wood. " Speaking to some little children one day about the danger

of taking shelter under trees during a thunder-storm, one of
them said that it was not so with all trees; 'For,' said he,
'you will be quite safe under an elder tree, because the cross
was made of that, and so the lightning never strikes it.'
The Bretons declare that the cross was made of the wood of
the aspen tree, and that the trembling of the aspen leaves
marks the shuddering of sympathetic horror."

The superstitious observances common amongst the cot-
tagers and the poorest of the inhabitants of the Eastern
Counties, are in many instances very similar to those that
are known to prevail over many of the counties of England.
Thus in the case of the following " Child's Prayer:"

> Matthew, Mark, Luke, and John,
> Bless the bed that I lie on!
> Four corners to my bed,
> Five angels there lie spread;
>   Two at my head,
>   Two at my feet,
> One at my heart my soul to keep.

The late Rev. E. S. Taylor of Martham said that he had
reason to believe that this prayer was in constant use among
the most ignorant of the rural poor in Norfolk. With a
variation, it is well known in the adjoining county of Suffolk,
and it is singular that such a prayer should have survived the
great change in religious opinions which took place in the
sixteenth century, and still remain in popular use.

WITCHES AND FAIRIES.

THE Eastern Counties of England were during the sixteenth and seventeenth centuries remarkably distinguished by the very prevalent belief in witchcraft. The cruelties that were practised and the executions that resulted from the influence of this superstition are at the present day distressing even to contemplate. When such a man as the learned Dr. Thomas Brown of Norwich is found to give his testimony in favour of the opinion that "the devil co-operates with the malice of these which we term witches, at whose instance he doth these villanies," we cannot expect that the mass of the people of the same era would be free from the superstition. I shall adduce proofs of the prevalence of this belief in Norfolk in past ages, and offer evidence that a belief in the power of witches prevails in this district at the present day.

The Editor of Forby's *Vocabulary* says that although witchcraft is not now so triumphant as in the days of "Hopkins, the witch-finder general," yet still, if a reward of ten pounds were again offered for the discovery of every witch, a sufficient number would be found to furnish a decent income to any modern Hopkins.

The soil of Norfolk and Suffolk appears to have been very favourable to the production of witches. As early as the reign of Henry VI., "Margery Jourdemayn, the famous witch of Eye," was employed by the Duchess of Gloucester, wife of the good Duke Humphrey. That there was a succession of "wise women" to fill the place of this celebrated professor cannot be doubted, but having had the good fortune to escape being burnt in Smithfield for high treason, their names are not recorded. In the latter part of the last century, however, the immediate neighbourhood of Eye was again distinguished by the residence of a sybil who, under the name of "Old Nan Barrett," enjoyed for more than forty

E

years a reputation only inferior to that of her renowned predecessor. She was not indeed sought after by royalty, nor probably much known out of Norfolk and Suffolk, but in those counties she was held in high veneration, and it was no unusual thing for people to go thirty or forty miles to consult her. We have perhaps had no person of equal celebrity since her time, but there have been many of humbler fame both in Norwich and in Yarmouth, who have been oracles in their respective districts.

Where the power of witches is generally acknowledged, it is natural to suppose that some precaution would be adopted to prevent its exercise. From enquiries that have been made, it does not appear that any other preventative has of late years been known to be in use in Norfolk than the very general one of nailing a horse-shoe to the threshold. The belief is that a witch cannot pass over the threshold on which a horse-shoe is nailed with the open part upwards, or at least that she cannot perform her diabolical feats within the house to which it belongs. That this belief is very prevalent in East Norfolk is evidenced by the number of horse-shoes which, even during the last twenty years, have been seen attached to doors, and wells, and fishing boats.

I learn from the *Transactions* of the Norfolk and Norwich Archæological Society that it is not many years since that a sound sea-worthy fishing boat was burnt, " stick and stern," near Northrepps, solely because it was held to be bewitched. Undoubtedly the number of cottage doors guarded by a horse-shoe is much less than it was some years ago, but the talisman is still to be seen, and sufficiently indicates the existence of the belief.

There is another prophylactic, which, however, from its nature, can only be resorted to in extreme cases. Where a witch is known to harbour resentment against any one, or to have expressed an intention of doing him or her an injury, it is held to be a sure preservation if the party threatened can draw blood from the sorceress, and many a poor old woman has been scarified in consequence of the received opinion that a witch will not "come to the scratch." A complaint was recently (1847) lodged before the bench of magistrates at Cromer by a poor woman, who was employed in carrying a letter bag along the coast, against some boys who pelted her with stones, and were not satisfied till they had "drawn blood," as they said, "from the old witch." The Rev. John Gunn, writing in 1847, says : " Applications have often been made to me for advice by persons feeling themselves aggrieved by the imputation of sorcery. In one instance, a labourer asked me what steps he should take to protect his wife from being called a witch. I persuaded him to let her treat the matter with contempt, and he resolved to do so, but a few days after he came to me in great agitation of mind, and declared that he could bear it no longer, for the people called his children 'devilings.' I have also known a farmer to complain of an old woman having an evil eye, and of her having fatally bewitched some of his horses and pigs as they passed her on the road."

Next to prevention comes the remedy, and the following is, as related by the Rev. Wm. Forby, considered to be a specific. If in the near neighbourhood, or anywhere indeed within the malignant influence of a known witch, a child is afflicted with an obstinate ague, a great many worms, or any pining sickness, if a calf be dizzy, or a cow be "tail shotten," or have "gargot," or "red water," so that it may reasonably be concluded to be bewitched, the most effectual remedy or mode of exorcism is to take a quantity of the patient's urine, and boil with it nine nails from as many old horse-shoes. The process is to begin exactly at midnight. The conductress of it is to have an assistant to obey orders, but is to touch nothing herself. The orders must be conveyed by signs, for a single word mars the whole charm. At a certain critical point in the process, when three, five, or seven of the nails have been put in motion at once by the force of the boiling fluid (for some cases are more difficult than others) the spirit is cast out, at which happy moment the child "squalls," the cow "blores," or the calf "blares," and convalescence immediately commences. The good woman from whom the rev. gentleman obtained this valuable information (not immediately indeed, nor without some little breach of confidence), confirmed it by recounting a failure that once befel herself. She had prevailed on a boy to sit up with her. All was going on most prosperously. The hobnails were in merry motion. The child in the cradle squalled. The boy, in a cold sweat, ventured to look behind him, and he was so overpowered with terror that he forgot all the cautions he had received, and called to his mistress to look at the little black thing which was endeavouring to escape through the keyhole. This was no doubt the evil spirit, which, thus recalled, must have entered the poor child again, for it certainly never recovered.

In Roberts' *Treatise on Witchcraft*, London, 1616, there is an account of "Norfolk Witches," and the mode of making a witch cake according to the prescription of a "cunning man" at Yarmouth. I quote from the reprint in *Halliwell's Anthology*: "It being firmly believed that Elizabeth Hancock, a widow, was bewitched by Maria Smith, her father, Edward Drake, unable to bear any longer the sight of his daughter in pain and torment, determined to go and consult a 'cunning man.' He told Edward Drake, as soon as he saw him, that he was come to seek help for his daughter, and added that she was so far spent that if he had stayed but one day longer, the woman that had wronged her would have placed her past recovery. He also showed Drake the face of his daughter in a glass, and told him that the witch had accused his daughter of stealing her hen, of which fact Drake was not previously aware. He then gave him the following directions, which, if strictly complied with, would be the means of giving the desired relief to his daughter. 'Make a cake with flour from the baker's, and mix with the same the patient's urine instead of other liquor, and bake it on the hearth. One half of this cake to be laid on the patient about the region of the heart, and the other half to be applied to the back directly opposite.' He also gave a box of ointment, like treacle, which must be spread upon that cake, and a powder to be cast upon the same, and certain words written in a paper to be laid on with the cake. He further told Edward Drake that if his daughter did not exhibit signs of improvement within six hours of the adoption of this remedy, then there was no health or recovery to be looked for. He also wished that silence should be kept, as the woman who had done this would know anything. The widow, it is said, was by this means freed from the languishing torments that she had endured for six weeks."

It was generally believed that a witch or wizard, whatever might be his size or corpulence, could not weigh down the church Bible, and the Rev. Robert Forby says many instances might be cited of persons who had been accused of witchcraft applying to the clergyman of the parish to be allowed to prove their innocence by this ordeal. This trial, however, is not considered quite satisfactory when the suspicion is very strong against the party accused.

The only sure criterion by which the guilt or innocence of a witch could be satisfactorily ascertained was believed to be by swimming. The actual experiment has been of rare occurrence during the present century, but the practice was once so common that tradition points out several pieces of water as having been customarily used for this purpose. In particular a deep hole in the river Waveney near Harleston, at a bend of the stream, is still known by the name of the "Witch Pool." The plan adopted was this:—The suspected person, generally an old woman, was wrapt in a sheet, having the great toes and thumbs tied together, and so dragged through a pond or river. If she sank, it was received in favour of the accused, but if the body floated (which must have occurred nine times out of ten if it was placed with care on the surface), the accused was condemned, on the

principle of King James, who, in treating of this mode of
trial, lays it down that as witches have renounced their baptism, so it is just that the element through which the holy
rite is administered should reject them.

Towards the middle of the last century a test of a much
more horrible kind was occasionally resorted to, which was
supposed to bring upon the witch herself the sufferings of
her victim. If an animal was supposed to be bewitched and
to be past hope of recovery, it was suspended by its four
feet over a large fire and burnt to ashes, and it was firmly
believed that the witch herself would consume away at the
same time and in exact proportion with the poor animal she
had tormented. Sometimes as soon as the fire was applied,
the suspected sorceress would come to the door of the house
in the utmost agony and alarm, and if she was admitted and
allowed to extinguish the fire, she would escape with no other
injury than a few kicks or curses, the natural consequence
of detection. If the animal, however, was consumed in the
fire, so was the witch also, at whatever distance she might
be, by a sympathetic combustion. That this belief is not
altogether extinct is proved by the following account, which
can be vouched for by a gentleman living on the spot:—A
young man residing not many miles from Yarmouth was
troubled in the year 1866 in rearing young chickens. Either
his eggs would not hatch or his broods died. He tried eggs
from various farms near at hand with no better success.
Provoked by repeated failures, he picked up the last two of
a brood that had died off, and which two seemed to be following their companions, and said to his wife, "If these
chickens are bewitched I'll find it out," and threw them
upon the fire. He says that his chickens after this ordeal
did as well as he could desire, but the old witch who had
done the mischief looked wonderfully scared next time he
saw her. This young man is a member of a Christian church,
has a good education, is a carpenter, skilful at his business,
and intelligent. His mother, however, is an oracle in super-

stitious lore, practised in blessing out fire, &c., and it is evident from his actually trying this cruel ordeal, that the young man, with all his intelligence and professed Christian principles, has not shaken off the influence of his early belief.

Mr. Henderson in his *Folk Lore of the Northern Counties* says that at Hurstpierpoint there is a cottage in which lived a witch of whom it was said that she could not die till she had sold her secret. Her end was dreadful. She was dying for weeks. At last an old man from Cuckfield Workhouse paid a halfpenny for the secret, and she died with the money in her hand. A blue flame appeared on the roof as she breathed her last. I have not heard of anything so marvellous as this, but that a similar belief prevails in the Eastern Counties is proved by information given to a clergyman in this district. The rev. gentleman says : " The ability to practise witchcraft is believed to be handed on from one to another, usually by the witch on her death-bed communicating the important secret to her chosen successor. A parishioner of mine said that she knew of an instance in which a box containing little imps was given by an old witch to a young woman whom she wished to succeed her in the art. The young woman, however, did not at all value the gift, but not knowing how to dispose of the disagreeable legacy, she called in the advice of a neighbour. The latter suggested that all the windows of the house should be closed, the shutters put up, and the doors locked and barred. This was only preliminary to what was to follow. After the windows were closed and the doors barred, a fire was lighted and the oven heated, and then the box which contained the imps was placed in the oven and the door tightly fastened. The yells which soon proceeded from the oven were said to have been frightful, for the imps proved to be no salamanders. At length all was silent, the two women cautiously re-opened the oven, and nothing was discovered to be left either of the box or the imps who had just before been so uproarious but a little dust."

It was believed that witches had the power of transforming themselves into the shape of certain animals. The cat, the hare, the mole, and the toad, have generally been selected for that purpose. The hare is the most common disguise of a witch in all the northern countries of Europe, and was well known in the Northern Counties of England, but I have not met with an account of such belief in these Eastern Counties. At the trial of the Lowestoft witches, 1664, one of the witnesses said that believing her child to be bewitched by Amy Duny, she, the witness, went to a man called Doctor Jacob, who lived at Yarmouth, who had the reputation in the country to help children who were bewitched. He advised her to hang up the child's blanket in the chimney corner all day, and at night when she put the child to bed, to put it into the said blanket, and if she found anything in it she was to be sure and throw it into the fire. The witness acted according to his directions, and at night when she took down the blanket with an intent to put her child therein, there fell out of the same a great toad, which ran up and down the hearth ; and she, having only a youth with her in the house, desired him to catch the toad and throw it into the fire, which the youth did accordingly, and held it there with the tongs. As soon as it was in the fire it made a great and terrible noise, and after a space there was a flashing in the fire like gunpowder, making a noise like the discharge of a pistol, and thereupon the toad was no more seen nor heard. The next day there came a young woman, a kinswoman of the said Amy, and told the witness that her aunt (the said Amy) was in a most lamentable condition, having her face all scorched with fire, and that she was sitting alone in her house, in her smock, without any fire. The witness in consequence went into the house to see Amy Duny, and found her in the condition just stated—her face, her legs, and thighs appeared to be very much scorched and burnt. The witness asked the said Amy how she came into that sad condition, and Amy replied that she might thank her for it, for that she (the witness) was the cause of it; but that she should live to see some of her children dead, and she upon crutches. The witness further stated that after the burning of the said toad her child recovered, and was well again.

For many years the power principally attributed to witches amongst us is that of foretelling future events, and of discovering the possessors of stolen goods. This is implicitly believed, and many a lass of the towns as well as the villages in this district has crossed the hand of the fortune teller with silver to learn the events of her future life. Even amongst those of a somewhat higher rank, it is not uncommouly the first thought that occurs after having been robbed, to consult a conjuror, either male or female. Despairing lovers, persons under the influence of the evil eye, and the owners of stolen goods, are the principal customers of the "conjurors." It is, however, a good symptom that this is seldom done openly. People entertain the belief, but are ashamed to own it; and there may be just grounds to hope that the superstition which nobody cares to avow is in a fair way of losing its influence. Several of the superintendents and inspectors of police could give very amusing particulars relating to persons who have applied to "cunning men or women," and which would show the prevalence of the belief among a certain class of persons in this county. As examples of this kind, I give a few of the statements that have been made known to me.

A man living at a village a few miles from Yarmouth went to a raffle and won some sausages. Upon eating them he was taken ill, and ultimately went into "a low way." Some friends persuaded him that he was bewitched, and advised him to consult Mrs. Mortimer, a well-known "cunning woman" at Yarmouth. His mother accompanied him on his visit to this woman, who at first alarmed them by the fierce way in which she received them, vowing that she would not have a man in her house. As they made their business

known to her, the old woman found that the man was likely
to prove a good customer, and she very soon cooled down
and admitted them. The mother, who related the adventure,
said, " I trembled from head to foot when I entered Mrs.
Mortimer's house. She took us upstairs, and my Charles
paid her a sovereign. She brought out her divining cup,
and wanted me to look, but I daren't." A written copy of
the Lord's Prayer was given to the man, and he was ordered
to wear this next his heart, and to take a mixture that the
old hag gave him. He was also required to send to her some
of his hair, cut from the nape of the neck, parings of his
toe and finger nails, and a bottle of his urine. These were
to be operated upon by her in order to complete the cure.
The man got better, and Mrs. Mortimer then demanded
another ten shillings, which he refused to pay, but finding
himself again in declining health, he paid the money, after
which he recovered, and continued well till the death of the
old hag. He has since that event felt it necessary to apply
to a " cunning man " at Norwich. The copy of the Lord's
Prayer was worn out on his person.

Another man in East Norfolk was troubled for a long period
by his pigs being bewitched. " If they didn't take it into their
heads to die outright, as some did, they wouldn't fatten."
He consulted a cunning man, and was told that one of his
own family had caused it, and that he must keep the pigs
in another man's sty. This he did with happy results, but
as that was an inconvenient arrangement for permanency, he
was advised to purchase the next lot in another person's
name, and to nail a stallion's shoe to his threshold. He acted
on this advice, and since then he has had no further trouble.

The following narrative has been given me by the Rev.
Edward Gillett of Runham Vicarage, near Filby. A few
years ago the Post Office authorities were informed that
several letters containing valuables which should have passed
through the Beighton Post Office (sub-office to Acle) were
missed. The usual plan was followed, a detective being sent

down, who posted a "test" letter containing a half-sovereign and stamps (both of course marked). The post-master, William Barker, fell into the trap, and was committed to Norwich Castle for trial. In company with a man committed for passing counterfeit coin, he effected his escape, and though the police came immediately to Beighton after him, and found some traces of him, they could not catch him. About three months after, nothing having been heard of him in the meanwhile, though advertised in the *Police Gazette*, the police in Liverpool took him into custody as he was in the act of posting a letter to his sister-in-law. It appears that he went from Beighton to Yarmouth, rather a difficult feat for one for whom the police are on the look-out, there being so few entrances to Yarmouth, to see Mrs. Mortimer, and paid her a sum of money for a " safe-conduct to Liverpool." This she gave him, insisting that he should go first to Leeds, work there at his trade for three months (he was a tailor), and then go to Liverpool. This artifice proves her right in one sense to the title of the " cunning" woman. He then went to Liverpool, keeping close by day and went out by night. This aroused the suspicions of the Liverpool police, and finding his description tally in some respects with that of some other person " wanted," they took him into custody. The letter that he was about to post at the time was written by his wife, urgently requesting her sister to go to Mrs. Mortimer and get " the protection for safe conduct to America" that was promised. Barker was tried, and received sentence of twelve months' imprisonment for the robbery, and six months for breaking out of gaol.

The following account of the tact of a cunning woman is related by the Rev. Wm. Forby: " Sometimes the revenge of witches was exercised rather in a sportive than a malignant spirit, and of this an instance was told and religiously believed in Norfolk towards the end of the last century. A farmer's wife having lost some feathers, consulted the celebrated ' Nan Barrett' on the surest mode of recovering them.

The sybil assured her that they should be brought back, but the niggardly housewife having obtained this assurance, refused to pay the old woman her accustomed fee.   Provoked, as she well might be, at being thus bilked, the prophetess repeated the assurance that the feathers should come back, but added 'that the owner should not be the better for them.'   The enquirer, however, fully satisfied that she should recover her goods, laughed at the threat, and returned in high glee, congratulating herself on having outwitted the witch and obtained the information so cheaply.   As soon as she got home, she called her maids to go to milking, and when they had about half done, hearing a slight noise, she raised her head, and saw her feathers come flying into the milking-yard like a swarm of bees; and to her great annoyance beheld them direct their flight towards the cows, and settle themselves snugly in the half-filled milk pails, thus spoiling at once both milk and feathers.   It will readily be imagined that after this catastrophe no one ever ventured to defraud Mrs. Barrett of her dues."

Before closing this chapter, I must briefly allude to an existing belief in another class of beings—a better kind of spirits than witches.   They are called fairies, and by some people "Pharisees."   They seem to stand midway between the purely spiritual and the natural, being able to go through a keyhole, and yet perform manual labour that is of great service to an industrious man.   They are rewarders of cleanliness and fond of fun, mostly, however, of a harmless character.   They have the power of making themselves seen, heard, and felt.   They interest themselves in man's affairs, now doing him a good turn, and, when offence is taken at some trifling incident, leading him into mischief and laughing heartily at his misadventures.   There are a few stories of fairy changelings.   Fairy children of some growth are said to be occasionally entrusted to human care for a time and recalled, and mortals are now and then kidnapped and carried off to Fairyland.   They are great enemies of sluttery, and if the kitchen floor is swept before going to bed and the sweepings not taken away, or if the broom is left on the floor without being placed standing on its handle, those well skilled in fairy lore will tell you that the fairies will come and punish the slatternly housewife. They are fond of singing, dancing in rings, moving hand in hand, and playing music together, and are said to ride horses and colts about meadows and fields, much to the farmers' chagrin. From the many aged persons who will occasionally evince their knowledge of the fairies, it is evident that this belief in the little folk— the remnant of a faded creed—is far from dead, though in the present generation it is held by a slighter tenure than formerly. A clergyman residing in the neighbourhood of Diss has recorded the following cases:—An old parish clerk told the clergyman that years ago he knew several houses where the fairies visited. They never appeared as long as any person was about. People used to lie hid to see them, but as soon as they saw anybody they vanished away. In the houses after they had fled, sparks of fire as bright as stars used to appear under the feet of the persons who disturbed them.

In another parish a man was ploughing in a field. A fairy, quite small and sandy-coloured, came to him and asked him to mend his peel (a flat iron with a handle to take bread out of an oven), and that if he did he should have a hot cake. The ploughman soon put a new handle in it, and soon after a smoking hot cake made its appearance in the furrows near him, which he ate with infinite relish.

A woman of 80, sister of the sexton of a parish near by the above-mentioned, told the clergyman that a house in the village was many years previous the scene of fairy visits and officiousness. The occupier was a clean and industrious man, and the fairies, who cannot abide dirt or slovenliness, used his cottage for their meetings. As his was kept tidy and clean, they cut and brought faggots for the good man, and filled his oven with nice dry wood every night. They also left a shilling for him under the leg of a chair. A fairy often came to him and warned him not to tell any one of it, for if he did the shilling, wood, and fairies would never come to him again. Unluckily for him he did tell his good luck, and then his little friends were never seen by him more.

The witty Dr. Corbet, Bishop of Norwich, has in his *Fairies' Farewell* given quite an epitome of the popular belief about fairies among the peasantry in his day. He says:

> Farewell, rewards and fairies,
>   Good housewives now may say;
> For now foul sluts in dairies
>   Do fare as well as they :
> And though they sweep their hearths no less
>   Than maids were wont to do,
> Yet who of late for cleanliness
>   Finds sixpence in her shoe ?
>
> Lament, lament, old abbeys,
>   The fairies lost command,
> They did but change priests' babies,
>   But some have chang'd your land.
> And all your children stol'n from thence
>   Are now grown Puritans,
> Who live as changelings ever since
>   For love of your domaines.
>
> At morning and at evening both
>   You merry were and glad;
> So little care of sleep and sloth
>   These pretty ladies had.
> When Tom came home from labour,
>   Or Cisse to milking rose,
> Then merrily went their tabor,
>   And nimbly went their toes.
>
> Witness those rings and roundelays
>   Of theirs which yet remain,
> Were footed in Queen Mary's days
>   On many a grassy plain.

*　　*　　*　　*　　*　　*　　*

A tell-tale in their company
  They never could endure,
And whoso kept not secretly
  Their mirth was punish'd sure.
It was a just and Christian deed
  To pinch such black and blue;
O! how the commonwealth doth need
  Such justices as you.

LEGENDS.

THE district of East Anglia is not noted for its legendary lore, but there are, nevertheless, many traditional tales of a legendary character that are still known and firmly believed by a number of the peasantry in the Eastern Counties. The Rev. John Gunn communicated a few years ago to the Norfolk and Norwich Archæological Society a very interesting paper on the Traditions and Superstitions of the parish of Irstead, of which he is rector, chiefly derived from Mrs. Lubbock, an old inhabitant, which showed how firm was the belief, and how much might be collected throughout the county by judicious enquiries among the aged and the ignorant.

HEARD'S SPIRIT.

Mrs. Lubbock said : " Before the Irstead enclosure in 1810, Jack o'Lantern was frequently seen here on a roky night, and almost always at a place called Heard's Holde, in Alder Carr Fen Broad, on the Neatishead side, where a man of that name, who was guilty of some unmentionable crimes, was drowned. I have often seen it there, rising up and falling and twistering about, and then up again. It looked exactly like a candle in a lantern." The lady evidently connected the "ignis fatuus" in that spot with the unhappy man's spirit, as if it were still hovering about, and Jack o'Lantern was in her apprehension endued with volition and intelligence, for she affirms that " if any one were walking along the road with a lantern at the time when he appeared, and did not put out the light immediately, Jack would come against it and dash it to pieces, and that a gentleman who made a mock of him, and called him ' Will of the Wisp,' was riding on horseback one evening in the adjoining parish of Horning, when he came at him and knocked him off his horse."

The Neatishead people were desirous to lay Heard's spirit, so annoyed were they by it, for it came at certain times and to certain places which he frequented when alive.   Three gentlemen attempted to lay the ghost by reading verses of Scripture, but he always kept a verse ahead of them, and they could do nothing, till a boy brought a couple of pigeons and laid them down before him.   He looked at them and lost his verse, and then they bound his spirit.

PHANTOM DOGS.

It is recorded that " a person named Finch of Neatishead was walking in the road after dark and saw a dog, which he thought was Dick Allard's, which had snapped and snarled at him several times.   Thinks he, ' You have upset me two or three times ; I will upset you now.   You will not turn out of the road for me, and I will not turn out of the road for you.'   Along came the dog, straight in the middle of the road, and Finch kicked at him, and his foot went through him as through a sheet of paper : he could compare it to nothing else.   He was quite astounded, and nearly fell backwards from the force of the kick."

The ordinary form which spirits are said to assume in East Norfolk is that of the phantom dog.   A headless dog with saucer eyes is said to pass nightly over Coltishall Bridge, while another, " Old Shuck " by name, travels between Beeston and Overstrand, the terror of the neighbourhood. A lane in the latter parish is called after him " Shuck's Lane."*

The late Rev. E. S. Taylor of Martham said : " Many persons in East Norfolk declare that they have seen a phantom in the shape of a black shaggy dog, with fiery eyes of immense size, that visits churchyards at midnight.   One

witness nearly fainted away at seeing it, and on bringing
his neighbours to see the place where he saw it, he
found a large spot as if gunpowder had been exploded
there. A lane in the parish of Overstrand is called after
this phantom 'Shuck's Lane.' The name appears to be a
corruption of 'shag,' as *shucky* is the Norfolk dialect for
'shaggy.' "*

SIR THOMAS BOLEYN'S SPECTRE.

Sir Thomas Boleyn, the father of the unfortunate Queen
of Henry VIII., resided at Blickling, distant about fourteen
miles from Norwich, and now the residence of the Most
Noble the Marquis of Lothian. The spectre of this gentleman is believed by the vulgar to be doomed on a certain
night in every year for a period of 1000 years to drive a
coach drawn by four headless horses, over a circuit of twelve
bridges in that vicinity. These are Aylsham, Burgh, Oxnead,
Buxton, Coltishall, the two Meyton bridges, Wroxham, and
four others. Sir Thomas carries his head under his arm, and
flames issue from his mouth. Few rustics are hardy enough
to be found loitering on or near those bridges on that night,
and the man who spoke of this belief says that he was on
one occasion hailed by this fiendish apparition, and asked to
open a gate, but " he warn't sich a fool as to turn his head;
and well a' didn't, for Sir Thomas passed him full gallop
like," and he heard a voice which told him that he (Sir
Thomas) had no power to hurt such as turned a deaf ear to
his requests, but that had he stopped he would have carried
him off. This tradition is familiarly known among aged
persons, but it is very seldom that you meet with anybody
who has *seen* the phantom.

The writer of the above in *Notes and Queries* says : " The
coach and four horses is attached to another tradition I have

---

* *Notes and Queries*, 1st Series, vol. 1, p. 468.

heard in the west of Norfolk, where the ancestor of a family is reported to drive his spectral team through the old walled-up gateway of his now demolished mansion on the anniversary of his death, and it is said that the bricks the next morning have ever been found loosened and fallen, though as constantly repaired."

Another vision of the headless horse is prevalent at Caistor Castle, the seat of the Fastolf family.

CHURCH BELLS.

Many legends of bells under ground and under water are known in various parts of England. Where the churches are said to have been swallowed up either by earthquake or the ravages of the sea, the old church bells are said to ring, deep, deep in the earth, every Christmas morning, and people go forth and put their ears to the ground, hoping to catch the music of the mysterious chimes in the subterranean temple.

The tradition in Norfolk is of a somewhat different character. In the village of Tunstall, distant a few miles from Yarmouth, there is a clump of alder trees familiarly known as " Hell Carr." Not far from these trees there is a pool of water having a boggy bottom that goes by the name of " Hell Hole." A succession of bubbles are frequently seen floating on the surface of the water in summer time, a circumstance to be accounted for very naturally, but the natives of the district maintain that these bubbles are the result of supernatural action, the cause of which is thus described :—The tower of the church is in ruins, and tradition says that it was destroyed by fire, but that the bells were not injured by the calamity. The parson and the churchwarden each claimed the bells, and while they were quarrelling for their possession, his Satanic Majesty came and carried off the disputed articles. The parson, however, not desiring to lose the booty, pursued and overtook his

Majesty, who, in order to evade his clerical opponent, dived through the earth to his appointed dwelling-place, taking the bells with him. Tradition points to "Hell Hole" as the spot where he made his exit, and the villagers consider that the bubbles on the surface of the pool are caused by the continuous descent of the bells in water to the bottomless pit.

THE HEART IN THE HAND.

The elder portion of the peasantry in and around Wickhampton are familiar with a strange legend. It is said that two brothers who owned respectively two adjoining parishes, disputed so strongly about their respective boundaries that they quarrelled and fought until they tore each others' hearts out. The Divine Being manifested his displeasure at such cruel conduct by turning them both into stone, and with their hearts in their hands they were placed in the church as monuments of Divine vengeance, and to deter others from similar acts of wickedness. A splendid monument in Wickhampton church to the memory of Sir Wm. Gerbygge and his lady is pointed at in confirmation of the legendary tale, as until the last few years the recumbent effigy of the knight held a small piece of stone in his hand shaped like a heart. It is said, in addition, that after the death of the brothers, one parish was called Wicked Hampton, since contracted into Wickhampton, and the other Hell Fire Gate, now known as Halvergate.

THE SWAFFHAM LEGEND.

Swaffham Church, noted for its architectural beauties, has furnished material for a legend worth recording. According to tradition, the entire expense of erecting this noble edifice was defrayed by a tinker or pedlar residing in the parish named John Chapman, who, if the voice of the legend is to be believed, was marvellously provided for by Divine Providence. It is said that this tinker dreamed that if he went to London Bridge he would, to use the phraseology of a certain class of advertisements, " hear of something greatly to his advantage." Nothing daunted by the difficulties of so long a journey five hundred years ago, when, not to utter a hint of railroads, even stage coaches had not been invented, the tinker heeded the voice of his good spirit, and went to London. After standing about the bridge for several hours— some versions of the legend mention the traditional three days—a man accosted him, and invited him to unfold the nature of his errand. With candour quite equal to his faith, John Chapman replied that he came there on the " vain errand of a dream." Now it appears that the stranger was a dreamer also, but, unlike the tinker, he was neither superstitious nor imprudent. " Alas ! good friend," said he, " if I had heeded dreams, I might have proved myself as very a fool as thou art, for 'tis not long since I dreamt that at a place called Swaffham in Norfolk dwelt John Chapman, a pedlar, who hath a tree at the back of his house, under which is buried a pot of money." John Chapman, of course, on hearing this hastened home, dug under his tree, and very soon found the treasure. But not all of it. The box that he found had a Latin inscription on the lid, which of course John Chapman could not decipher. But though unlettered, he was not without craftiness and a certain kind of wisdom, so in the hope that some unsuspicious wayfarer might read the inscription in his hearing, he placed it in his window. It was not long before he heard some youths turn the Latin sentence into an English couplet :

> Under me doth lie
> Another much richer than I.

Again he went to work, digging deeper than before, and found a much richer treasure than the former. With a heart overflowing with gratitude for his good fortune, the tinker shortly afterwards, when the inhabitants of Swaffham wished to re-edify their church, astonished the whole town by offering to defray the expense of a large portion of the works. On the ends of the oaken bench nearest the pulpit, there is the carved effigy of John Chapman on one side and that of his dog on the other, and this is sufficient to establish the truth of the legend in the minds of the credulous of the district.

THE TREASURE OF CALLOW PIT.

Among the old inhabitants of the neighbourhood of Southwood, a small village between Yarmouth and Norwich, there still lingers a curious tradition respecting a golden treasure that lies at the bottom of " Callow Pit "—an old cavernous opening on the boundary of the parish that has evidently been in existence for many centuries. To ascertain for me particulars of this legend, a clergyman of the district called at the cottage of an old shepherd—one of the thirty-nine inhabitants of the parish ; and his daughter, a middle-aged woman, immediately gave him all she had heard from childhood about the Callow Pit and its golden treasure. It may be as well to premise that the pit is in a secluded district, and was formerly a place that was avoided by young people at night time, as it was reported that a headless horseman was to be seen riding in its vicinity ; but the clue to the mystery attached to this spot may be found in the fact that it was formerly used by a gang of desperate men as a place of deposit for smuggled goods. The tale current in the neighbourhood is that a large quantity of gold is enclosed in an iron chest that lay submerged at the bottom of Callow Pit, for although the pit is at the present day almost always dry— so dry, indeed, that the old shepherd above alluded to has cleaned it out two or three times without finding the treasure—it was formerly filled with water.

Once upon a time two daring men filled with a firm belief in the legend determined to try and obtain this wondeful chest. Having, with due regard to secresy, made all the necessary preparations for the adventure, they one night took advantage of a low state of the water to put their scheme into execution. Accordingly they placed ladders across the pit to form a bridge. By means of a strong staff with an iron hook, they caught hold of the ring in the lid of the chest, and by dint of great exertion drew up the golden treasure to their temporary platform. The staff was then put through the ring and placed on their shoulders, preparatory to carrying off in triumph the chest of hoarded wealth. Whether dealing with fairies or demons, the popular belief is that silence is essential to success, and in this case, unfortunately, one of the men was so elated at the possession of the much-coveted prize, that he cried out, "We've got it safe, and Old Nick himself can't get it from us." The pit was in a moment enveloped by a dense vapour, having a strong sulphurous smell, and a black hand and arm, supposed to belong to his Satanic Majesty, was thrust through the water and seized the chest. A desperate struggle between the arch fiend and the bold adventurers ensued for the possession of the chest, the result of which was that the chest, unable to withstand the supernatural grasp, separated from the ring and sunk into the water to be seen no more, while the ring remained on the staff of the courageous adventurers, who, baulked of the reward of their daring, determined to affix their only trophy to the door of Southwood Church, where it still remains as a handle to the door, and a convincing proof in the minds of believers of the truth of this extraordinary legend.

LEGENDS OF KING EDMUND.

A remarkable legend relating to Edmund, King of East Anglia, that has been handed down for centuries, is worthy

of record here.   Edmund, who lived in the ninth century,
resided at Thetford, his capital, but being driven from thence
by the Danes and overpowered by numbers in battle, he sur-
rendered to save the destruction of life and property among
his faithful subjects.   The Danish Princes, his conquerors,
ordered him to be bound to a tree and beat with " short
bats."   They then cruelly made him a mark for the soldiers,
and his body was covered with arrows, after which he was
beheaded, and his head and body were then cast into the
thickest part of the wood at Hoxne.   When the departure
of the Danes removed the terror their presence inspired, the
East Anglians assembled in considerable numbers determined
to pay the last duties of attachment to the corpse of their
beloved King.   The body was discovered and interred at
Hoxne, but the head could not be found.   His zealous subjects in consequence divided themselves into small parties,
and resolved to search every part of the wood.   Terrified by
the obscurity of the place they traversed, some of them called
out, " Where are you ? "   A voice answered, " Here ! Here !
Here ! "   They hastened to the place whence the sound proceeded, and found a wolf holding the head between his fore
feet.   The animal politely delivered up his charge, and the
people, almost overpowered with joy, carried the royal head
to the body, to which, as soon as it came in contact with it, it
united itself so exactly that the juncture was not visible
except when closely examined.   The friendly wolf joined in
the procession, and after seeing the precious treasure that he
had with so much care protected joined to the body whence
it had been severed, he, without showing any fierceness, returned to the woods.

There is on the border ground of Norfolk another legend
respecting King Edmund, which, though it does not exactly
agree with the one just related, inasmuch as instead of sur-
rendering it makes the King get betrayed, we give here as it
is told.   After the disastrous battle near Thetford above
alluded to, the Monarch, it is said, concealed himself under

the arch of a bridge in Hoxne now called " Gold Bridge," and so named from the brilliant appearance of the gilt spurs which he happened to wear, and which proved the means of discovering his retreat. A newly-married couple returning home in the evening, and seeing the reflection of the spurs in the water, betrayed him to the Danes. Indignant at their treachery, the King is said to have pronounced, in the warmth of his resentment, a dreadful curse on every couple who should afterwards pass over this bridge on their way to or from the altar of Hymen. Even to this day, after an interval of nearly a thousand years, such is the superstitious regard paid to this denunciation, that a wedding party proceeding to or coming from the Church never fail to avoid the bridge, even if obliged to take a circuitous route.†

MR. NAYLOR'S APPARITION.

The following, though not exactly a legend, is too curious a story to be allowed to pass unnoticed. The original will be found in the register of the Church named, from which it has been copied :

Extract from the register in Brisley Church, Norfolk.

Dec. 12th, 1706. I, Robert Withers, M.A., Vicar of Gately, do insert here a story which I had from undoubted hands, for I have all the moral certainty of the truth of it possible :

" Mr. Grove went to see Mr. Shaw on the 2nd of August last. As they sat talking in the evening, says Mr. Shaw, ' On the 21st of the last month, as I was smoking my pipe and reading in my study between eleven and twelve at night, in comes Mr. Naylor (formerly Fellow of St. John's College, but had been dead full four years). When I saw him I was not much affrighted, and I asked him to sit down, which accordingly he did for about two hours, and we talked to-

---

* Yates' *History and Antiquities of Bury St. Edmund's.*

gether. I asked him how it fared with him. He said, "Very well." "Were any of our old acquaintances with him?" "No" (at which I was much concerned), "but Mr. Orchard will be with me soon, and yourself not long after." As he was going away I asked him if he would not stay a little longer, but he refused. I asked him if he would call again. "No; he had but three days' leave of absence, and he had other business." '

" N.B.—Mr. Orchard died soon after. Mr. Shaw is now dead. He was formerly Fellow of St. John's College, an ingenuous good man. I knew him there, but at his death he had a College living in Oxfordshire, and here he saw the apparition."

THE WISHING WELLS AT WALSINGHAM.

I close my collection of the superstitious beliefs of the peasantry by a notice of the wishing wells at Walsingham. Amongst the slender remains of Walsingham, once the celebrated seat of superstitious devotion, are two small circular basins of stone, a little to the north-east of the site of the conventual church. The water of these wells had at the time of Erasmus a miraculous efficacy in curing disorders of the head and stomach, the special gift no doubt of the Holy Virgin, who has probably since that time resumed it, for the waters have no such quality now. She has substituted, however, another of far more comprehensive virtue. This is nothing less than the power of accomplishing all human wishes, which miraculous property the water is still believed to possess. In order to attain this desirable end, the votary, with a due qualification of faith and pious awe, must apply the right knee bare to a stone placed for that purpose between the wells. He must then plunge to the wrist each hand, bare also, into the water of the wells, which are near enough to admit of this immersion. A wish must then be formed, but not uttered with the lips, either at the time or afterwards, even in confidential communication to the dearest friend. The hands are then to be withdrawn, and as much of the water as can be contained in the hollow of each is to be swallowed. This silent wish will certainly be accomplished within twelve months, if the efficacy of the solemn rite be not frustrated by the incredulity or some other fault of the votary.

Curious Customs, &c.

THE CHURCH.

PRIVILEGE OF SANCTUARY.

THE " Privilege of Sanctuary," by which a thief or a murderer fleeing from justice to a church was allowed to go free on condition of his voluntarily abjuring the realm, is one of the mediæval curiosities which are known to have been in full practice in Norfolk. The privilege appears to have been introduced into England at a very early date. Ina, King of the West Saxons, in a Code of Laws promulgated in 693, expressly recognised it. By the laws of Alfred the Great (A.D. 887), the privilege is given for three nights to any one flying to a church, and William the Conqueror in his fourth year made express laws for protecting the privilege.

It seems that in such churches as were more particularly known as places of sanctuary, chambers were provided over the belfry door in which men slept for the purpose of admitting fugitives at any hour of the night. As soon as any one was so admitted, the Galilee bell was immediately tolled to give notice that some one had taken sanctuary. The culprit then placed himself before the shrine of the patron saint, and begged for a coroner. The coroner attended and heard his confession. The culprit, in the presence of the sacrist, the sheriff, the under-sheriff, and others, renounced the kingdom. He then stripped himself to his shirt and gave up his clothing to the sacrist as his fee. The sacrist restored the clothing, and placed a white cross of wood in the culprit's hand. He was then consigned to the under-sheriff, who committed him to the care of the nearest constable, with whom he marched until he was handed over to the next, and by him to the next, in the direction of the coast. It devolved on the last constable to see that the culprit was placed on board a ship, where he bade an eternal farewell to his country.

From the records of the corporate bodies of Norwich and of Great Yarmouth, Mr. Harrod obtained the following illustrations of the exercise of this privilege:

"William Lot of Hemstede placed himself in the church of St. Gregory, the Monday before St. Bartholomew's Day, in the year 51 [1251]. The coroners and bailiff went and interrogated him why he placed himself there, and he confessed before them that he did so because of certain robberies he had committed, namely, on account of certain clothes he had stolen at Hemstede, and he was taken to Yarmouth and there incarcerated, from whence he escaped, and therefore placed himself in sanctuary. And he abjured the realm, and had protection to Sandwyz."

For three centuries the disputes between the monks and the citizens of Norwich about their respective jurisdictions led on many occasions to very serious disturbances, and even to loss of life, and this continued down to the dissolution of the monasteries. One of these contests offers an illustration of the right of "sanctuary." A serjeant-at-mace arrested a felon on Palm Sunday, 1507, on Tombland, in the "disputed territory," and was taking him off to the Guildhall prison. The Prior Bronde (afterwards Wolsey's successor at St. Alban's) with many of the monks attempted a rescue. The citizens, and subsequently the sheriff, joined in the fight. The sheriff had just succeeded in laying hold of the prisoner, when one of the monks drew the sheriff's gown tight behind, pulled him down backward, and held him, while others got the prisoner from his clutch, and led him off to sanctuary in the Cathedral.

The records of the Corporation of Great Yarmouth give the following :

"The 23rd Edward I.—John Schot of St. Edmund's placed himself in the church of the Friars' Preachers, the Friday after the Conception of the Blessed Mary, in the year 23, acknowledged to have stolen goods and chattels of merchants of Wincelse and Flanders to the value of £30, and to have broken prison at Yarmouth; abjured the kingdom the Monday following, and a port is given him at Portsmue within three weeks.

"Geffrey Gom of Lynn placed himself in the church of the Friars' Preachers same day, and acknowledged to have killed Richard **** of Vascony, and to have broken prison at Yarmouth the day and year aforesaid. He abjured the kingdom the Monday aforesaid, and port is given him at St. Botolph's [Boston] in fifteen days.

"Richard Clerk of Norwich placed himself in the church of St. Nicholas the same day, and acknowledged to have killed John Russell, and to have broken prison at Yarmouth; abjured the kingdom the Wednesday after the Feast of St. Lucy the Virgin in the year of King Edward 23, and port is given him at Southampton in a month."

"Under a due administration of justice," says Mr. Hallam, "this privilege would have been simply and constantly mischievous, as we properly consider it in those countries where it still subsists. But in the rapine and tumult of the middle ages, the right of sanctuary might as often be a shield to innocence as an impunity to crime. We can hardly regret, in reflecting on the desolating violence which prevailed, that there should have been some green spots in the wilderness where the feeble and the persecuted could find refuge. How this right must have enhanced the veneration for religious institutions! How gladly must the victims of internal warfare have turned their eyes from the baronial castle, the dread

and scourge of the neighbourhood, to those venerable walls
within which not even the clamour of arms could be heard to
disturb the chaunt of holy men and the sacred service of the
altar."

REFUGE IN THE CHURCH PORCH.

Closely connected with this privilege of sanctuary seems
to have been the custom of taking refuge in the church
porch as a temporary home until a lodging could be found
elsewhere. Mr. S. W. Rix of Beccles furnishes the following
illustration :—" In an old ' Towne Booke' for the parish of
Diss, I found among the disbursements of Samuel Foulger,
one of the churchwardens in 1687, the following :

> To the wench Ellener that laye in the church
> porch at severall times   ...   .   £00 7s. 0d.;"

and Mr. Goddard Johnson found the following entry in the
Corporation Book of the city of Norwich, under the year
1662 :

> Thomas Corbold, who hath a loathsome disease, have with his
> wife and two children layne in the porch of St. Peter's per Mounter-
> gate above one year. It is now ordered by the Court that he be put
> into some place in the pest houses during the pleasure of the Court
> until the lazar houses be repaired.

These extracts prove the existence of the custom in the
17th century; and that a remnant of this custom still prevails among the poor of Norfolk—viz., that any person may
lodge in the church porch and is not removable—is evidenced
by the following testimony from the Rev. A. Sutton, Rector
of West Tofts, Brandon :—" In proof of the idea being
current among the lower orders that the church porch is a
place of refuge for any houseless parishioner, I beg to state
that a poor woman of the adjoining parish came the other
day to ask whether I as a magistrate could render her any

assistance, as in consequence of her husband's father and mother having gone to America, she and her family had become houseless, and were obliged to take up their abode in the church porch."

BENEFIT OF CLERGY.

" Benefit of clergy," which exempted ordained persons from civil jurisdiction, is another relic of the past of which Norfolk affords examples. Thus Blomefield says :—" On an appeal of death in the King's Bench, 38th Henry III., the defendant pleaded that he was a clerk, and would not answer; and the Dean of Blofield came into Court on behalf of the Bishop of Norwich, and demanded him as a clerk of the diocese by letters patent of the Bishop, testifying that he constituted the said Dean to require and receive him of the Court as a clerk, and he was accordingly delivered to him, the Court exhorting to quick and full justice."

BURNING OF HERETICS.

The burning of heretics, as all were anciently termed who denied the doctrines of Transubstantiation, the Mass, &c., was of such frequent occurrence at Norwich in the sixteenth century, that in an old map of the city examined by the Rev. Richard Hart, the following was printed on the portion of Mouschold that was immediately under St. Leonard's Priory :

Ye place where ye Heretickes are custumably burned.

Bishop Nykke was a cruel persecutor of all those who professed the doctrine of the Reformation, and during his episcopate Robert Adams, clerk, also Thomas Ayers, Thomas Bingy, Thomas Norrice, and Thomas Bilney, priests, sealed their profession with their blood.

A folio manuscript in vellum preserved in the Guildhall at Norwich among the city archives, contains among other chronological memoranda the following :

1579.—Matthew Hamonde for denying Christ Jesus to be the Son of God, and asserting that by His death none can be saved, and also denying the New Testament to be the Scripture of God, was convicted of heresy, and burned the xxth of May, 1579.

1582.—This year, the xviij day of September, before these new Sheriffs (Henry Pye and Edward Johnson) were sworn, one Abydall Lewis, an heretic, for denying the divinity of Christ, was burnt in the Castle Ditch, where Doctr. Gardener, Deane of Xt. Church, preached, and the said Lewis died most obstinately without repentance or any speech.

1588.—This year, upon Tuesday, being the 14th day of January, Francis Knight, alias Ket, Master of Arts, was burnt in the Castle Ditch for most horrible heresy, denying that Christ was God before His ascension, and denying also the divinity of the Holy Ghost, and for many other erroneous opinions.

POOR'S BOX IN CHURCHES.

"Before the Reformation," says Anthony Wood, "in every church was a poor man's box." Poor boxes are often mentioned in the twelfth century. At that period Pope Innocent III. greatly extended Papal power, and among other things he ordered hollow trunks to be placed in all the churches to receive alms for the remission of the sins of the donors. The common poor box in the churches appears to have been a shaft of oak hollowed out, at the top covered by a hinged lid of iron, with a slit in it for the money to fall through into the cavity, and secured by one or two iron locks.

One of the most curiously constructed of the ancient poor boxes now remaining is that in the church of Cawston, near Aylsham. The church was built between 1385 and 1414. The poor box was provided with three keys, two of which were for the churchwardens, and the third was most probably for the clergyman, as one of the keyholes was more orna-

mented than the others. The most singular part of this box
is an inverted iron cup for preventing the money from being
taken out by means of any instrument through the holes on
the top of the box.

The church of Loddon, near Bungay, built about 1495,
also contains a depository of this description. It is rude in
make and bulky, upon a stand. It consists of two partitions,
both of which admit of being fastened with padlocks. In
the cover of one is a slit for the offerings, the other cover is
solid. This has been explained on the supposition that one
was the receiving box and the other the treasury or store.
Hone says that when a sufficient sum was collected, it was
taken out of the receiving box and placed in the adjoining
box in the presence of the two churchwardens.

Ben Jonson in his masque of the *Metamorphosed Gipsies*,
as it was thrice presented before King James, 1621, &c.,
makes a gipsy tell Tom Ticklefoot, a rustic musician :

> On Sundays you rob the poor's box with your tabor;
> The collectors would do it, you save them a labour.

Whereunto a countryman answers :

> Faith, but, a little, they'll do it now upstant.*

From this we gather that it was customary at that time to
put money in the parish poor's box on Sundays, and that the
trustees of the poor were sometimes suspected of misapply-
ing it. The neglect of this mode of public contribution is
noted in Hogarth's Marriage Scene of the *Rake's Progress*
by a cobweb covering the poor's box in the church. There
is an intimation to the same effect in Beaumont and Fletcher's
play of the *Spanish Curate*, which further intimates that
poor's boxes had posies :

> The poor man's box is there too; if ye find anything
> Besides the posy, and that half rubb'd out too,

* Notwithstanding.

> For fear it should awaken too much charity,
> Give it to pious uses : that is, spend it.

The posies or mottoes on poor's boxes were short sentences to incite benevolence, such as "He that giveth to the poor lendeth to the Lord," &c.

SOLITARY SERMON.

The one solitary sermon preached in the "open air" to the inhabitants of a city in which more than fifty discourses are delivered every Sunday now, forms a striking contrast between the present and the past. After the celebration of mass in their respective churches, the various congregations of Norwich used to assemble in an open space before the Palace and to the north of the Cathedral, called *Le Grene-yard*. The mayor and aldermen, with their families, had a covered seat or booth erected for them against the walls of the Palace ; the dean, prebendaries, and clergy sat in balconies or galleries attached to the north wall of the Cathedral. The bishop and his chancellor sat in the Palace near the open window, and the people congregated round the Cross at which the sermon was preached, erected in the centre of the area.

A CURIOUS SERMON.

The following appears to us a curiosity in theological literature. It was preached in the parish church of Burston, a small village near Diss, in Norfolk, about the beginning of last century, by the Rev. Hugh Moor :

"Fight the good fight," &c., 1 Timothy, 6 ch., 12 v.

Beloved, we are met together to solemnize the funeral of Mr. Proctor. His father's name was Mr. Thomas Proctor, of the second family ; his brother's name also was Mr. Thomas Proctor. He lived some time at Burston Hall, in Norfolk, and was high constable of

Diss Hundred. This man's name was Mr. Robert Proctor, and his wife's was Mrs. Buxton, late wife of Mr. Matthew Buxton; she came from Helsdon Hall, beyond Norwich.

He was a good husband and she a good housewife, and they got money; she brought a thousand pounds with her for portion.

But now, beloved, I shall make it clear by demonstrative arguments—first, he was a good man, and that in several respects: he was a loving man to his neighbours, a charitable man to the poor, a favourable man in his tithes, and a good landlord to his tenants. There sits one Mr. Spurgeon can tell what a great sum of money he forgave him upon his death-bed: it was four score pounds. Now, beloved, was not this a good man, and a man of God, and his wife a good woman?—and she came from Helsdon Hall, beyond Norwich. This is the first argument.

Secondly, to prove this man to be a good man and a man of God. In the time of his sickness, which was long and tedious, he sent for Mr. Cole, minister of Shimpling, to pray for him. He was not a self-ended man, to be prayed for himself only; no, beloved, he desired him to pray for all his relations and acquaintances: for Mr. Buxton's worship, and for all Mr. Buxton's children, in case it should please God to send him any; and to Mr. Cole's prayers he devoutly said, "Amen, amen, amen!" Was not this a good man, and a man of God, think you, and his wife a good woman?—and she came from Helsdon Hall, beyond Norwich.

Thirdly and lastly, beloved, I come to a clear demonstrative argument to prove this man to be a good man, and a man of God, and that is this—there was one Thomas Proctor, a very poor beggar-boy; he came into this country upon the back of a dun cow: it was not a black cow, nor a brindled cow, nor a brown cow; no, beloved, it was a dun cow. Well, beloved, this poor boy came a begging to this good man's door. He did not do as some would have done, give him a small alms and send him away, or chide him and make him a pass and send him into his own country. No, beloved, he took him into his own house, and bound him an apprentice to a gunsmith in Norwich. After his time was out he took him home again, and married him to a kinswoman of his wife's, one Mrs. Christian Robertson, here present. There she sits. She was a very good fortune, and to her this good man gave a considerable jointure. By her he had three daughters; this good man took home the eldest, brought her up to a woman's estate, married her to a very honourable gentleman, Mr. Buxton, here present—there he sits—gave him a vast portion with her, and the remainder of his estate he gave his two daughters.

Now, was not this a good man, and a man of God, think you, and his wife a good woman ?—and she came from Helsdon Hall, beyond Norwich.

Beloved, you may remember some time since I preached at the funeral of Mrs. Proctor, all which time I troubled you with many of her transcendent virtues, but your memories perhaps may fail you, and therefore I shall now remind you of one or two of them.

The first is, she was a good knitter as any in the county of Norfolk. When her husband and family were in bed and asleep, she would get a cushion, clap herself down by the fire, and sit and knit. But, beloved, be assured she was no prodigal woman but a sparing woman, for, to spare candle, she would stir up the coals with her knitting pins, and by that light she would sit and knit, and make as good work as many other women by daylight. Beloved, I have a pair of stockings upon my legs that were knit in the same manner, and they are the best stockings that ever I wore in my life.

Secondly, she was the best maker of toast in drink that ever I eat in my life, and they were brown toasts, too ; for when I used to go in a morning, she would ask me to eat a toast, which I was very willing to do, because she had such an artificial way of toasting it— no ways slack, nor burning it. Besides, she had such a pretty way of grating nutmeg and dipping it in the beer, and such a piece of rare cheese, that I must needs say that they were the best toasts that ever I eat in my life.

Well, beloved, the days are short, and many of you have a great way to your habitations, and therefore I hasten to a conclusion. I think I have sufficiently proved this man to be a good man, and his wife a good woman, but fearing your memories should fail you, I shall repeat the particulars, viz. :

1. His love to his neighbour.
2. His charity to the poor.
3. His favourableness in his tithes.
4. His goodness to his tenants.
5. His devotion to his prayers, in saying, " Amen, amen, amen ! "
to the prayers of Mr. Cole, Mr. Gibbs, and myself.

With reference to the above, the Rev. Henry Temple Frere, Rector of Burston, writes me (May, 1868) : " The only notices that I can find in the Burston Register at all relevant are these :—' September, 1713. Uxor Stephain Buxton de Diss Haywood '—possibly Thomas Proctor's daughter ;

and '1662· Elizabeth Moor, the wife of Hugh Moor *(sic)*, Rector of Burston, buried January 10th.' Hugh Moor's name is not signed to any page of the Register, nor is his burial recorded. The entries to the end of 1672 are written in a fine bold hand. They change for 1673, when probably we must place Hugh Moor's death or resignation. It is traditionally said that when he commended Mrs. Proctor's knitting, he stuck his leg out of the pulpit and slapped his calf for emphasis, but this is really all I can add."

Sir Thos. Beevor, Bart., says : " I find from Blomefield that Hugh Moor *(sic)* held Burston from 1626 to 1674; Robert Proctor held Gissing from 1613 to 1668 ; Thos. Cole held Shimpling from 1649 to 1684."

The sermon is quoted as extracted from the *British Magazine* for November, 1750.

HOUR GLASSES IN PULPITS.

In St. Edmund's Church, South Burlingham, stands an elegant pulpit of the fifteenth century. It is painted with diaper pattern, in red, green, and gold, and it is in Norfolk the only specimen of its kind. On it there still remains an old hour glass, though such appendages were in all probability not introduced until some centuries after the erection of this pulpit. In Salhouse Church, near Norwich, an iron hour-glass stand still remains, and at Edingthorpe Church, near North Walsham, there is also the hour-glass stand on the right hand side of the pulpit.

Hour glasses are relics of Puritanic times, and appear to have constituted in those days part of the furniture of the pulpit. Butler in his *Hudibras* speaks of "gifted men preaching by a carnal *hour* glass," and Gay in his *Pastorals* writes :

> He said that Heaven would take her soul no doubt,
> And spoke the hour glass in her praise quite out.

Hogarth in his " Sleeping Congregation " has introduced an hour glass on the left side of the preacher, and Wilkie has painted one in his " John Knox preaching before Mary Queen of Scots."

FEMALE PARISH CLERKS.

In the memoir of Bishop Blomfield it is mentioned that when he was presented to the rectory of Dunton, in Buckinghamshire, the parish clerk was a woman over seventy years of age, who could not read, and who, when she stole the communion plate of the church, took it to the nearest pawnbroker, in ignorance that the name of the parish was engraved in conspicuous letters upon it. The majority of our readers are doubtless quite unaware that until very recently a female parish clerk existed in Norfolk. The parish was Ickburgh, near Brandon. It is the parish church to Buckenham Hall, the seat of the Hon. Francis Baring. The woman was appointed in 1822, and the anomaly ceased only in 1866, the female parish clerk having had a reign of 44 years.

THE SHRINES AND PILGRIMAGES OF NORFOLK.

Many places in Norfolk were during the mediæval period noted as the resorts of pilgrims from all parts of Great Britain, although but very little is now known relative to the shrines which caused these localities to be so attractive. In a few cases, however, local traditions and ancient documents have combinedly furnished particulars of considerable interest to the public generally as well as to the antiquary ; and to the industry of the Rev. Richard Hart of Catton we are indebted for the chief details relating to the " Shrines and Pilgrimages of Norfolk " which we here give.

In the church of EAST DEREHAM, in this county, were anciently deposited the relics of St. Withburga, natural daughter of Anna, King of the East Angles, who was revered for her extraordinary sanctity as well as her royal descent. It was in the ninth century that the Abbot and monks of Ely conceived and executed the *pious* theft of these relics, laying down their plans with a tact and precision that might have put the most accomplished London burglar to the blush. They cleverly managed to *intoxicate* the East Deréham clergy, and having divided the entire distance into stages, with relays of men and horses, got far beyond the reach of pursuit before the rightful owners awoke to a sense of their great loss.

In the church of TRIMMINGHAM-NEAR-THE-SEA was anciently deposited the alleged head of St. John the Baptist. Visitors to this church, if they asked questions about this relic, were sometimes directed to a strip of brass, which it was said "would tell them all about it." This was a remarkable proof of the fallibility of local tradition, inasmuch as on this brass were the words only: "Praye for the soule of William Paston," &c.

St. Walstan of Bawburgh (or Baber) was held in deep reverence by our ancestors, and his effigy, with a scythe for his emblem, is still to be seen on the rood screens at Burlingham St. Andrew, Ludham, Barnham Broom, Sparham, and Denton. Although born of respectable parentage, and according to the legend even of royal descent, St. Walstan voluntarily embraced a life of poverty, and hired himself as a common labourer to a farmer at Taverham in this county. Walstan is alleged to have given away his food, and the very shoes off his feet, in charity to the poor; but when his mistress came to rebuke him for his thoughtlessness and want of thrift, she found him barefooted loading a cart with thorns, yet totally unhurt. The time of his death having been miraculously revealed to him, Walstan's last request to his master was that his body might be placed in a cart drawn by two unbroken oxen, and they should be left entirely to themselves. On two occasions they are said to have stopped with the sacred body, viz., once on the top of a hill, from which a fountain gushed forth ; it is further said that they crossed over a deep pond of water as if it had been a solid mass of earth or stone. At last they are said to have reached Bawburgh, the place of Walstan's birth, where the saint was buried, and a church built over his mortal remains. Walstan's shrine and altar in the north aisle of this church were constantly served by six chantry priests, and the offerings were so considerable that in 1309 the church was totally rebuilt and splendidly adorned. There was a chapel on Bawburgh bridge, and it was the duty of a hermit who constantly dwelt there to sprinkle the pilgrims with holy water before they approached the sacred shrine. In those times St. Walstan was looked upon as the patron saint of agriculture, and diseased cattle used to be brought thither to be blessed.

In a chapel at the upper end of the church at WINFARTHING was preserved a sword called "the good swerde of Win-farthing," to which numerous pilgrims are said to have resorted. One of its alleged properties was sufficiently curious, for it is said that when the yoke of matrimony galled a woman (or, to speak less metaphorically, when any woman longed to be a widow), she had nothing else to do but to cause a light to be burnt continually before this sword for a whole year ; but the omission even of a single day was sure to break the charm, and if a suspicious husband examined his chandler's bills this might of course occasionally happen, and the illumination be brought to a full stop.

According to the legend, this relic originally belonged to a robber, who once took sanctuary in the church of Win-farthing, but escaped through the negligence of the watch-men, leaving his sword behind him.

Matthew Paris has given us a long and interesting account of the Holy Cross of Broomholme, strikingly characteristic of the age in which he lived. He says that Baldwin, Earl of Flanders, had been elected Emperor of Constantinople, where he reigned honourably for many years, but he on one occasion rashly went forth to battle without those precious relics which the patriarchs and bishops were always wont to carry before him when he fought against the enemies of the Cross. On that disastrous day the infidel force was ten times more numerous than his own. The Christian army was surrounded by the barbarians, Baldwin himself was slain, and all his followers were either taken prisoners or put to the sword.

When the melancholy news reached Constantinople, the Emperor's chaplain, who was an Englishman, and had all the relics under his care, taking with him those which were held most sacred, and many valuable jewels besides, secretly fled to his native country. On his arrival in England, he immediately repaired to St. Alban's, the most celebrated abbey in the kingdom, and sold to one of the monks a silver gilt crucifix, two of the fingers of St. Margaret, and several gold rings set with precious stones.

He then took from his cloak-bag a certain wooden cross, which he affirmed with an oath was undoubtedly made of the wood of that cross on which our Saviour died, but the monks did not believe him, and he was allowed to depart with this inestimable but unrecognised treasure. Now this chaplain had two little sons, respecting whose maintenance and education he was extremely anxious, and with this object in view he visited many abbeys, offering the said cross on the condition of their receiving himself and his children as monks. Having suffered many repulses from the richer monasteries, he at last arrived at the priory of Broomholme, which was then miserably poor, and its buildings were of the most humble and inconvenient description. Requesting to see the prior and brethren, he showed them the aforesaid cross, made of two pieces of wood placed transversely, tho one over the other, the entire length being that of a man's hand. He humbly implored them to receive himself and his children as monks in compensation for this and other relics. The prior and brethren rejoiced at the acquisition of so valuable a treasure, and reverently taking this blessed wood into their oratory, placed it there with all becoming devotion. In the year of our Lord 1223 miracles began to be wrought in this monastery, to the honour and glory of the cross. Life was restored to the dead, sight to the blind, the lame were enabled to walk, lepers were cleansed, and devils were cast out. This cross was visited, adored, and worshipped, not only by the English people, but by natives of the most distant lands, who heard of these wonderful miracles.

But WALSINGHAM, it is said, stood at the head of all the Norfolk pilgrimages. Kings Henry III., Edward I., Edward II., Henry VIII., and a multitude of illustrious pilgrims from all parts of the world, visited "The Sacred Milk." King Henry VIII., who in the year 1539 desecrated the shrine of Walsingham, had in the earlier part of his reign twice visited it as a devotee, walking barefoot, it is said, from the palace of East Barsham to this place; and if we are to believe Sir Henry Spelman, King Henry on his death-bed bequeathed his soul to the care of our Lady of Walsingham!

Down even to recent times, aged Norfolk peasants have been known to term the Milky Way of the heavens "The Walsingham Way," as if specially created to point out the road to that once celebrated shrine; and in the days of Erasmus few Englishmen thought that they could prosper throughout the year unless, according to their means, they should have made some offering to the shrine of our Lady at Walsingham,

A chapel had been founded at Walsingham a little before the Conquest. The Virgin Mother was alleged to have appeared in person to the widow of Ricoldie de Faverches, and the chapel was said to have been built after the exact model of the *Sancta Casa* at Loretto—the sacred cottage which, according to the legend, had been miraculously transported by angels from Nazareth till it found its last resting-place at Loretto. According to an ancient narrative, the foundations of this chapel were originally laid where "The Wishing Wells" are now seen, but they were continually disarranged in a most unaccountable way, till the founders at last recognised this circumstance as a token of the will of Heaven, and the site was removed to the north-west, where the chapel afterwards stood.

For upwards of five centuries from that date Walsingham flourished gloriously, having been resorted to by numerous pilgrims from all parts of the world, and enriched by their benefactions. In one year the offerings at this shrine amounted to £260, which cannot be estimated at less than £3,000 of our present currency, and in one week (while the visitors were there) the gifts amounted to 133 shillings, or about £61 10s. present value, independently of donations in wax, which were a considerable source of revenue. From the Paston Letters we learn that when John Paston lay ill at the Inner Temple, his mother (in addition to a former offering) presented *an image of his weight in wax* to the shrine of our Lady of Walsingham.

Walsingham Priory has been for many years a mere wreck of what it once was, but with the help of Erasmus, who visited it just previous to its being dismantled, we may in some measure be enabled to see it in its ancient glories. After praising in general terms the beauty of the church, he describes more particularly the chapel of the Blessed Virgin Mary, which was then in an unfinished state, or, in other words, with the doors and windows open to the weather. Nevertheless it enclosed a small wooden chapel of exceeding splendour, to which pilgrims were admitted through small wickets at the sides. It had no windows, but a multitude of wax tapers continually burning supplied the want of natural light, while the fumes of incense breathed forth the most delicious perfume. "You would pronounce it," says Erasmus, "the very dwelling-place of the Gods, such is the blaze of silver and gold and jewels on every side!"

One of the canons was always in attendance to receive the
oblations of the faithful, not that it was compulsory to give
anything, but he says many gave because he was looking on,
while others pretended to give but actually stole.

He describes this magnificent chapel as having then contained many statues of the saints—some of silver, others of
solid gold; and they exhibited to him at the same time
altar plate, jewels, and other valuable treasures, which he
says would have taken the whole day even to enumerate.

Closely adjacent to the church was a building which,
according to the legend, had, like the *Sancta Casa* at
Loretto, been suddenly transported by a miracle from a
great distance in the very depth of winter, and when the
ground was thickly covered with snow, while at the same
time two wells gushed forth from the ground beneath at the
command of the Blessed Virgin Mary. They were wonderfully cold, and said to be endowed with healing virtues as
far as regarded all diseases of the head and stomach. When
he heard these things, Erasmus looked around him with
amazement. Everything that he saw appeared to be new,
and yet this legend extended into a very remote antiquity.
He says, "Looking around me, I enquired how many years
had elapsed since the house was brought thither, to which
the canon replied, 'Several centuries.' 'And yet,' I rejoined, 'these walls do not appear to be old!' The guide
assented. 'Nor yet these wooden columns!' He did not
deny that they had been very recently erected, and indeed
the thing spoke for itself. 'And then again,' I said, 'the
roof and reeds appear to be even still more recent.' This
he readily allowed. 'And as to these beams and cross-beams,
they do not seem to have been put up many years.' He
acknowledged the fact. And now, when no part of the
building had eluded this scrutiny—'Whence then,' I
asked, 'do it appear that this house was brought from
so great a distance?' Immediately the guide pointed
out a very ancient bear's skin, nailed to the roof, and

laughed at my dulness for having overlooked so manifest an argument."

In the large gate of the priory, the guide pointed out to Erasmus a very small wicket, about an ell high and three-quarters of an ell wide, through which even a foot passenger could only pass by stooping and stepping carefully over the lower ledge. They assured Erasmus that in the year 1314 a knight on horseback, fleeing from the eager pursuit of his enemies, called upon the Blessed Virgin in his extremity, and that, without dismounting, he and his steed were miraculously and instantly conveyed through this narrow opening. A brass plate is said to have been fastened to the gate in perpetual memory of this wonderful event.

They exhibited to Erasmus a finger joint of gigantic proportions, telling him that it had belonged to St. Peter. He enquired of the attendant whether he was to understand the Apostle of that name? and being answered in the affirmative, "Then," exclaimed Erasmus, "St. Peter must have been a man of prodigious stature!" at which one of the pilgrims unfortunately laughed, and the guide was only to be appeased by the payment of an extra fee.

The most illustrious relic which this monastery possessed was "The Sacred Milk." This was produced with great solemnity. The canon in attendance put on his surplice and stole, and having prostrated himself before the altar in prayer, drew forth with much reverence the crystal ampoule in which it was contained, and held it to the pilgrims, who kissed it as they knelt. He at the same time received their oblations on a wooden tablet, such as were then used to collect tolls in Germany. Erasmus read on an inscription in the Lady Chapel that a certain pious man named William, a native of Paris, a most diligent collector of relics, went in the course of his travels to Constantinople, of which his brother happened to be then Patriarch. This brother told him about "The Sacred Milk," earnestly advising him to beg, buy, or *steal it*, as being far more valuable than any of his other relics, or even the whole of them put together. William, however, obtained the relic honestly after all. He persuaded a nun to give him a portion of the milk, but on the journey homewards he was death-stricken. In his last mortal agony, William conjured a friend to convey this precious relic to the church of St. Genevieve at Paris. This his friend faithfully promised to do, but he also was assailed by a deadly malady, and being at the point of death, entrusted the sacred deposit to an English earl, who religiously fulfilled the injunction, but solicited and obtained from the clergy to whom he conveyed the relic that portion which was subsequently enshrined at Walsingham.

The Rev. Richard Hart, in reviewing some of the above facts, says : "Most assuredly we have but little cause to regret the circumstance that pilgrims are no longer matters of daily experience. In too many instances we know that they degenerated into a fashionable lounge—the refuge of frivolity—and very gross and flagrant abuses were the natural result. In other instances, he who had violated the laws of God and man visited the shrine, either as an imposed penance or as a voluntary expiation of his guilt; while the superstitious devotee, in utter forgetfulness of the duties which he owed to his family and his home, wandered about from shrine to shrine, laying up for himself, as he fondly imagined, a large stock of merit against the time to come. Still it would be unjust to deny that some beneficial results may have arisen out of this exploded system. When the whole continent of Europe was convulsed with war, the person of the pilgrim was held sacred; and shielded by a common religion, he could travel even through a hostile country fearlessly and unmolested. Pilgrimages also materially tended towards the structure and decoration of our churches. England was in those times much less wealthy than she is at the present day, yet the most magnificent churches, still the glory of our land, were erected and endowed with an unsparing liberality."

FEASTS AND PAGEANTS.

THE city of Norwich has for many centuries been celebrated
for its shows, its festivals, and its pageants. Prior to and
during a portion of the Tudor period of Norwich history,
Whit-Monday and Tuesday were perhaps the most popular
of all the festival days in the year. Miracle plays were exhibited by a procession in the streets on these anniversary
days, and not merely the inhabitants of the city assembled,
but the people also from all the surrounding districts may
be said to have flocked into the city to witness these rude
dramatic entertainments. They possess considerable interest
at the present day in consequence of the excellent illustrations which they give of the life and amusements of the
people in the middle ages.

In the dark ages, when the Bible was not permitted to
circulate among the people, these miracle plays constituted
an attempt on the part of the monks—some of whom were
authors and others were actors—to supplant the Pagan revels
of the olden time by amusements that more particularly
referred to Christian beliefs and church usages. The passion
for dramatic representation has ever been a strong one among
the masses of the people, and those rude and irreverent stage
amusements which delighted our ancestors have through
the force of social progress had to make way for the elabo-
rate stage mechanism and dramatic display of the 18th and
19th centuries.

The miracle plays were performed at Norwich and elsewhere in the open air, and they were got up at such an enormous cost that the St. Luke's Guild—a fraternity composed
of the pewterers, braziers, plumbers, bell founders, and other
trades of the city—which had for many years the entire
management and burden of these Whit-Monday exhibitions,

H

was almost ruined by the expense. To relieve themselves, the brethren of this guild addressed a petition to the Mayor and Corporation of Norwich, praying that every occupation in the city should be compelled to set forth and bear the expense of one pageant in the Whitsuntide dramatic procession entertainments. As each branch of trade had then its own company or trade guild, bound together on the " protection " principle for their own common advantage, and governed by laws of their own, it was easy to make such an arrangement, and the Mayor and Corporation, after hearing the petition, agreed that henceforth every occupation in the city should find and set forth one such pageant in the procession on Monday in Pentecost week as should be appointed by the Mayor and Aldermen.

Mr. Henry Harrod found in the *Assembly Book* in the Record Room of the Corporation, the following list of the early Norwich pageants :

1. Mercers, Drapers, Haberdashers   ...   Creation of the World.
2. Glasiers, Steyners, Screveners, Pchemyters, Carpenters, Gravers, Caryers, Colermakers, Whelewrights ...   .   Helle Carte.
3. Grocers, Raffemen (Chandlers)   ...   Paradyse.
4. Shermen, Fullers, Thik Woollen Weavers, Coolightmakers, Masons, Lyme Bruers   ...   .   Abell and Cain.
5. Bakers, Bruers, Inkepers, Cooks, Millers, Vynteners, Coupers ...   Noyse Shipp.
6. Taillors, Broderers, Reders, and Tylers   Abraham and Isaak.
7. Tanners, Coryors, Cordwainers   Moises and Aaron, with the Children of Israel, and Pharo with his Knyghts.
8. Smythes   ...   .   Conflict of David and Golias.
9. Dyers, Calaunderers, Goldsmythes, Goldbeters, Saddlers, Pewterers, and Brasyers   ...   .   The Birth of Christe, with Shepherds and Three Kyngs of Colen.

10. Barbers, Waxchandlers, Surgeons, Fisitians, Hardwaremen, Hatters, Cappers, Skinners, Glovers, Poyntemakers, Girdelers, Pursers, Bagmakers, "Scapps," Wyre-drawers, Cardmakers ... ... } The Baptysme of Christe.

11. Bochers, Fishmongers, Watermen ... Resurrection.

12. Worsted Weavers ... ... The Holy Gost.

This bare list of pageants and the trades by whom they were performed is all that Mr. Harrod found respecting the matter in the archives of the Corporation ; bu' as the same Miracle Plays were represented in other cities and towns, a very fair idea of the pageants that drew thousands of our ancestors to Tombland and Castle Hill may be obtained by a reference to other accounts that have been published.

The pageants were performed on movable stages, constructed for the purpose. Each company brought forth its pageant and the carriage or stage in which they played. These carriages were high places, made like two rooms, one above the other, open at the top. The lower room was used as a dressing room, the higher room was the performing place. By an excellent arrangement, to prevent crowding, each play was performed in the principal streets and public places in the city, and scaffolds were erected to enable some of the spectators to sit during the performance. The first probably begun on Tombland, and then moved on to the Market Hill, which was most likely the Mayor's position at the show. By the time this pageant was ended, the second was ready to take its place, and then it moved forward to another street, and then to another, &c., so that all the pageants were being exhibited at different places in the city at the same time. Order was thus, to a great extent, well preserved, in spite of the great concourse of people from all places round who came to enjoy the spectacle.

The pageants were introduced by proclamation made by three heralds, who, after a flourish of trumpets, announced in a lengthy prologue the various parts of the Miracle Play that were to be shown. As these rude dramas for the most part followed the Bible narrative very closely, it will only be necessary to describe particular portions, and notice a few of the legends and peculiarities mixed up with them.

The first of the Norwich pageants, the *Creation of the World,* was most likely the same as that played at Chester, Wakefield, and other places. The performance at one of these is thus described by an eye-witness :—" The end of a barn being taken away, a dark hole appeared, hung with tapestry the wrong side outwards, a curtain running along and dividing the middle. On this stage the Creation was performed. A stupid-looking Capuchin personated the Creator. He entered in a large full-bottomed wig, with a false beard, wearing over the rusty dress of his order a brocade morning gown. He first came on, making his way through the tapestry, groping about, and purposely running his head against posts, exclaiming, with a sort of peevish authority, ' Let there be light,' at the same time pushing the tapestry right and left, and disclosing a glimmer through linen cloths from candles placed behind them. The creation of the sea was represented by the pouring of water upon the stage, and the making of dry land by the throwing of mould. Angels were personated by girls and young priests, habited in dresses (hired from a masquerade shop), to which the wings of geese were clumsily attached near the shoulders. The angels actively assisted the character in the flowered dressing gown in producing the stars, moon, and sun. To represent winged fowl, a number of cocks and hens were fluttered about, and for other living creatures some cattle were driven on the stage, with a well shod horse and two pigs with rings in their noses. Soon after, Adam appeared. He was a clumsy fellow in a strangely-shaped wig, and, being closely clad with a sort of coarse stocking, looked quite as grotesque as in the worst of the old woodcuts, and something like Orson, but not so decent. He stalked about wondering at everything, and was followed from among the beasts by a large ugly mastiff with a brass collar on. When he reclined to sleep preparatory to the introduction of Eve, the mastiff lay down by him. This occasioned some strife between the old man in brocade, Adam, and the dog, who refused to quit his post; nor would he move when the angels tried to whistle him off. The performance proceeded to the supposed extraction of the rib from the dog's master, which being brought forward and shewn to the audience, was carried back to be succeeded by Eve, who, in order to seem rising from Adam's side, was dragged up from behind his back through an ill-concealed and an equally ill-contrived trap-door by the performer in brocade. As he lifted her over, the dog, being trod upon, frightened her by a sudden snap, so that she tumbled upon Adam. This obtained a hearty kick from a clumsy angel to the dog, who consoled himself by discovering the rib produced before, which being a beef bone he tried his teeth upon."

The next pageant was *Paradise*, provided by the grocers and raffemen. In the grocers' books, now lost, were the items of expenditure about this pageant, among others for painting clothes for Adam, Eve, &c. In the French collections, a legendary incident is introduced in this play. When Adam attempts to swallow the apple, it will not stir, and, according to the legend, this was the cause of the lump in the man's throat, which has been preserved ever since.

The third pageant, *Helle Carte*, was brought forth by the glaziers, &c., and was certainly the most singular one of the series. In some places where this pageant was represented, it took the form of a monstrous and grotesque head, having a sort of crown of spikes across the forehead, above which sat a devil with four spotted wings as porter of hell, holding in his hand a hook with three prongs, of the form usually depicted in all infernal scenes from a very early period. A devil behind held a torch, and the scene was enlivened by male and female demons in grotesque costumes, who danced with comic evolutions to the music of a third demon, who lustily plays on an infernal bagpipe, the chanter of which assumes the form of a serpent. On some occasions drunkards were forced to swallow burning wine, and the whole scene was specially designed to impress the spectator with a horror of hell torments. An illuminated drawing in the British Museum shows that the huge painted hell mouth was made to open and shut, and demons are represented dragging into it a variety of classes of dishonest people. The devils that busied themselves in the most grotesque fashion about this pageant were especial favourites with the people, and indulged in many a jest with the unfortunates who fell into their clutches; and the authors of the old mysteries sometimes gave them an opportunity to display their vagaries by introducing a little episode, such as the "cheating hostess of Chester," in the mystery there performed, with whom the audience could have but little sympathy, and would therefore exceedingly enjoy the welcome given her by Satan and the demons:

> Welcome, dear darling, to endless bale,
>   Using cards, dice, and cups small,
> With many false oaths to sell thy ale;
>   Now thou shalt have a feast.

At Coventry in 1556 persons were paid for "keepynge" or attending at hell mouth, probably to open and shut it. The devils were dressed in coats and hose of canvas, and were covered with hair. It is found from the payments that these demons, like the modern theatrical clowns, were paid extra wages for the extra exertion required from them.*

---

* Some of the payments in the old books are very curious, and others, although very absurd, are set down as matters of account with the utmost gravity. Thus we have "Payd to ye demon, xxi.d.," while the bishops have but one shilling each, and the angels only eightpence. Again: " Payd Pilate, the bishop, and knights, to drink between the stages, ix.d; payd for setting of the world on fyer, v.d.; payd for half a yard of rede sea, vi.d.; payd for kepyn of fyer at hell mouthe, iiij.d." These last items show that some attention was paid to theatrical effect in these pageants, though the charges read oddly enough now.

The fifth pageant, *Noyse Shipp*, was brought forth by the bakers. This was a very popular play, as a considerable portion consisted of disputes between Noah and his wife, and her rebellious disposition afforded much amusement to the people. Noah's wife preferred staying with her gossips to entering the Ark, and, as one writer says, with the characteristic perverseness of women, had to be dragged into it by her son Shem, when she gives her husband a box on the ear.

Of the details of several of the other pageants, no records have been found, and of the others the details are too meagre or uninteresting to be repeated here.

No information has come to us as to the time when these Miracle Plays were first performed in Norwich, but we know that the Reformation had not the immediate effect of annihilating these observances, for the Corpus Christi procession was kept up years after. Mr. Harrod says that the plays were put down in Norwich, and that in about ten or twelve years the Grocers' Company broke up and sold a dilapidated stage, the last of their pageant carriages.

Of the provincial mayoralty processions, that of Norwich was well known as one of the most interesting. It exhibited some peculiar features of " pomp and antique pageantry," even until the year 1835, when the old Corporation was legislatively abolished. In the olden time all the trade guilds or confraternities, preceded by their banners, marched through the principal streets to the Cathedral. By the statutes of 31 Henry VIII. and 1 Edward VI., all the guilds except that of St. George's Company were abolished, but the pageant of St. George and the Dragon and St. Margaret always appeared until that once opulent and important brotherhood was dissolved in 1731. Their annual processions were generally very grand, and they invariably exhibited their patron saint in great glory. Blomefield has furnished us with many items on this subject, showing their great liberality. Thus, in 1534, Philip Foreman is ordered " to be George this year, and to have £10 for his labour and finding apparel;" a very large sum when the value of money at that time is considered. In 1537 was "bought for the apparel of the George and Margaret eight yards of tawny and four yards of crimson velvet, to be in the custody of the aldermen," so that St. Margaret,* who is always painted with the Dragon as well as St. George, also appeared in the procession, and was called the Lady of the Guild. In 1468, in the inventory of the goods belonging to the guild, is "a scarlet gown for the George, with blue garters"—(in the reign of Edward IV. the colour of the gown or surcoat of the Knights of the Garter was changed from blue to purple, and it was embroidered all over with blue garters; the hood was similarly decorated)—" a coat of armour for the George, beaten with silver; a chaplet for St. George, with a brooch of common gilt; and all the horse's furniture, a dragon, a basnet, a pair of gauntlets, two white gowns for the hench-men, and a sword, the scabbard covered with velvet and bossed."

In 1549 the company sold their old pageant-dresses, and among them a black velvet vestment, a jerkin of crimson velvet, a cap of russet velvet, a coat of armour of white damask, with a red cross; a horse harness of black velvet, with copper buckles, gilt, for the George; and a horse har-ness of crimson velvet, with flowers of gold, for the Lady. In 1556, "a gown of crimson velvet, pirled with gold," was bought for the George. In 1558, it was ordered " that ther shall be neither George nor Margaret, but for pastime the Dragon to come in and show himself as in other yeres."

---

* The legend of this saint assures us that, in answer to her prayer for a conflict face to face with her secret and hidden enemy, the devil, he ap-peared to her in the shape of a dragon and swallowed her alive, and that while in his stomach she made the sign of the cross, which caused him to burst asunder, and she thus "issued out all whole and sound." There is a painting by Raffaelle of this event, in which the saint is represented with her foot on the head of a gigantic dragon, and holding a palm branch.— Fairholt's Introduction to *The Civic Garland.*

When the company dissolved itself in 1731, the inventory of their goods contained the following items connected with pageants, and the value set upon them :

One large silver-headed staff, with the effigies of St. George on horseback trampling the Dragon under his feet	£5	5	0
One new dragon, commonly called Snap-Dragon	3	3	0
Two standards, one of St. George and the Dragon and the other the English colours	1	1	0
Four sashes for the standard-bearers	0	10	6
Two habits for the standard-bearers	2	2	0
Five habits for the wiflers	2	12	6
Two habits, one for the club-bearer, another for his man, who are now called *fools*	0	10	6

The club-bearers and whifflers were always seen in the London pageants, their duty being to clear the way, and the Norwich Corporation retained their whifflers to the last. The frontispiece to the first part of my *Lord Mayors' Pageants* represents the London civic whiffler of the time of Charles I., and the last of his race appeared at Norwich previous to the operation of the Reform Bill in 1832. His costume was curious, and had been handed down from the age of the Tudors. It consisted of white stockings, gartered below the knee with crimson ribbons, capacious trunk breeches of blue plush, a doublet of white cotton, with full sleeves, trimmed with light blue ribbons and ornamented with gilt buttons, a hat made of crimson cloth and edged with white ribbon, having a large blue bow and white feather; his shoes were decorated with large white rosettes. There were four whifflers employed, and each held a sword, broad and short in the blade, but having a long handle grasped by both hands. It was blunt at the point and without edge, and with this harmless but dexterously-flourished weapon, which they frequently threw up into the air and caught in its descent with unerring precision, they contrived by a sort of half-leaping, half-pirouetting movement, without hurting any one, to make all bystanders cautious how they came within reach of their varied evolutions, and thus effectually did the business of pioneering for the cavalcade, they being, like the heralds of ancient Rome, held sacred from personal insult or violence, which not even the lowest of the populace ever attempted.*

Next these men, and at the head of the procession, appeared the Dragon, familiarly known as Snap. The universal popularity of the Dragon in public shows and on great festivities has been frequently noted, both in England and on the Continent. The last of the Dragons that figured at Norwich has been thus described. The body of the monster was formed of light materials, being composed of canvas stretched over a frame-work of wood; the outside was painted of a sea-green colour, with gilt scales, picked out with red. The body was five feet in length, and was sometimes used to secrete wine abstracted from the mayor's cellars. The neck was capable of elongation (measuring three feet and a-half when extended), was supported by springs attached to the body, and was capable of being turned in any direction at the will of the bearer. From between the ears the whole outer extremity of the back was surmounted by a sort of mane of crimson colour, tied in fantastic knots around the juncture of the enormous tail, which extended about five feet, curling at the further extremity. Between the wings was a small aperture for air, and beneath the body was hung a sort of petticoat to conceal the legs of the bearer, whose feet were furnished with large claws. The Dragon's head had its lower jaw furnished with a plate of iron resembling a horseshoe; it was formerly garnished with enormous nails, which produced a terrible

---

* The office had been held in the family of the last of the whifflers, William Dowsing, for more than two centuries, and mention is made in Kemp's *Nine Days' Wonder* of their being employed when he danced into Norwich in 1599. A coloured print of this whiffler was published in 1841 by Mr. C. Muskett of Norwich.

clatter when the jaws met together. They were made to open and shut by means of strings, and the children amused themselves by throwing halfpence into the gaping mouth, which turned to the right and left during the whole of the journey, noisily clashing its jaws, from which the Dragon's popular name of Snap was probably derived.

The company of St. George of Norwich was founded in 1385, being a society of brethren and sisters in honour of the martyr St. George, who by voluntary subscriptions provided a chaplain to celebrate service every day before the high altar on the south side of the Cathedral for the welfare of the brethren and sisters of the guild when alive, and the repose of their souls when dead; and thus they continued until Henry V. granted them a charter, by which they were incorporated by the name of the aldermen, masters, brethren, and sisters of the fraternity or guild of St. George in Norwich, and they annually chose one alderman, four masters, and twenty-four for the assembly or common council. The company having dwindled to poverty, gave up their charter, books, and goods to the city in 1731, in consideration of their debts, which amounted to £236 15s. 1d., being paid by the Corporation.

THE NORWICH GUILD—A MAYOR'S FEAST : TEMP. ELIZABETH.

The Earls of Northumberland and Huntingdon, the Lords Thomas Howard and Willoughby, with many other noblemen and knights, paid a visit to the Duke of Norfolk, and were entertained, with their retinue, at the Duke's Palace in Norwich in 1561. The guild happening at this time, William Mingay, Esq., then Mayor, invited them and their ladies to the feast, which they accepted, and expressed the greatest satisfaction at their generous and hospitable reception. At the entertainment the Duke and Duchess of Norfolk sat first, then the three Earls of Northumberland, Huntingdon, and Surrey, Lord Thomas Howard, Lord

Scroop and his lady, Lord and Lady Bartlet, Lord Aberga-venny, with so many peers, knights, and ladies, that the hall could scarcely contain them and their retinue. The Mayor's share of the expense was one pound twelve shillings and ninepence, the feast-makers, four in number, paying the rest. The Mayor's bill of fare was as follows:

Eight stone of beef, at 8d. a stone, and a sirloin	0	5	8
Two collars of brawn	0	1	0
Four cheeses, at 4d. a cheese	0	1	4
Eight pints of butter	0	1	6
A hinder quarter of veal	0	0	10
A leg of mutton	0	0	5
A fore quarter of veal	0	0	5
Loin of mutton and shoulder of veal	0	0	9
Breast and coat of mutton	0	0	7
Six pullets	0	1	0
Four couple of rabbits	0	1	8
Four brace of partridges	0	2	0
Two Guinea cocks	0	1	6
Two couple of mallards	0	1	0
Thirty-four eggs	0	0	6
Bushel of flour	0	0	6
Peck of oatmeal	0	0	2
Sixteen white bread loaves	0	0	4
Eighteen loaves of white wheat bread	0	0	9
Three loaves of Meslin bread	0	0	3
Nutmegs, mace, cinnamon, and cloves	0	0	3
Four pounds of Barbary sugar	0	1	0
Sixteen oranges	0	0	2
A barrel of double strong beer	0	2	6
A barrel of table beer	0	1	0
A quarter of wood	0	2	2
Two gallons of white wine and canary ...	0	2	0
Fruit, almonds, sweet water, perfumes	0	0	4
The cook's wages	0	1	2
Total	£1	12	9

After dinner, Mr. John Martyn, a wealthy citizen of Norwich, made the following speech: "Maister Mayor of

Norwich, and it please your worship, you have feasted us like a king. God bless the Queen's grace. We have fed plentifully, and now whilom I can speak plain English, I heartily thank you, Maister Mayor, and so do we all. Answer, boys, answer. Your beer is pleasant and potent, and will soon catch us by the *caput* and stop our manners; and so huzza for the Queen's Majesty's Grace, and all her bonny-browed dames of honour. Huzza for Maister Mayor and our good dame Mayoress, his noble Grace *—there he is, God bless him—and all this jolly company. To all our friends round county who have a penny in their purse and an English heart in their bodies to keep out Spanish dons and papists with their faggots to burn our whiskers. Shove it about, twirl your capcases, handle your jugs, and huzza for Maister Mayor and his brethren their worships."

ST. VALENTINE'S DAY.

The old-fashioned festivals of mirth and good fellowship, wherein all classes delighted to join, are being rapidly dispelled by the cold and formal conventionalities of modern society. May Day, with its glorious sylvan customs, is now a thing of the past. Christmas and Easter festivals have lost their joyous character; and even St. Valentine's Day— the day of days in our villages and small towns for fun and frolic, in the shape of tender messages in verse and doggrel rhymes—has altogether altered its characteristic features during the last half-century. In Norwich and the towns of Norfolk the celebration of St. Valentine is somewhat peculiar, and demands a notice at our hands.

It is customary at Norwich for valentines to be received, not on the 14th of February as in other districts, but on the evening of the 13th, St. Valentine's Eve. Another peculiar feature connected with this festival in Norfolk is that the valentine, instead of being an ornamental billet-doux, is

* The Duke of Norfolk.

some article of intrinsic value. The Norwich papers for some two or three weeks prior to St. Valentine's Day contain a number of advertisements attracting attention to goods that are declared suitable for valentine presents. Life-size walking dolls, performing acrobats, clock-work trains, vases, lustres, workboxes, desks, clocks and watches, jewellery and electro-plated goods of every kind, shawls and mantles, furs and muslins, dressing bags and albums, attractive gift books, all sorts of fancy articles, and even a guinea knife cleaner, have been advertised as suitable for valentine presents. Tradesmen anxiously obtain all kinds of novelties for the season, and many of the shops most noted for the variety of their stocks are literally besieged by customers on Valentine's Eve. The mode of delivering these valentines is also peculiar. The parcel containing the valentine is placed on the doorstep on Valentine's Eve, and a thundering rap being given at the door, the messenger takes to his heels, and is off instantly. Those in the house, knowing well enough the purpose of such announcing rap, quickly fetch in the various treasures. Where there is a young family, the raps are likely to be frequent, and the juveniles get into a perfect furore of excitement on such evenings.

PLOUGH MONDAY.

Plough Monday was the name given to a rustic festival held on the Monday after the feast of the Epiphany, commonly called Twelfth Day, on which day, after the festivities of Christmas, it was in olden time customary to resume the labour of agriculture. There is in the tower of the church at Cawston a gallery called the Plough Rood, and on this the following lines are carved :

> God spede the plow, and send us ale corn enow,
> 　Our purpose for to make
> At . . . . of the plow lite of Lygate,
> 　Be merry and glad;
> What good ale this work mad.

This is believed to refer to those celebrations of Plough Monday which prior to the Reformation were not unusual in connection with guilds in agricultural districts. The members of the guild would go on Plough Monday to church, and kneeling before the plow rood, pray " God spede the plow, and send us ale corn enow our purpose for to make ;" that is, to carry on their labours on the land, and to spend a joyful day at the plow light of Lygate, and there to show their belief in the need of good ale to enable them to work, they say, " Be merry and glad, 'twas good ale this work mad." After which they, gaily dressed, passed in procession through the village, dragging a plough that had been blessed and censed with incense by the priest, and gathering largess as they went along. It seems strange to us to pray for ale, but in those times ale was everywhere the common beverage of the country, and was thought as necessary for the support of life as bread, and therefore it was thought as natural to pray for ale corn to make ale with, as to pray for daily bread. Bread and ale gave them strength to plough the land.

HARVEST CATCH.

A gentleman of Norfolk writing in 1827 to Mr. Hone, the Editor of *The Table Book*, gave some amusing particulars of the old customs in the county connected with the harvest supper. The health-drinking catch, which was the last thing before parting, he has given us. The first had relation to the mistress, and was as follows :

Now supper is over, and all things are past,
Here's our mistress's good health in a full flowing glass;
She is a good mistress, she provides us good cheer;
Here's our mistress's good health, boys—come drink *half* your beer.
She is a good mistress, she provides us good cheer;
Here's our mistress's good health, boys—come drink *off* your beer.

During the time the catch is going round, the whole party are standing, and with the exception of the drinker they join in chorus. The glass circulates, beginning with the "Lord," in regular succession through the "company," after that it is handed to the visitors, the harvestmen of gone-by days, who are not forgotten on the occasion. If the drinker be taken off his guard, and should drink off his beer at the pause in the catch, he is liable to a forfeit. If one of the chorus misplaces the words half and off, which not unfrequently happens at the heel of an evening, he incurs a similar penalty.

After the mistress comes the master :

Here's health to our master, the Lord of the feast,
God bless his endeavours and send him increase,
And send him good crops, that we may meet another year;
Here's our master's good health, boys—come drink *half* your beer.
God send him good crops, &c.—come drink *off* your beer.

Where the beer flows very freely, and there is a family, the catch is sometimes carried on through the different branches with variations composed for the purpose, perhaps at the spur of the moment, and some of them have been very happily conceived.

CHRISTMAS CUSTOM IN NORFOLK.

During the last century it was the custom on large farms to make a great quantity of cider of two qualities, and at Christmas the best cider was tapped, and so long as the yule log, or Christmas block, was burning, say for some ten or twelve days, the servants had the cider in common. The worst or slowest burning log was held in reserve by the servants till Christmastide; and till that was consumed, a small piece excepted, which was retained till another year for the purpose of setting fire to the new yule log, the general beverage of the family was the best cider, of which one or more casks were made expressly for the occasion twelve months before it was required. Master, mistress, and servants took their meals together.

CUSTOMARY VIANDS FOR PARTICULAR DAYS.

On certain days of the year it was the custom of old times to prepare a particular kind of food, which was considered peculiar to that day. Some of these customs are still in use amongst us. On Michaelmas Day, for instance, many persons who can afford it have a roast goose for dinner. Christmas is a season of festivity in all parts of the kingdom, but in Norfolk that festival was formerly begun in a way which was not general in other parts. On the morning of Christmas Day, in many farmhouses, a large quantity of frumerty used to be prepared, and the labourers on the farm, with their wives and children, were invited to breakfast upon it. It is considered a great treat, and is really a most nourishing and delicious food. Ale or mead, with a toast and nutmeg, was appropriated to Christmas Eve. Hot elderberry wine with spice was the usual regale for holiday friends. On Shrove Tuesday, pancakes and "coquilles" are indispensable, but the "fat hen" is now never threshed, nor indeed is there any tradition of that barbarous sport having been practised in these counties for many years. On Easter Sunday, a tansey pudding is provided in Norfolk, and on Whit-Sunday cheese cakes. Whitsuntide is always celebrated with baked custards, and, if possible, with gooseberry pies, and these delicacies are standing dishes throughout the whole of the festive season.

MAY DAY.

It was an old custom in Norfolk in most farmhouses that any servant who could bring in a branch of hawthorn in full blossom on the first of May, was entitled to a dish of cream for breakfast.

CURIOUS DOCUMENTS, &c.

THE PETITION OF THE NORFOLK REBELS IN 1549.

THE petition here printed is copied from the incomplete and charred M.S.* in the British Museum, from which Mr. Russell also printed it in his "*Kett's Rebellion in Norfolk; being a History of the great Civil Commotion that occurred at the time of the Reformation, in the reign of Edward VI:*"

THE LIST OF THE HUNDREDS AND THEIR REPRESENTATIVES.

[The hundred] of [N]orwich	
the hundred of ffourehoo†	Robert Kett
	Thomas Rolff
	William Kett
The hundred of north grenehowe‡ ...	Edmond fframyngham
	William Tydde
The hundred of South erpyngham ...	Reynold Thurston
	Iohn wolsy
the hundred of est fflegge and west flegge	Symond englysshe
	William pecke
The hundred of landryche§	George blomefild
	William herryson
the hundred of Eynsforth‖	Edmond belys
	Robert Sendall
the hundred of humbleyard	Thomas prycke
	henry hogekynges
the hundred of [nor]th erpyngham ...	Rychard Bevis
	William Dowty
[th]e hundred [of T]auerham¶	Thomas Garrod
	William petyr
[the h]undred of brothercrosse	Robert Mans[....]
	Robert Ede
The hundred off Blowfeld	John Spregey
	Elys hyll

* Harl. M.S., 204, leaf 75.   † Forehoe.   ‡ Greenhoe.
§ Launditch.   ‖ Eynesford.
¶ The hundred of Taverham occurs in Blomefield's *Norfolk* (ed. 1809),
p. 467.

The hundred off walsham	John Kytball
	Thomas Clerke
The hundred of Tunsted	John herper
	Richard lyon
The hundred of happyng	Edward Joye
	Thomas Clocke
the hundred of hensted	William Mowe
	Thomas hollyng
the hundred of holt	Iohn Bossell
	valentyn moore
The hundred of loudon and knaveryng* ...	Robert Ierold
	Richard ward
the hundred of north grenehowe	Edward Byrd
	Thomas tudenhn†
the hundred of metforth‡	Symond Nevell
	william howlyng
The hundred off ffrebrygge§	william heydon
	thomas Iacher
The hundred of Callowe	Robert Cottes
	Iohn Oxwyk
The hundred of depewade	William Browne
	Symond Sendall
. . . . . . Suff Co [?] ...	. . . .
	Richard wright

We pray your grace, that where it is enacted for Inclosyng, that it be not hurtfull to suche as have enclosed saffren groundes for they be gretly chargeablye to them, and that ffrome hensforth no man shall enclose eny more.

We certifie your grace, that where as the lordes of ther manours hath byn Charged with certen ffre rent, the same lordes hath sought meanes to charge ther ffre-holders to pay the same rent, contrarye to right.

We pray your grace, that no lord of no manner shall comon vppon the Comons.

We pray that prestes from hensforth shall purchase no londes, neyther ffre nor Bond; and the londes that they haue in possession may be letten to temporall men, as they wer in the ffyrst yere of the reign of kyng henry the vijth.

We pray that Rede-grounde and medowe grounde may be at suche price as they wer in the ffyrst yere of kyng henry the vijth.

---

* Loddon and Clavering.   † ? ham.   ‡ Mitford.   § Freebridge Lynn.

We pray that all marshysshe that ar holden of the kynges maiestie by ffre rent, or of eny other, may be ageyn at the price that they wer in the ffirst yere of kyng henry the vijth.

We pray that all Busshelles within your realme be of on scice, that is to sey, to be in mesure viij gallons.

[We] pray that [the parsons] or vicars that be notable to preche and sett forth the woorde of god to hys parissheners may be clerely putt from hys benyfice, and the parissheners there to chose an other, or elles the pateron or lord of the towne.

We pray that the paymentes of castillward rent, and blanche fferme, and office landes, whiche hath byn accostomed to be gathered of the tenamentes, where as we suppose the lordes ought to pay the same to ther balyffes for ther rentes gatheryng, and not the tenantes.

We p[r]ay that no man vnder the degre of a knyght or esquyer kepe a dowe house, except it hath byn of en ould aunchyent costome.

We pray that all ffreholders and copieholders may take the profightes of all comons, and ther to comon, and the lordes not to comon nor take profightes of the same.

We pray that no ffeodorye within your shires shalbe a counceller to eny man in his office makyng, whereby the kyng may be trulye serued, so that a man beeng of good consyence may be yerely chosyn to the same office by the comons of the same sheyre.

We pray your grace to take all libertie of lete into your owne handes, whereby all men may quyetly enioye ther comon with all profightes.

We pray that copiehould londes that is onresonable rented, may go as it dyd in the ffirst yere of kyng henry the vij; and that at the deth of a tenante, or of a sale, the same landes to be charged with an esey ffyne, as a capon, or a resonable some of money, ffor a remembrance.

[We] pray that no prest [shall be a chaplain residential, steward], nor no other officer to eny man of honor or whorshyppe, but only to be resydent vppon ther benefices, wherby ther parissheners may be enstructed with the lawes of god.

We pray that all bonde men may be made ffre,* for god made all ffre with hys precious blode sheddyng.

---

* The time had not yet come for "bonde men" to obtain their freedom. Many years of fierce contention and of deadly strife were passed before this precious boon was secured to all. It was not till after the great Puritan struggle that the iniquities and oppressions that had been grafted on to the feudal system were abolished.

We pray that Ryvers may be ffre and comon to all men for ffysshyng and passage.

We pray to no man shalbe put by your Eschetour or ffeodarie to ffynde eny office, vnles he holdeth of your grace in cheyff or capite aboue x.li. by yere.

We pray that the pore mariners or ffyssheremen may haue the hole profightes of ther ffyshynges, as purpres, grampes, whalles, or eny gret ffysshe, so it be not preiudiciall to your grace.

We pray that euery propriatorie parson or vicar havyng a benifice of x.li. or more by yere, shall eyther by them selues or by some other person teche pore men's chyldren of ther parisshe the boke called the cathykysme* and the prymer.†

We pray that it be not lawfull to the lordes of eny manner to purchase londes frely, and to lett them out ageyn by copie of court roll, to ther gret advaunchement, and to the vndoyng of your pore subiectes.

We pray that no propriatorie parson or vicar (in consideracion of advoydin[g] trobyll and sute bet[w]yn them and ther pore parisshners, which they daly do procede and attempt), shall from hensforth take for the full contentacion of all the tenthes which now they do receyve, but viij.d. of the noble, in the full discharge of all other tythes.

[We pray that no man u]nder the degre of a [knyghte?] shall kepe any conyes vpon any of his owne ffrehold or copiehold, unless he pale them in, so that it shall not be to the comons noysoyns.

We pray that no person, of what estate degre or condicion he be, shall from hensforth sell the adwardshype of any chyld, but that the same chyld, if he lyve to his full age, shalbe at his owne chosyng concernyng his mariage, the kynges wardes only except.

We pray that no manner of person havyng a manner of his owne, shall be no other lordes balyf, but only his owne.

We pray that no lord, knyght, nor gentleman, shall have or take in ferme any spirituall promocion.

We pray your grace to gyve lycens and aucthorite by your gracious comyssion vnder your grett seall, to suche comyssioners as your pore

* "A Briefe Catechisme and Dialogue betwene the Husbande and his Wiffe;" also "The Instruccyon of the Truthe, wherein he teacheth the unlearned man." N. d., but published 1545.

† "A goodly prymer in Englysshe, newly corrected and prynted, with certeyne godly meditations and prayers added to the same very necessarye and profytable for all them that ryghte assuredlye understande not the latine and greke tongues." N. d., but published in 1535.

comons hath chosyn, or to as many of them as your maiestie and
your counsell shall app̄ynt and thynke mete, for to redresse and
refourme all suche good lawes, statutes, proclamacions, and all other
procedynges, whiche hath byn hydden by your Iustices of your
peace, Shreues, Escheatoures, and other your officers from your pore
comons synes the ffirst yere of the reign of your noble grandfather
kyng henry the seventh.

We pray that those your officers that hath offended your grace and
your comons, and so proved by the compleynt of your pore
comons do gyve onto those pore men so assembled iiij.d. euery day
so long as they have remayned ther.

We pray that no lorde, knyght, esquyer, nor gentleman, do grase
nor fede eny bullockes or shepe, if he may spend fforty poundes a
yere by his landes, but only for the provicion of his howse.

> By me Robert Kett
> By me Thomas Aldryche   Thomas Cod

RHYMING WILL.

The following rhyming will is transcribed from a *Common-
place Book* of· about the year 1740. The date of Ray's
Philosophical Letters (from which it was copied) is not
given :

From Mr. Ray's Philosophical Letters, p. 102.

Sr. Phil. Shippon to Mr. Ray.—An humoursome Rhythming will
of one More, who died not long since, about Mershland, in Norfolk,
and gave his estate to his Grand-daughter, now married to one Mr.
Shelton, a gentleman of this county that hath a good estate near
Bury.

> " In the name of God, Amen ! I, Thomas More,
> The 4th year of my Age above Three score,
> Revoking all the Wills I made before,
> Making this my last ; and First, I do implore
> Almighty God into his hand to take
> My Soul, which not alone himself did make,
> But did redeem it with the precious Blood
> Of his dear Son ; that Title still holds good.
> I next bequeath my Body to the Dust
> From whence it came, which is most just,
> Desiring yet that I be laid close by
> My eldest Daughter, tho' I know not why.

I leave my Grand child, Martha, her full due,
My Lands and all my Cattle, save a few
You shall hereafter in this Schedule find,
To piety or Charity design'd ;
Whom I my sole Executrix invest,
To pay my debts, and so take all the rest.
But since that she is under Age, I pray
Sir Edward Walpole* and her father may
The Supervisors be of this my Will ;
Provided that my Cousin Colvil still
And Major Spensly her assistants be :
Four honest men are more than two or three.
Then I shall not care how soon I die,
If they'll accept it, and I'll tell you why ;
There's not a man of them but is so just,
With whom almost my Soul I dare to trust.
Provided she doth make her son
Heir to my house at least, and half my Land ;
If she hath such, and when she hath so done,
She be a means to let him understand
It is my Will his name be written thus,
I, A. B. C. or D. Moore, *alias*

EPITAPH.

Here lies in this cold monument,
As appears by his last Will and Testament.
He was very rich, his name was More,
Who never knew poet die rich before ?
But to speak Truth, his Verses do shew it,
He liv'd a rich Man, but dy'd a poor poet.

MEDICAL CHARGES (1681—1732).

Surgeons connected with the Poor Law Board frequently
complain, and ofttimes not without reason, of the miserably

---

* It has been thought that some idea may be formed of the date of the
will from the mention of Sir Edward Walpole, but there have been *three*
of this name—1. Sir Edward Walpole of Houghton, born 1621, created
1661, died 1667 ; 2. Sir Edward Walpole of Pinchbush and Spalding, of
same family as above, created 1663, died 1669 ; 3. Sir Edward Walpole, son
of Sir Robert Walpole, born 1706, created 1753, died 1784. The reference is
probably to the first, who was M.P. for Lynn for many years.

small sums that are allowed at the present day for attendance on pauper patients, but the following items of medical charges, which appear in old account books of the parish of Pulham St. Mary Magdalen, Norfolk, not only contrast very curiously with the professional fees of modern times, but show that parochial surgeons were no better paid in the 17th than they are in the 19th century. The list of items cannot fail to interest the majority of my readers :

		£	s.	d.
1681.	It. Allowed for phisicke and Chirurgery for several poore people	00	16	06
1682.	It. Pd. Dr. Tubby for healing of Barber's thigh	0	2	6
	It. Pd. for getting ye widd. Hammond bled, & other charges for her & ym yt helpd and looked to her	0	2	6
1687.	Payd to dockter Tubby for setting Eliz. Newman's boyes arme	0	3	6
	To dockter Tubby for Administring fissake to John Bolton In siknes	0	2	0
1688.	Itm. To Richard goodwin's wife when sicke, & paid for her bleding and fissake and woode ...	0	5	0
	It. Pd. for bleding will Willby	0	0	6
	It. Pd. Tho. Tubby for heleing of Richard Goodwin's Boyes Arme	0	4	0
1689.	It. Pd. to Tho. Tubby for surgery for the poore as appears	00	7	0
1699.	Pd. to Doctor Yull for heeling old John Bowen leg last yeare	00	10	00
	Pd. for small things for Widdo Allen	00	01	04
	Pd. More for bleeding her 2 times	00	01	06
	Pd. Doctor Yull for looking to old John Bowen being bruised by a fall	00	05	00
1701.	Pd. Mr. Yull for a plaister for Miller's wife ...	00	01	00
1703.	Itm. Payd to Doctor Yull, he being fetcht from Norwich* for John Hines his wife when in Travaile of Child Birth	00	05	00
1710.	Paid Doctor Yull for curing young Tiler of the eyche	00	01	06
1722.	Item. Paid Mr. Yull for plaisters and salve for the poore	00	04	00

* A distance of fifteen miles.

1723. Item. Paid Mr. Yull for plaisters and salve for
the yeere 03 00 00
1732. Item. Paid Doctter Yull His bill for Robert
Kerrison when He was Ill 00 07 06

The original bills of Dr. Yull to which the last two items refer, were found pinned to the leaves of the book, apparently as vouchers for the entries. They are as follows:

Aprell the aiten, 1723

Rasaved of thon. dixe sen., the som of 3 pound fore the Ceure of Batlye, and godye Boise arme, and godye whipe, wich is in fooll.

By me Thomas Yull.

Robert Cearison his bill, augt. ye 7, 1732.

					s.	d.
Item, a purg					1	0
ye 8, a cordle					3	6
ye 10, a purg					1	0
ye 11, ditto					1	0
ye 13, ditto					1	0
					7	6

Oct. 26. Recd. the Contents of this bill p' me Tho. Yull.

No intimation is given of the nature of the disease with which Kerrison was afflicted, but it is presumed that the doctor's treatment was successful, as no record of his death at that time appears in the parish register.

HERRING PIES.

Prior to modern alterations in municipal laws, the customary duty or service rendered to the Crown by the city of Norwich on account of fee farm, consisted in the yearly delivery at Court of "twenty-four herring pies." This remarkable feudal tenure originated in times before the foundation of Yarmouth, when the valley of the Yare was still an estuary, and Norwich, now some eighteen miles from the

sea, an important fishing station. The course of procedure
was this : Out of their official allowance, the sheriffs of the
city for the time being annually made provision, according
to a prescribed formula, for the manufacture of these pies,
which were forthwith transmitted to the lord of the manor
of Carleton, to be by him or his tenant carried to the royal
palace and placed on the sovereign's table. The following
indenture, being the identical one to which Blomefield
(*Hist. Norw.* fol., 1741, pp. 263, 264) refers, will explain the
rest :

THIS INDENTURE, made at Norwich, at the Guildhall there, the
twenty seventh of September, at ten of ye clocke of ye forenoon of
ye same day, in ye twenty fifth year of ye reign of our Lord Charles
the 2nd, by ye grace of God of England, Scotland, France, and
Ireland, King, Defender of ye Faith, &c., and in ye year of our
Lord 1673, BETWEEN John Leverington and Robert Freeman,
sheriffs of ye city of Norwich, on one part, and Edward Eden,
gentleman, tenant of Thomas Lurd Richardson, Baron of Cramond,
&c., of ye other part, WITNESSETH, that ye aforesaid sheriffs, on ye
day, houre, and place aforesaid, delivered to ye said Edward Eden
one hundred herrings (viz., of ye large hundred), of ye first new
herrings that came to ye said city, in twenty four pies, well seasoned
with ye following spices, viz., halfe a pounde of ginger, halfe a
pounde of pepper, a quarter of cinnamon, one ounce of spice of
cloves, one ounce of long pepper, halfe an ounce of grains of paradise, and halfe an ounce of galangals, to be brought to ye King's
palace, wherever he is in England, and there to be delivered. AND
be it known that ye said Edward Eden or his attorney carrying ye
said pyes, shall receive at the king's house six loves, six dishes out of
ye kitchen, one flaggon of wine, one flaggon of beer, one truss of
hay, one bushel of oats, one prickett of wax, and six candles of
tallow; IN TESTIMONY of whiche ye parties aforesaid have alter-
nately set their seals to this Indenture, ye day, houre, and place, and
yeare aforesaid.

Blomefield gives at length a curious letter, dated
"Hampton Court, iiij. of Oct., 1629," from the household
officers of the king to the mayor and sheriffs of Norwich,
on the subject of these pies, which it seems in the instance

referred to "were not well baked in good and strong pastye as they ought to have been." Divers of them, also, were found to contain no more than "four herrings," whereas the tenure required five to be put into every pye at the least." Neither were they made of the *first* new herrings that reached the city. And other "just exceptions against the goodness of them" were likewise taken, to which a particular answer, "for his Majesty's better satisfaction," was demanded. The cost to the sheriffs of these pies in 1754 was £2, independently of carriage, &c.

TRIAL BY WAGER OF BATTEL.

Trial by wager of battel—a relic of feudal times which was not finally abolished in England till the year 1818—was practised in Norfolk upon many occasions, such trials being permitted for civil as well as criminal cases. Thus, in the 34th Henry III., Agnes, wife of Adam de Rattlesden, impleaded Richer de Reymes for the fourth part of a fee in Overstrand and Northrepps. Richer had released it to Roger de Herleberghe for eighty marks of silver. Roger was called to warrant it, and a duel, or combat of trial, was fought on this account between the said Roger and a freeman of Simon son of Hugh, in behalf and right of Agnes, and after that they came to an agreement.

The manner in which the barbarous trial of "wager of battel" was conducted, may be thus briefly stated. The battle was fought in the presence of the Court, and in the following form. At sunrise the parties assembled, and the lists were set out by the Court. The accuser and accused were to be bare-armed and bare-legged, and each of them armed with a wooden truncheon an ell long, and a square wooden target. All being ready, they took each other's hands, and supposing the case to be one of murder, each swore, the accuser that the accused did kill the deceased, and the accused swore that he did not. Each man was also required to swear that he had about him no bone, no stone, no charm of any sort, whereby the law of the devil may be exalted or the law of God depressed; after which they fought it out. If the accused could defend himself till the stars appeared in the evening, he was held to be acquitted, but if he was beaten or cried out so as to surrender, he was condemned to be hanged.

DUCKING STOOLS.

Blomefield, referring to the fact that St. George's Guild had a tenement in Norwich which they sometimes used as a Guildhall, adds, they had also customs at Fyve Brigge Stathe, and were obliged to find a cucke stool there. From the Court Book, he further notices two instances of the use of the cucke stool:

1562. A woman, for whoredom, to ryde on a cart with a paper in her hand, and tynklyd with a bason; and so at one o'clock to be had to the cokyng-stool, and ducked in the water.

1597. Margaret Grove, a common skould, to be carried with a bason rung before her, to the cucke stool at Fye Bridge, and there to be three times ducked.*

There was also a cucking stool at Harleston.

From the numerous references to the cucking stool in the ancient records of many boroughs, we have abundant proof that the ladies were in former times very frequently subject to visitations of ill tongue, and that their lords and masters were sufficiently ungallant to consider no remedy so effectual for preventing a recurrence of the disorder as the cold-water cure administered by means of the cucking or ducking stool.

The cucking or ducking stool was a means adopted for the punishment of scolds and incorrigible women by ducking them in the water, after having secured them in a chair or

* Blomefield's *History of Norfolk,* 1741, vol. 2, p. 739.

stool fixed at the end of a pole, serving as a lever by which they were immersed in some pond or river.

The practice continued till within the last century, and corporate bodies were required to furnish themselves with these appliances, as they are now enforced to provide and maintain fire engines.

PUNISHMENT OF BOILING TO DEATH.

The horrible punishment of boiling criminals to death for such a crime as poisoning, was inflicted in the time of Henry VIII., but this barbarous mode of executing justice did not, it is said, remain on the statute book for any lengthened period. A cauldron filled with water was fixed in the most public spot in whatever town the execution took place—in London Smithfield was the spot selected—and a fire being placed under, the culprit was plunged into the water as soon as it boiled. To increase the barbarity, a chain was affixed to the body, and by means of a gibbet the man or woman was pulled up and down in the boiling water until life was entirely extinct. An instance of this mode of punishment occurred at KING'S LYNN in the sixteenth century, as may be seen by the following record :

1531. This year here was a maid boiled to death in the Market Place for poisoning her mistress.*

PRESSING TO DEATH.

"Pressing to death" was a sentence passed upon the accused should he obstinately refuse to plead to the indictment, he not being "mute by the visitation of God." The Rev. Richard Hart says that this obsolete punishment was certainly practised in the county of Norfolk, though from having mislaid his notes, he was unfortunately unable to pro-

* *Notes and Queries*, vol. 5, p. 355, 1st Series.

duce any direct evidence of the fact. This most cruel sentence was actually pronounced upon a man of the name of Spiggott, accused of highway robbery, at the Old Bailey in the January of 1720, and there may have been still later examples.*

OBSOLETE PUNISHMENTS.

In many parts of England the scold's bridle, "to curb women's tongues that talk too idle," was in use in the sixteenth and seventeeth centuries. The machine was made of thin iron, and so contrived as to pass over and round the head, when the whole clasped together, and was fastened at the back of the neck by a small padlock. The bridle bit, as it was called, was a flat piece of iron about two inches long and one inch broad, which went into the mouth and kept down the tongue by its pressure. We have no evidence to offer of the use of such an instrument as this in Norfolk, but iron collars were used as a mode of punishment in Norfolk as late as the commencement of the present century. The description given of a case in the Norwich Workhouse in 1805 is horrifying as to the use of these instruments of torture. The statement emanated from the benevolent James Neild, and although an attempt was made to contradict it, his statement as to all the main facts remains unimpeached, and this mode of punishment was probably in consequence given up.

One boy particularly attracted Mr. Neild's attention. "He had round his neck an iron collar called a yoke, with four projecting prongs, secured by a large clumsy iron padlock. Upon examining his neck, it was slightly galled. Upon one leg was a strong iron ring fastened near the ankle like a handcuff, to which was attached a massy chain about four feet five inches long; at the end of this chain was a log of wood two feet two inches in circumference,

* *Norwich Spectator*, vol. 4, page 263.

weighing altogether twenty-two pounds. With this encumbrance he slept every night, but during the hours of work in the day the chain and log were taken off that he might have the use of his legs to spin ; but the yoke round his neck had never been taken off during the three weeks in which he had been in this state of punishment. As soon as he had finished his work, the chain and log were regularly fastened on his leg, and in that state he regularly passed the night. Every Sunday he was locked up by himself all the day with his irons on. He told me in the presence of the mistress of the house that this punishment was to continue for six months, and this was not contradicted by her. He complained that the ring had made his leg sore, and on taking his stocking off, there appeared some scabs and slight excoriations upon it. He was twelve years of age, his name William Rayner, his father dead, his mother run away.

" Under these circumstances," continued Mr. Neild, " I requested the Worshipful the Mayor would have the goodness to order his irons to be taken off, and that he would oblige me with permission to take them to his house.

" It was said that this boy had been frequently sent to the city bridewell for petty thefts, and that he was incorrigible. This, however, did not turn out to be the truth, for the next morning I went to the bridewell, and together with the keeper examined the books for ten years past, when it appeared that the boy was sent to bridewell for two days, the 18th April, 1804, for running away from the workhouse, not for theft, and the keeper told me that he never was in custody there before or since. That he is not incorrigible I am inclined to believe, for he had both sense and gratitude to come running after the Mayor and myself, and thank us feelingly for his deliverance."

MISCELLANEOUS.

TRADE AND COMMERCE.

THE HUGUENOTS IN NORFOLK.

A COLONY of Flemings settled in the reign of Henry II. at Worsted and Norwich, and "Worsted" stuffs soon became common. These colonists were the first to introduce into England water-driven corn mills, wind mills, and fulling mills. They also re-introduced the art of building in brick, which had not been practised in England since the time of the Romans. Traces of their early brickwork are still observable in several of the old churches at Norwich and Worsted. Norwich and the neighbouring towns derived many advantages from the influx of foreign artisans in the reign of Edward III., the "Father of English Commerce." To the trade of spinning worsted was added that of manufacturing it into cloth in 1336, after which date the latter branch became the leading manufacture of the city. Norwich was appointed by royal edict one of the ten staple towns for the sale of wool, woolfells, and cloths, to which merchants resorted from all parts for purposes of business. Enjoying such privileges, Norwich became a centre of busy industry, and the adjoining towns of Worsted and Wymondham shared in its prosperity; "every one," says an ancient chronicler, "having combers, carders, spinsters, fallers, dyers, pressers, packers, and fleece sorters."

THE ORIGIN OF THE SPINNING AND OTHER TRADES AT NORWICH.

One of the most important of the settlements made by Protestant refugees in England in the sixteenth century was that formed at Norwich, where they founded and carried on many important branches of trade.

Although Norwich had been originally mainly indebted to foreign artisans for its commercial and manufacturing importance, the natives of this city were among the first to turn upon their benefactors. The local guilds, in their usual narrow spirit, passed stringent regulations directed against the foreign artisans who had originally taught them their trade. The jealousy of the native workmen was also roused, and riots were stirred up against the Flemings, many of whom left Norwich for Leeds and Wakefield in Yorkshire, where they prosecuted the woollen manufacture free from the restrictions of the trades' unions; while others left the country for Holland, to carry on their trades in the free towns there.

As an instance of the treatment which the early refugees experienced at the hands of the citizens, it is mentioned that in the reign of Henry VII. an attempt was made by a body of Flemings to establish the manufacture of felt hats at Norwich. To evade the fiscal regulations of the guilds they settled outside the boundaries of the city, but an act having been passed enjoining that hats were only to be manufactured in some city, borough, or market town, the Flemings were thereby brought under the bondage of the guilds, the making of hats by them was suppressed, and the Flemish hat-makers left the neighbourhood.

The consequence was that Norwich, left to its native enterprise and industry, gradually fell into a state of stagnation and decay. Its population rapidly diminished, a large proportion of the houses stood empty, riots among the distressed work-people were of frequent occurrence, and it was even mooted in Parliament whether the place should not be razed. Under such circumstances the corporation determined to call to their aid the skill and industry of the exiled Protestant artisans now flocking into the country. In the year 1564 a deputation of the citizens, headed by the Mayor, waited on the Duke of Norfolk at his palace in the city, and asked his assistance in obtaining a settlement in the place of a body of

K

Flemish workmen. The Duke used his influence with this object, and succeeded in inducing some 300 Dutch and Walloon families to settle in the place at his charge, and to carry on their trades under a licence granted by the Queen. The exiles were very shortly enabled, not only to maintain themselves by their industry, but to restore the city to more than its former prosperity. The houses which had been standing empty were again tenanted, the native population was again fully employed, and the adjoining districts shared in the general prosperity. In the course of a few years as many as 3,000 of the foreign workmen had settled in the city, and many entirely new branches of trade were introduced and successfully carried on by them. Besides the manufacture of sayes, bayes, serges, arras, mouchade, and bombazines, they introduced the striping and flowering of silks and damasks, which shortly became one of the most thriving branches of trade in the place. The manufacture of beaver and felt hats, before imported from abroad, was also successfully established. One Anthony Solen introduced the art of printing, for which he was awarded the freedom of the city. Two potters from Antwerp, Jasper Andries and Jacob Janson, started a pottery, though in a very humble way. Other Flemings introduced the art of gardening in the neighbourhood, and culinary stuffs became more plentiful in Norwich than in any other town or city in England. The general result was abundant employment, remunerative trade, cheap food, and great prosperity; Bishop Parkhurst declaring his persuasion that "these blessings from God have happened by reason of the godly exiles who were here so kindly harboured."

TOO MANY ATTORNEYS.

In the fifteenth century Norfolk seems to have become remarkable for litigation, and the quirks and quibbles of its attorneys were complained of in the House of Commons as a grievance. The Act of 33 Henry VI., c. 7, says that not long since in the city of Norwich, and in the counties of Norfolk and Suffolk, there were only six or eight attorneys at the most coming to the King's Courts, in which time great tranquillity reigned in those places, and little vexation was occasioned by untrue and foreign suits. But now, says the Act, there are in these places four score attorneys or more, the generality of whom have nothing to live upon but their practice, and besides are very ignorant. It complains that they came to markets and fairs, and other places where there were assemblies of people, exhorting, procuring, and moving persons to attempt untrue and foreign suits for small trespasses, little offences, and small sums of money, which might be determined in Courts Baron, so that more suits were now raised for malice than for the ends of justice, and Courts Baron became less frequented. These are the motives which the act states for making a reformation, which was that in future there should be but six common attorneys in the county of Norfolk, the same in the county of Suffolk, and in the city of Norwich two. These were to be admitted by the two Chief Justices of the most sufficient and best instructed, and persons acting as attorneys in these parts without such admission were subjected to heavy penalties.

WAGES IN NORFOLK IN 1430-1.

At a meeting of the Norfolk and Norwich Archæological Society held in December, 1853, Hudson Gurney, Esq., communicated, from a document received from Sir Henry Ellis, the following particulars of labourers' wages, as fixed by the justices of the peace in Norfolk in the 9th Henry VI. (1430-1) :

It is ordered that a plowman, a shepherd, a carter, a maltester, the best shall take 13s. 4d. in the yere, and mete, and drynk, and clothyng, and the secoudary 10s. and mete and drynk.

A woman servant of husbondrye, the best shall take 10s., and mete, and drynk, and clothyng.

A laborer, a dycher, a waller, an higger, a dawber, shall take in the wynter's day 1½d., and in the somer's daye 2d.; and a secondary laborer, a waller, an higger, a dawber, shall take in the wynter day 1d., and in the somer's day 1½d. and mete and drynk.

A baylly of husbondrye shall take in the yere 20s., and mete, and drynk, and clothyng.

A thatster shall take in the wynter's day 1½d., and on the somer's day 2d., and mete and drynk.

Masons, leyers, reders, tylers, sall take on the wynter's dayes 2d., and on the somer's day 2½d., and mete and drynk.

A carpenter and sawer shall take on the wynter's dayes 2d., and on the somer's day 3d. A secundary carpenter, a sawer, shall take on the wynter's daye 2d., and on the somer's day 2½d., and mete and drynk.

The thressyng of a qrtr. whete, rye, mestelyon, peson, and benes, and the syeng of the same, 4d., without mete.

The thressyng and the syeng of a qrtr. barley and ote, 2d., wythoute mete.

TAVERN SIGNS.

THE WHITE HART AT SCOLE.

The White Hart at Scole had the most extensive and expensive public-house sign ever produced. It is thus mentioned by Sir Thomas Brown, March 4, 1663: "About three miles further I came to Scole, where is a very handsome inne, and the noblest sighnepost in England, about and upon which are carved a great many stories, as of Charon and Cerberus, Actæon and Diana, and many others; the signe itself is a White Hart, which hanges downe carved in a stately wreathe." A century later it is again mentioned. Speaking of Osmundestone or Scole, Blomfield says:—
" Here are two very good inns for the entertainment of travellers. The White Hart is much noted in these parts, being called by way of distinction Scole Inn. The house is a large brick building, adorned with imagery and carved

work in several places, as big as the life; it was built in 1655 by James Peck, Esq., whose arms impaling his wife's are over the porch door. The sign is very large, beautified all over with a great number of images of large stature carved in wood, and was the work of Fairchild. The arms about it are those of the chief towns and gentlemen in the county. There was lately a very round large bed, big enough to hold twelve or twenty couples, in imitation, I suppose, of the remarkable great bed at Ware. The house was in all things accommodated at first for large business, but the road not supporting it, it is in much decay at present." A correspondent in *Notes and Queries* says :—" I think the sign was not taken down till after 1795, as I have a recollection of having passed under it, when a boy, in going from Norwich to Ipswich."

The following details of this wonderful erection are obtained from an engraving made in 1740, entitled *The North-East Side of ye sign of ye White Heart at Schoale Inn, in Norfolk, built in the year 1655 by James Peck, a merchant of Norwich, which cost £1,057. Humbly dedicated to James Betts, Gent., by his most obt. servt., Harwin Martin.*

The sign passed over the road, resting on one side on a pier of brickwork, and joined to the house on the other; its height was sufficient to allow carriages to pass beneath. Its ornamentation was divided into compartments, which contained the following subjects, according to the numbers in the engraving :—1. Jonah coming out of the fish's mouth. 2. A lion supporting the arms of Great Yarmouth. 3. A Bacchus. 4. The arms of Lindley. 5. The arms of Hobart. 6. A shepherd playing on his pipe. 7. An angel supporting the arms of Mr. Peck's lady. 8. An angel supporting the arms of Mr. Peck. 9. A white hart (the sign itself), with this motto, " Implentur veteris Bacchi Pinguisque Fermæ. Anno Dom. 1655." 10. The arms of the Earl of Yarmouth. 11. The arms of the Duke of Norfolk. 12. Neptune on a dolphin. 13. A lion supporting the arms

of Norwich. 14. Charon carrying a reputed witch to Hades.
15. Cerberus. 16. A huntsman. 17. Actæon (addressing
his dogs, with the words, "Actæon ego sum, dominum cog-
nosciti vestrum.") 18. A white hart couchant (underneath
the name of the maker of the sign, Johannes Fairchild,
struxit). 19. Prudence. 20. Fortitude. 21. Temperance.
22. Justice. 23. Diana. 24. Time devouring an infant
(underneath, "TEMPUS EDAX RERUM.") 25. An astronomer,
who is seated on a "circumfenter, and by some chemical
preparations is so affected that in fine weather he faces that
quarter from which it is about to come."

There is a ballad on this sign in *Songs and other Poems*,
by Alexander Brome, Gent., London, 1661, p. 123.

POETICAL SIGNBOARDS AND TAVERN RHYMES.

In King Street, Norwich, there was for years a house
combining the double attractions of a barber's shop and a
beer shop. By the side of the pole, the barber's recognised
sign, appear the following lines :

> Rove not from pole to pole,
>   But step in here ;
> Where nought exceeds the shaving
>   But the beer.

This witty inscription, attributed to Dean Swift, is said to
have been penned by him for a barber who at the same time
kept a public-house.

Sir Walter Scott in his *Fortunes of Nigel*, as a motto to
one of his chapters, gives the following version :

> Rove not from pole to pole—the man lives here
> Whose razor's only equall'd by his beer ;
> And where in either sense the Cockney put,
> May, if he pleases, get confounded cut.

At Swainsthorpe, a village five miles from Norwich, is a

public-house known as the Dun Cow. Under the portrait of the cow there was formerly the following couplet :

> Walk in, gentlemen, I trust you will find
> The Dun Cow's milk is to your mind.

A writer in the first volume of *The East Anglian* gives the following lines, as copied by him from a fly sheet in a public-house at Mulbarton, in Norfolk :

THE LANDLORD'S KIND CAUTION TO HIS CUSTOMERS.

> Right welcome all who visit here,
> I'll treat you with good wholesome cheer;
> I deal in ale, as chrystal clear,
> In porter brown, in good strong beer.
> I've rum and gin, and brandy too,
> They suit myself and will please you ;
> My wines would make a Nabob smile ;
> My whiskey will your hearts beguile ;
> My chairs are easy, fires are bright,
> So take a seat, yourselves delight ;
> My tobacco's rich, pipes white as snow,
> Alike they're formed to soothe your woe.
> I'm ready to attend your call,
> But I've no chalk to spoil my wall;
> Chalk ever does sweet peace destroy,
> Stirs up foul anger, stifles joy.
> My liquor's good, my dealing just,
> My profit's small—I cannot trust.
> I'm sure these lines can cause no sorrow,
> So pay to-day, I'll trust to-morrow.
> If I refuse to trust a friend,
> Or if I trust or money lend,
> The one he takes it in disdain,
> The other will my house refrain.

The same writer says that he saw the following written in paint over the fire-place in a house some three or four parishes from Mulbarton :

All you that stand before the fire,
To see you sit is my desire;
That others may, as well as you,
See the fire, and feel it too.

Since man to man is so unjust,
None can tell what man to trust;
I've trusted many to my sorrow,
Pay to-day, trust to-morrow.

In the kitchen of the Crown Inn, at Banham, near Attle-borough, in one of those large, old-fashioned, open fire-places, which were once so common but are now seldom met with, and above the mantel-piece, the following lines are painted:

Take not abroad a lighted pipé,
Or else a pot you're fined;
But stay till your tobacco's out,
Or leave your pipe behind.

At the village of Great Cressingham, more than sixty years since, below the sign of the Robin Hood, was this couplet:

Robin Hood is not at home,
But pray walk in and drink with little John.

The landlord was a little man and his name was John.

FRAGMENTS.

ROADS AND TRAVELLING.

Happily, says the Rev. Richard Hart, those who have been born within the last fifty years will find it difficult to understand how very, very bad nearly all the English roads used to be, even in my own individual experience; yet, with the evidence before us, we can have no reasonable doubt that in moving about from place to place, our ancestors must have had still greater difficulties to contend with, for there were then very few roads of any description, and public conveyances were utterly unknown. The turnpike road from Hethersett to Fettlebridge, beyond Attleborough, constructed between the years 1694 and 1707, is indeed reputed to have been the very earliest in the whole kingdom.

Even in "the golden days of good Queen Bess," Kempe thought that he had accomplished a prodigious feat in walking from London to Norwich in nine successive days, at the rate of about fourteen miles a day.* About the same period we read of a Queen's Messenger "riding in hast" from London to Yarmouth "in the space of ten dayes."† From this and other similar documents, we learn that the day's journey scarcely ever exceeded twenty miles, although the messengers "rode in hast, and with like spede returned."

Almost two centuries earlier than this, when Henry Duke of Lancaster, afterwards Henry IV., rode with his unfortunate kinsman Richard II. from Conway to London, in such extreme haste that he would not even allow the deposed monarch time to change his clothes, the journey occupied eleven days actually upon the road. They rested the whole of the Sunday at Lichfield. The greatest distance that they accomplished in any one day was twenty-four miles, but fourteen miles was the usual average.‡

It was in 1568 that post horses were first established in Norwich, and it was then expressly provided that no horse should be used for more than twelve or fourteen miles together, and the hire of a hackney for a journey was fixed at twelvepence the first day and eightpence each day after. No one was to hire any post horses in the city unless he was licensed by the Queen's Majesty's warrant, or that of the Duke of Norfolk, the Privy Council, or the Mayor.

---

* Kempe's *Nine Days' Wonder*, republished by the Camden Society.

† *Original Papers*, 2, 104, &c. ‡ See Hollingshed.

Mail coaches from Norwich to London were not established till 1785, more than two centuries later, but private enterprise anticipated this luxury at least fifty-one years before this period, as will be seen in " Gleanings from Old Newspapers."

PHENOMENA IN NORFOLK, A.D. 1646.

The following extracts relating to strange phenomena in Norfolk are taken from a rare tract, entitled *Signes from Heaven, or severall Apparitions seene and hearde in Ayre in the Counties of Cambridge and Norfolke, on the 21st day of May last past, in the Afternoone;* 1646. 4to., Lond., 1646, four leaves :

"Also at Brandon, in the County of Norfolke, the inhabitants were forced to come out of their houses to behold so strange a spectacle of a spire steeple ascending up from the earth, and a pike or lance descending downwards from Heaven. The Lorde in Mercy blesse and preserve His Church, and settle peace and truth among all degrees, and more especially among our churchmen."

" In Brandon, in the county aforesaid, was seen at the same time a navie or fleet of ships in the ayre, swiftly passing under sayle, with flags and steamers hanged out, as if they were ready to give an encounter."

" In Marshland, in the county of Norfolk aforesaid, within three miles of King's Linne, a captain and a lieutenant, with divers other persons of credit, did heare, in the time of thunder, a sound as of a whole regiment of drums beating a call, with perfect notes and stops, much admired at of all that heard it."*

THE NORFOLK WONDER.

The Norfolk Wonder, or the Maiden's Trance, being a strange and true relation of one Sarah Barker, of Elsom, in

* Halliwell's *Norfolk Anthology.*

Norfolk, of sixteen years of age, who on the 2nd of this instant May (being in perfect health) fell into a trance, and lay as dead for three days and nights together, when, just as they were going to bury her in the church, she came to life again, to the amazement of all that saw her, and declared what strange things she had seen in the other world, as the joys of Heaven and the dismal terror and amazing torments of Hell ; and lastly, how an angel all in white told her what should happen in England and France betwixt this and December next, and it would as surely come to pass as she should die three days after, which happened accordingly ; with her last prayer, written by her own hand a little before she died, which she left as a legacy to all young persons of both sexes, to put them in mind of mortality. Licensed according to Order. Printed for T. Wells, in Holborn, 1708.

This little tract contains seven pages besides the title, which is sufficient to explain the whole, being, in fact, a copious analysis of it.*

THE KING SHALL HAVE WRECK OF THE SEA.

One of the King's prerogatives was and still is " The King shall have wreck of the sea throughout the realm ; whales and great sturgeons taken in the sea or elsewhere within the realm, except in certain places privileged by the King," so reads statute 1, c. 2, of the 17 Edward II. Charles John Palmer, Esq., F.S.A., the accomplished anti-quary and historian of Great Yarmouth, writing in May, 1857, says " Whales, sturgeons, porpoises, dolphins, and other fish, having in them a great or large thickness of fat-ness, are called ' Fishes Royal,' and from ancient time have, by right of custom, belonged to the Crown. In 1559 Queen Elizabeth, by charter, made a grant to the town of Yar-mouth of all fishes royal taken between Winterton Ness in

* Halliwell's *Norfolk Anthology.*

Norfolk, and Easton Ness, in Suffolk, which grant was confirmed by James I. in 1608, and the town enjoyed the privilege, such as it was, till 1835, when the Municipal Corporation Act abolished all local admiralty jurisdictions.

"A few years since (1857) a whale came on shore at Winterton, and I, as receiver of droits for the Crown, reported
the circumstance, and was instructed to assert the Queen's
right to the same, which I did, although the parties who had
got possession of it were allowed to retain it."

KITTY WITCH ROW.

Brand in his *Popular Antiquities* says that a woman
dressed in a grotesque and frightful manner was otherwise
called a kitch witch, probably for the sake of a jingle. It
was customary many years ago at Yarmouth for women of
the lowest order to go in troops from house to house to levy
contributions, at some season of the year and on some pretence which nobody now seems to recollect, having men's
shirts over their own apparel, and their faces smeared with
blood. These hideous beldams have long discontinued their
perambulations, but in memory of them one of the many
rows in that town is called Kitty Witch Row.

HUNTING SQUIRRELS ON CHRISTMAS DAY.

The Rev. Robert Forby, writing of the end of the last
century, says that in many parts of the country, particularly
where there is much wood, the custom prevails of hunting
squirrels on Christmas Day. Why this pretty, harmless
animal should be selected for this barbarous diversion, or
why this particular festival should be chosen for the *grande
chasse*, does not appear to be known; but on a Christmas
morning half the idle fellows and boys in a parish assemble
in any wood or plantation where squirrels are known to harbour, and having started their game, pursue it with sticks

and stones from tree to tree, hallooing and shouting with all their might, till the squirrel is killed. It is a cruel sport, and is very properly discountenanced and falling into disuse; but on a fine morning the shouts of the hunters echoing through the woods, with occasional bursts of laughter and rustic merriment, have a very lively and exhilarating effect.

POT DAY.

Within the memory of many persons now living, it was the custom, amongst even very substantial farmers, to cook only three times a week, of which Sunday was always one. These days of periodical cookery were called "pot days," and as their friends were usually acquainted with them, a person intending to go to the house uninvited, would calculate accordingly, and say "I will go on such a day, for I know that is pot day."*

HOLLOW MEAT.

Before the improved system of husbandry was introduced into Norfolk, there were many warrens, and the country was very much overrun with rabbits. In the light-land farms these formed a considerable part of the diet of the farming servants, and were known by the name of "hollow meat;" and as the servants in Scotland are said to have stipulated against salmon, so it was the practice here when a servant let himself to a farm, to make a proviso that he should be fed upon "hollow meat" only a certain number of days in the week.

* Forby's *Appendix*.

EPITAPHS AND EPIGRAMS.

EPITAPHS.

THE following epitaph in Haddiscoe Church is worthy of record :

WILLIAM SALTAR,
YARMOUTH STAGE COACHMAN,
DIED OCTOBER 9TH, 1776,
AGED 59 YEARS.

Here lies Will Saltar, honest man,
Deny it envy if you can;
True to his business and his trust,
Always punctual, always just.
His horses, could they speak, would tell
They lov'd their good old master well.
His up-hill work is chiefly done,
His stage is ended, race is run ;
One journey is remaining still,
To climb up Sion's holy hill.
And now his faults are all forgiv'n,
Elijah like, drives up to Heav'n,
Takes the reward of all his pains,
And leaves to other hands the reins.

The following, certainly in very bad taste, was formerly in Thetford churchyard :

My grandfather was buried here,
My cousin Jane, and two uncles dear;
My father perished with a mortification in his thighs,
My sister dropped down dead in the Minories ;
But the reason why I am here, according to my thinking,
Is owing to my good living and hard drinking.
Therefore, good Christians, if you'd wish to live long,
Beware of drinking brandy, gin, or anything strong.

The following is in Bacton Church, near North Walsham:

To the memory of MICAIAH GAZE, who departed this life November 4th, 1751, aged 61 years.

> You that pass by this place may think on me,
> For as you are so once you did me see;
> What I am now will quickly be your doom;
> My house is straight, but by my side there's room.
> And if your dust should fall into my grave,
> 'Tis no great matter, ev'ry man shall have
> His very dust, and neither new nor more,
> For he that made it keeps it all in store.

The following epitaph is to be seen in the churchyard of the village of Mundesley, near North Walsham, and on the coast. It is scarcely necessary to remark that the person commemorated by this epitaph was drowned at sea, and washed upon Mundesley beach. The date on the stone is September 8th, 1832:

> Sleep, stranger, sleep, within thy narrow bed,
> Till earth and sea shall both give up their dead;
> Up! seek the Saviour—Lo! the Judge in sight;
> Wake, reader, wake, and Christ shall give thee light.

At Stow Bardolph there is the following to the memory of Sir Thomas Hare, Bart., who died July 1st, 1693, aged 35:

> The glorious sun which sets at night
> Appears next morning clear and bright;
> The gaudy deckings of the earth
> Do every spring receive new birth;
> But life, when fled, has no return,
> In vain we sigh, in vain we mourn.
> Yet does the turtle justly grieve her fate
> When she is left behind without her mate;
> Nor less does she who raised this tomb,
> And wishes here to have a room
> With that dear he who underneath doth lie,
> Who was the treasure of her heart, the pleasure of her eye.

On an altar tomb in Ditchingham churchyard there is the following epitaph to an unknown person:

> Without a name, for ever senseless, dumb;
> Dust only now contains this silent tomb;
> Where 'twas I liv'd or died it matters not,
> To whom related, or of whom begot.
> I was, but am not, ask no more of me,
> 'Tis all I am, and all that you must be.

In Wheatacre Church, near Beccles, there is the following:

> Here lies the body of Beatrice, the beloved wife of John Guavor, clerk, Rector of this parish, and . . . . . [obliterated] in the county of Suffolk.
>
> > She was truly religious,
> > Meek in apprehension,
> > Expert in geography,
> > Compassionate and charitable.
>
> > Born 24th Sept., 1699, died 27th April, 1740.

Mr. Orchard, in his select collection of epitaphs, gives the following from Attleborough:

JOHN DOWE.

> Here lieth the Dowe who ne'er in his life did good,
> Nor would have done though longer he had stood.
> A wife he had, both beautiful and wise,
> But he ne'er would such goodness exercise.
> Death was his friend to bring him to his grave,
> For he in life commendam none could have.

In Witchingham Church, Norfolk, the following is on Thomas Allyn and his two wives, 1650:

> Death here advantage hath of life, I spye,
> One husband with two wives at once may lye.

The following inscription is in Cantley Church :

Here lyeth the body of Robert Gilbert, of Cantley, in the county
of Norf., Gent., who dyed on the 5th of November, 1714,
aged 59 years.

> In wise frugality luxuriant,
> In justice and good acts extravagant,
> To all the world an universal friend,
> No foe to any but the savage kind.
> How many fair estates have been eras'd
> By the same gen'rous means that his increas'd.
> His duty thus perform'd to heaven and earth,
> Each leisure hour fresh toilsom sports gave birth;
> Had Nimrod seen he would the game decline,
> To Gilbert's mighty hunter's name resign.
> Tho' hundreds to the ground he oft has chas'd,
> That subtle fox Death earth'd him here at last,
> And left a fragrant scent so sweet behind
> That ought to be pursu'd by all mankind.

The following are in Norwich Cathedral :

> Depositum
> Johanni Spendlove,
> Prebendarii,
> Julii 8, Anno Domini
> 1666.

> Dean Suckling's daughter,
> Prebend Spendlove's wife,
> For a far better
> Chang'd this present life,
> March the 21st, 1656.

Richardus Corbet, Theologiæ Doctor, Ecclesiæ Cathedralis Christi,
Oxoniensis, primum alumnus, inde decanus, exinde episcopus, illinc
huc translatus, et hinc in Cœlum, Julii 28, 1635.

TRANSLATION.

Richard Corbet, D.D., first student of Christ Church, Oxford,
then dean, and next bishop of that place, thence translated hither,
and from thence to heaven, on the 28th of July, 1635.

Here WILLIAM INGLOTT, organist, doth rest,
Whose art in musick this Cathedral blest;
For descant most, for voluntary all,
He past on organ, song, and virginall.
He left this life at age of sixty-seven,
And now 'mongst angels all sings St. in Heaven;
His fame flies far, his name shall never die,
See, art and age here crown his memorie.

> Non digitis, Inglotte, tuis terrestria tangis,
> Tangis nunc digitis organa celsa poli.

Anno Dom. 1621.

Buried the last day   This erected the 15th
of December, 1621.   day of June, 1622.

Here lies the body of Honest Tom Page,
Who died in the 33d year of his age.

EPIGRAMS BY DR. SAYERS.

In 1803 Edward Whetstone, the old clerk of Trowse
parish, gave an organ to the church. Originally he had
only bequeathed the purchase money, but having mentioned
his intention to the vicar and other principal inhabitants,
and wishing to hear his own organ, they agreed to allow
him an annuity out of the rates equivalent to the interest of
his legacy, which was thus made available in his lifetime.
Soon after the organ was placed in the church the following
epigrams by Dr. Sayers found their way into the *Norfolk
Chronicle:*

ON TROWSE ORGAN.

Fungar vice cotis acutem.—Horace.

I, Whetstone, clerk of this good parish,
   Having no organ fit for singing,
And wishing much my breath to cherish,
   Bought pipes to set the church a ringing.

Now, though I ne'er could hum a stave,
   To some renown I still aspire,
For this brave organ which I gave
   Is deem'd the Whetstone of the choir.

On the Same.

Ned Whetstone to Trowse parish left
   An organ, which in giving,
He thought that when of breath bereft,
   He'd make more noise than living.

But fearing that if he should go,
   The choice might be ill-suited,
He chose to live to witness how
   His will was executed.

PROVERBS.

THE student of humanity can never afford to neglect or pass by the proverbs of a people. They generally inculcate patience, frugality, manly independence, and perseverance, and embody good sense, natural equity, and a spirit of kindness. The following are some of the most popular proverbs in this county:

If the hen does not prate she will not lay—*i.e.*, scolding wives make the best housewives. ₒ

If it won't pudding it will froize—*i.e.*, if it won't do for one thing it will for another.

His religion is copyhold, and he has not taken it up.—This is said of one who never goes to any place of worship.

A wheelwright's dog is a carpenter's uncle—*i.e.*, a bad wheelwright makes a good carpenter.

I'll give him a kick for a culp—*i e.*, a Rowland for an Oliver.

Laurence has got hold of him—*i.e.*, he is lazy.

Hitty missy, as the blind man shot the crow—*i.e.*, accidentally.

You must eat another yard of pudding first—*i.e.*, you must wait till you grow older.

It is a good thing to eat your brown bread first—*i.e.*, if you are unfortunate in the early part of life, you may hope for better success in future.

The dog that fetches will carry—*i.e.*, a talebearer will tell tales of you as well as to you.

I was not born in a wood to be scared by an owl—*i.e.*, I am not so easily frightened as you may imagine.

Little knocks rive great blocks—*i e.*, steady perseverance with little means gets through great difficulties.

I will come when the cuckoo has picked up the dirt—*i.e.*, in the spring.

What's hers is mine, what's mine is my own, quoth the husband.

Nip a nettle hard and it will not sting you—*i.e.*, strong and decided measures prevail best with troublesome people.

You may know a carpenter by his chips.—This is usually applied to great eaters, who leave many bones on their plates.

Elbow grease gives the best polish—*i.e.*, hard rubbing makes furniture look brighter.

The miller's boy said so—*i.e.*, it was a matter of common report.

She is fond of gape seed—*i.e.*, of staring at everything that passes.

He has got his jag—*i.e.*, as much drink as he can fairly carry.

To go down the red lane—*i.e.*, to be swallowed.

The beard will pay for the shaving.—This is used when a person is paid for his labour by taking part or the whole of that which he is employed about, as cutting bushes, &c. In general it means the work will produce enough to pay itself.

There is a good steward abroad when there is a wind frost—*i.e.*, you have no occasion to look to your labourers, they must work to keep themselves warm.

God's lambs will play.—An apology for riotous youth; probably it was originally a sneer at some unlucky Puritan who had been detected in some indiscretion.

I gave it him as it came from mill, undressed—*i.e.*, the bran and flour mixed together. It means, I spoke my mind plainly, and without dressing up.

When the cat is away the mice will play—*i.e.*, if the master is out of the way servants will be idle.

To make one eat humble pie—*i.e.*, to make him lower his tone and be submissive.

You can't make a silk purse out of a sow's ear—*i.e.*, you cannot make a handsome thing out of base materials. It is frequently applied to a stupid fellow upon whom education is thrown away.

It will take the gilt off the gingerbread—*i.e.*, it will reduce his profits.

To give one the seal of the day—*i.e.*, to be commonly civil to him, but nothing more.

Little fish are sweet.—It means small gifts are always acceptable.

You will catch more flies with a spoonful of honey than with a gallon of vinegar—*i.e.*, kind language prevails more than sharp reproof.

A lame tongue gets nothing.

Go to Bungay to get new bottomed.—The explanation given of this common saying is that people broke at Beccles and removed to Bungay and throve there.

I made my obedience to him, but he would neither speak nor grunt.—This is said when a superior passes without returning your civility.

A ground sweat cures all disorders—*i.e.*, in the grave all complaints cease from troubling.

Give him that which costs you nothing—*i.e.*, civility.

He does not know great A from a bull's foot.

It is better to rub than rust.

He was meant for a gentleman, but was spoilt in the making.

He lies bare of a suit—*i.e.*, he has no money.

He will make a tight old man.—This is said of a lazy fellow, who does not hurt himself with work.

He has laid a stone at my door—*i.e.*, in modern cant phrase, he has cut me.

He has a Friday look—*i.e.*, sulky, downcast.

He has made a hole in his manners.

Ill weeds grow apace.

A Scotch mist will wet an Englishman to the skin.

It's an ill wind that blows nobody good.

Choose a wife on Saturday instead of Sunday.

It does not rain but it pours.

A green Christmas makes a fat churchyard.

Winter's thunder is summer's wonder.

There's good land where there's a foul way.

There's a scabby sheep in every flock.

God tempers the wind to the shorn lamb.

Don't lose the ship for a ha'porth of tar.

It's a pity fine weather should do harm.

The darkest hour is nearest dawn.

One hour's sleep before midnight is worth two after.

Of a ragged colt cometh many a good horse.

Never offer your hen for sale on a rainy day.

Happy is the bride the sun shines on.

As white as the driven snow.

After a storm comes a calm.

Make your hay while the sun shines.

> Friday night's dreams on Saturday told,
> Are sure to come true, be they never so old.

THE WEATHER AND THE CROPS.

A writer in the *Fortnightly Review* has remarked that the upper and middle classes seldom trouble themselves much about the weather except for conversational purposes, unless a journey or a party of pleasure is involved. But with the poor, whose comforts depend upon the weather, it is very different. The farm labourer, whose day's wage often depends on the clouds, and the fisherman, whose meal rests with the winds, naturally pay great attention to the weather, and hence we find that their proverbs smack of the fierceness of men who have struggled with the storm, and their vocabulary teems with words expressive of every shade and variety of weather. Such expressions as "being under a cloud" and "laying up for a rainy day" are common, and when a north-east wind blows it is said "there's a good steward abroad." Among their weather terms we have the "rime frost," the "dag," the "smur," and a gentle but long-continued rain is "a regular sop."

The peasant in his rude fashion is a meteorologist. From living almost constantly abroad he gets a habit of studying

the clouds, and speaks confidently of those "water-carts,"
"Noah's Arks," forerunners of continued rain. More than
half a century has passed since Howard first reduced the
forms of clouds to a systematic nomenclature, and his suc-
cessors have so far improved upon his plans that there is not
a cloud which cannot be scientifically named and defined.
But our fishermen and the shrewdest of our peasants knew
these facts long ago. They name the clouds after natural
objects, and you may hear them talk of " bullfinch skies "
to express the lovely vermillion tints of sunset clouds, and
the " shepherd's flock " to denote what one of our poets has
described with so perfect a touch :

> Detached in ranges through the air,
> Spotless as snow and countless as they're fair,
> Scattered immensely wide from east to west,
> The beauteous semblance of a flock at rest.

Weather rhymes and proverbs are treasured up in almost
every village, and that they contain some germs of truth is
pretty certain, or they would not have held their ground so
long. Thus :

> Candlemas Day, the good housewife's goose lay ;
> Valentine's Day, yours and mine may.

That is, geese if kept warm and properly taken care of, the
common practice of good housewives, will lay eggs by the
2nd of February ; if not, they will in any case do so by
the 14th.

> If Candlemas Day be fair and clear,
> The shepherd would rather see his wife on a bier.

> As far as the sun shines into the cottage on Candlemas Day,
> So far will the snow blow in afore Old May.

A cold and late spring is anticipated if Candlemas Day is
fine, and mortality among ewes and lambs result from incle-

ment weather. Sir Thomas Brown in his *Vulgar Errors* speaks of a general tradition that inferreth the coldness of the succeeding spring from the shining of the sun on Candlemas Day. In other parts of England we hear it said:

> If Candlemas Day be fair and bright,
> Winter will have another fight.

> If Candlemas Day be fair and clear,
> There'll be two winters in the year.

The Germans say the badger peeps out of his hole on Candlemas Day, and if he finds snow, he walks abroad; if he sees the sun shining, he draws back again into his hole. The French have a similar saying of the bear.

> The farmer should have on Candlemas Day
> Half his turnips and half his hay.

> You should on Candlemas Day
> Throw candle and candlestick away.

Daylight being sufficient by this time.

> When Candlemas Day is come and gone,
> The snow won't lie on a hot stone.

This means that the sun on Candlemas Day has too much power for the snow to lay long without thawing. We must not forget, however, that these weather proverbs were applied during the "Old Style," when Candlemas Day was twelve days later in the year than it is now.

> So many fogs in March,
> So many frosts in May.

If the bushes hang of a drop on St. Matthias' Day before sunrise, it will be a dropping season. If the bushes be dry, we may look for a dry summer.

March comes in like a lion and goes out like a lamb.

A bushel of March dust is worth a Jew's eye or a king's ransom.

Mad as a March hare.

In April the cuckoo shows his cold bill,
In May he sings both night and day,
In June he change his tune,
In July away he fly,
In August go he must.

If the cock moults before the hen,
We shall have weather thick and thin;
But if the hen moult before the cock,
We shall have weather as hard as a rock.

If the robin sings in the bush,
Then the weather will be coarse;
But if the robin sings on the barn,
Then the weather will be warm.

If the cuckoo the last week before he leaves chatters and "cuckoos" on the tops of the oaks, it is a sure sign of a fine harvest. If bad weather is coming, he sings low among the bushes, and can scarcely get his cuckoo out. If he comes in April, there will be an early harvest; if he does not come till May, then the harvest is into October. If he sings after Midsummer, the harvest will last till Michaelmas.

Sow in the slop,
Heavy at top.

That is, wheat sown when the ground is wet is most productive.

The weather will fine when the rooks play pitch half-penny.

That is, if flying in flocks some of them stoop down and pick up worms, imitating the action of a boy playing pitch half-penny.

A rainbow at morning
Is the shepherd's warning;
But a rainbow at night
Is the shepherd's delight.

The philosophy of this rustic proverb is clear enough. In the morning the rainbow is seen in the clouds westward, the quarter from which we get most rain, and of course in the evening in the opposite quarter of the heavens.

> First comes David, then comes Chad,
> And then comes Winneral as though he was mad;
> White or black,
> Or old house thack.

This alludes to the stormy weather commonly experienced at the beginning of March. St. David's Day is the 1st of March, St. Chad's the 2nd. The first two lines of this weather proverb are known in Suffolk, but St. Winwaloe, whose anniversary falls on the 3rd of March, is there called Winnold, and not, as in genuine Norfolk, Winneral. The Norfolk proverb means that at this period there will be either snow, rain, or wind, which latter is intended by " old house thack."

> When the wind's in the east,
> It's neither good for man nor beast;
> When the wind's in the south,
> It's in the rain's mouth.

> If red the sun begins his race,
> Expect that rain will flow apace.

> When clouds appear like rocks and towers,
> The earth's refreshed with frequent showers.

> A sunshiny shower
> Won't last half-an-hour.

Rain at early morn brings out the proverb :

> If it rains before seven
> 'Twill hold up before eleven.

Another couplet on a rainy morning is :

> Between twelve and two
> You'll see what the day will do.

It will clear up if you can see enough blue sky to make a pair of breeches.

> Many haws, many sloes,
> Many cold toes.

> Many hips and haws,
> Many frosts and snaws.

> A swarm of bees in May
> Is worth a load of hay;
> A swarm of bees in June
> Is worth a silver spune;
> A swarm of bees in July
> Is not worth a fly.

> The first cock of hay
> Frights the cuckoo away.

> He who bathes in May
> Will soon be laid in clay;
> He who bathes in June
> Will sing a merry tune;
> He who bathes in July
> Will dance like a fly.

> Cast not a clout till May is out.

> Mist in May and heat in June,
> Makes the harvest right soon.

> As welcome as flowers in May.

> March dust and May sun
> Makes corn white and maids dun.

When a sun-dog comes on the south side of the sun there will be fair weather, when on the north side there will be foul weather.

If you see the old moon with the new there will be stormy weather.

When the new moon happens on a Saturday it is believed to be a sign of unfavourable weather, and if the full moon falls on a Sunday the belief is greatly strengthened. The proverb is :

> Saturday's new and Sunday's full,
> Never was good and never wool.

The new moon "lying on its back," with the horns of its crescent pointing upwards, is believed to indicate a dry moon; and, on the contrary, when the new moon appears with the horns of the crescent pointing downwards, or, as it is locally expressed, "when it hangs dripping," it will be a wet moon.

There is also a saying with reference to the new moon that

> When early seen,
> 'Tis seldom seen.

A "burr," that is a halo, round the moon is a sign of rain. The sun rising clear in the morning and going to bed again, as it is called, immediately, is a sure indication of a foul day.

If there be bad weather and the sun does not appear all the week, it is firmly believed that it will shine on Saturday. Many country people maintain that the sun always peeps through the clouds on that day, if only for a minute, just as it were to show his face.

> If woolly fleeces spread the heavenly way,
> No rain be sure disturbs the summer's day.

> Sow beans in the mud,
> And they'll grow like a wood.

> Sow beans and peas on David and Chad,
> Be the weather good or bad.

> When the sloe tree is white as a sheet,
> Sow your barley whether it be dry or wet.

> Many frosts and many thowes,
> Make many rotten yowes (ewes).

If the ice will bear a goose before Christmas it will not bear a duck afterwards.

> Plough deep while others sleep,
> And you shall have corn to sell and to keep.

> This rule in gardening never forget,
> To sow dry and plant wet.

> After a famine in the stall,
> Comes a famine in the hall.

> When the wind doth feed the clay,
> England woe and well-a-day ;
> But when the clay doth feed the sand,
> Then it is well for Angle-land.

Gleanings from Old Newspapers.

ONE of the most distinctive features of modern times, and the most indubitable sign of the broadening intelligence of the people, is the number and volume of the newspapers that are required to satisfy the appetite of the public. No greater contrast is afforded by the narrow winding streets and alleys, and the quaint projecting gables and low storeys of an old city, when compared with the broad ways and stately fronts of our own time, than is presented to our view when comparing the dingy leaf of a century and half ago called a newspaper with the broad sheet and its seventy columns that is found scarcely adequate to satisfy the wants of the reader of the present day, but which has to be supplemented by a daily issue.

Newspaper literature seems to have had its rise in Norwich very early in the eighteenth century. *The Norwich Postman*, a small quarto foolscap, published for a penny a number in the year 1706, was the first newspaper published in the city. One of the earliest publications of this kind was the *Weekly Courant or Weekly Packet*, printed by a Mr. Collins near the Red Well in St. Andrew's. This was a small folio, containing only a very small quantity of news, and appeared in 1714. In 1721 appeared the *Norwich Weekly Mercury or Protestant Packet*, and about the same time the *Norwich Gazette*. From some old volumes of these papers I have selected a few advertisements and announcements as calculated to give my readers an insight into the manners and customs of our forefathers in Norfolk a century and half ago.

STAGE COACHES.

In these days, when one may breakfast in Devonshire, dine in London, and sup in Edinburgh, and all in the same day, it will be interesting to read some of the old advertisements exhibiting the methods of locomotion in use by our steady slow-going forefathers. The first to which I direct my readers' attention is taken from the *Norwich Gazette* of May 19, 1722, and refers to the setting out of an "empty coach," a rather unprofitable speculation one might suppose for the proprietor, who, however, seemed to think that it might notwithstanding be filled with passengers.

> ON Saturday, 26th Instant, an Empty COACH will Set out from Bartholomew Hunton's in St. Giles', in Norwich, for Cambridge, and will go by the Way of Bury St. Edmund's: And a Week after another Coach will set out from Bartholomew Hunton's aforesaid for Leeds in Yorkshire, and will go by Way of Wisbich, Spalding, and Lincoln. All Persons who intend to go by either of these Coaches are desired to apply themselves to Bartholomew Hunton aforesaid, who will use them Very Reasonably.

I hope Bartholomew Hunton was as good as his word, and used his passengers "very reasonably," and that he likewise got them safely to their destination.

The next advertisement is copied from the *Norwich Weekly Mercury or Protestant Packet,* in which it appeared in 1727. The advertisement is interesting for two or three reasons. In these days, if your conveyance is announced to start at 9·35, and you get to the starting-place at 9·36, you will indubitably find that the snorting monster has left you in the lurch, and is already speeding on its destination a mile off. In 1727 the fortunate traveller had a margin, not of a few moments merely, but of two days. To be sure it then took three days to get from Norwich to London; now we may do it in little more than .

three hours. Now we are bound by iron necessity to one route ; then the passengers might choose any route they pleased—it was a.1 the same to the coachman. Here is the advertisement :

> NOTICE is Hereby Given that on Thursday or Friday next, the 6th and 7th of June, a COACH AND HORSES will set out for London from Mr. Thomas Bateman's in St. Giles's Parish, in Norwich, and will perform the same in 3 Days. The said Coach will go either by Newmarket or Ipswich as the Passengers shall Agree upon.

The next advertisement shows that in 1741 some little improvement had taken place in the matter of travelling, for in the summer—the time, it will be observed, to which the foregoing refers—the proprietors actually undertake to accomplish the journey in two days, although they stipulate for three in the winter. The date of the announcement is May 30, 1741 :

> THIS is to Give Notice that the London Stage Coach sets out on Thursday, the 11th of June, from Mr. John Godfrey's, at the Duke's Palace, in Norwich, and sets up at the Bull Inn, in Bishopsgate Street, in London. The said Coach sets out every Thursday Morning from the Duke's Palace for London, and every Thursday Morning from the Bull Inn for Norwich, and meets at the White Swan in Bury St. Edmund's, and so continue going and coming in Two Days during the Summer, and in Three Days the Winter. Parcels are taken in at Reasonable Rates at the abovesaid Places. To be performed from Bury to London and London to . Bury by 4 sets of able Horses. Performed [if God permit]
>
> By us
> { Thomas Goodchild.
> St. George Norman.
> Alexander Appleyard.
> Benjamin Pottinger.

That the honest quartett whose signatures are attached to the above announcement had reason for the grave doubt suggested by the pious phrase at the end, " if God permit," is shown by a paragraph in the same paper of Sept. 19th of the same year, in which the Editor, Mr. Henry Crossgrove, quaintly says :

> I hear that on Friday Night, the 11th Instant, the Norwich Stage Coach and the Lynn Stage Coach, were both robbed by the Devil's Ditch on Newmarket Heath by a single Highwayman, as they were returning Home.

The last advertisement of this class that I shall print is one that shows that Norfolk more than a century ago furnished its quota of poultry to the Christmas feasts of the metropolis. Every year the Great Eastern Railway Company whirls along in a few hours tens of thousands of geese, turkeys, &c., for the London Christmas market. In 1741 Mr. James Nasmith and Mrs. Elizabeth Beecroft did the same thing on a smaller scale in three days, as set forth below :

> THIS is to Give Notice that on Tuesday, the 22nd of this Instant, there will be a Coach go from Mrs. Beecroft's, on Tombland, in Norwich, on purpose to carry Fowls to get into London on Christmas Eve.
>
> Performed by us { James Nasmith. Eliz. Beecroft.

TRADE AND COMMERCE.

The busy spirit of competition—the very soul of trade and commerce—whose existence is so prominently manifested in the advertising columns of modern Norfolk newspapers, began to display itself in Norwich as early as a century ago through the same medium. The following is as good a specimen of candour and self-assertion as we shall find in our days, even on the other side of the Atlantic. It seems, moreover, to indicate the commencement of the gun-smith trade in Norwich :

THESE are to acquaint all Gentlemen and Others that in the Shop in the Haymarket over against the Star, in Norwich, late in the occupation of Mr. Edward Daffey (the ingenious London Gunsmith), are to be Sold, Made, or Mended all Sorts of fine Flying Guns or Marsh Guns, all Sorts of Steel Bows against the Season of Rook Shooting, all sorts of Pistols, Holster and Screw, by HENRY KEMP, who served his Apprenticeship with the said Mr. Henry Daffey. Here likewise may be observed that the right bred in all Faculties are the most capable, and for their Credit sake most willing to show their Ingenuity, first in the Performance, next in their Candour in fair Dealing. What Umbrage soever this may give to such as are but Pretenders to Arts or Trades (to which they have no right by Nature or Servitude), I must yet by their Leave tell 'em that I am the only Person that ever was an Apprentice to the Gun Smith Trade in Norwich.

HENRY KEMP.

Here is another specimen of vigorous competition in the interest of a professor of an art not now frequently obtruded before the public eye in the advertising sheet. Its date is November 20th, 1722 :

ROBERT GEDNEY, who Served his Time with a London Chimney Sweeper upon Tombland in Norwich, now lives in Saint Paul's Parish, and will Sweep a Chimney as well as Any One in Town. If any Chimney should happen to be on Fire, he will put it out without any Danger to House or Chimney. And as he served his apprenticeship in Norwich he hopes the Citizens will make use of him sooner than of one that is a Stranger. NOTE: He has a large Quantity of SOOT to dispose of to any countryman that wants.

In the issue of the *Norwich Gazette* of November 17th, 1711, we find one William Gray propounding and practising a unique method for the recovery of old debts. It may be recommended to the attention of the tradesmen of the Norfolk towns :

> NOTICE is Hereby Given, that all Persons indebted for Strong Beer to Mr. WILLIAM GRAY (commonly called Major Gray), at the Sign of the Fountain in Saint Benedict's Parish, in Norwich, that if they will come to his House in the Parish aforesaid, and spend Six Pence in Jorams of Beer Ready Money, for every six pence they so spend, six pence more shall be set off of everyone of their respective Debt or Debts, provided the Persons so indebted do in that manner drink themselves out of such Debts within the Space of one Six Months from the Date hereof; but upon Failure thereof they shall be prosecuted according to Law. As witness my Hand,
>
> > WILLIAM GRAY.

The following from the *Norwich Gazette* of April 28th, 1722, is enigmatical as well as curious. One would think, as the gravedigger in *Hamlet* says concerning the grave, that the coffin was a house that lasted its tenant "till doomsday." It appears, however, that formerly it was possible for a coffin to serve two occupants in succession. How Robert Robinson came into possession of his gloomy chattels I am unable to say, but one cannot read the announcement without being haunted with grim visions of a midnight trade now happily rarely practised.

> Robert Robinson, in Saint Peter's Parish, in Norwich [near BEDLAM], has great Choice of good SECOND-HAND COFFINS to Sell for Ready Money.

Here is another, almost as curious in its way as any of the foregoing. Norfolk was in 1722 blessed with a " famous rat-catcher," and this is what he said of himself in the public prints :

> WILLIAM HUNT, of Woodrising, Taylor and Rat Catcher, in April last past, at the House of Mr. Robert

Adley in Woodton, catch'd in one Fortnight no less than 1418 Rats, the Truth of which will be attested by the Neighbourhood. The famous rat catcher is now to be spoken with at Woodton Hall.

AMUSEMENTS, FESTIVITIES, &c.

Nothing perhaps has undergone a greater change during the last century than the character of the amusements and sports of the people. Modern newspapers teem with accounts of the matches of the cricket clubs of which every village and hamlet in the country can now boast. In the old newspapers we find no indications of the game, but in place thereof we meet with a number of advertisements relating to the old-fashioned and now almost obsolete game of "camp." Here is one copied from the *Norwich Gazette* of May 2nd, 1741:

> To be Camp'd for Free, at Brundwell White Horse, near Blofield, on the 10th of May, Ten Hats with Silver Buttons and hoops: To hand up at One o'clock and play between Two and Three.

The famous Lynn Mart had sometimes some curious visitors. The following was in the same paper as the above of February 3rd, 1722:

> By His Majesty's Permission.
> THIS is to Give Notice to all Gentlemen, Ladies, and Others, that on Monday next, at Mr. Green's, in the Market Place, in Lynn, will be acted an excellent new Play called DIDO and ÆNEAS, or the wonderful Prince of Troy, with the enchantments of CIRCE, the Queen of Magic Art, where you will see her drawn in her chariot by Two Dragons, and how she flew away with the wondrous Prince of Troy. Likewise, a Young Woman that Dances with Swords, who turns round several Hundred Times together with incredible Swiftness, and carries Quart Pots and tankards on the hilts

of the Swords with the Points in her Mouth to Admiration. Also a Dance performed by an Italian, Scaramouch, and Harlequin, called the Hoop'd Petticoat Dance, with several other Entertainments too tedious to mention here. Also the Noble Wax Work, performed to a greater Curiosity than ever was before, representing the Court of Queen Eleanor and Fair Rosamond, the Figures as large as Men and Women. And lastly, several live creatures which tumble and Show you Variety of Comical Actions at the Word of Command. Performed by JOHN KIRBY, who will continue his Diversions there during the Mart.

The following news paragraphs show that the loyal and patriotic feeling, which appears to be a strong characteristic of the Norfolk people, and which was so enthusiastically manifested on the occasion of the visit of the Prince and Princess of Wales, with the Queen of Denmark and the Duke of Edinburgh, in 1866, existed and made itself apparent early in the eighteenth century. An old newspaper, dated June 2nd, 1722, gives the following narrative:

Tuesday last being the Anniversary of the Happy Restauration, the same was celebrated here with greater Demonstrations of Joy than has perhaps ever been known before: For besides ringing of Bells, firing of Guns, Bonfires, &c., the Streets were almost generally strewn with Sand, Thyme, Greens, and Flowers, Oaken Boughs set up at the Doors, Garlands and Pictures hung out, and Variety of Comick and Antick Dances performed in the Streets.

Admiral Vernon's successes were thus celebrated:

Saturday, May 23: On Thursday last, upon receiving the glorious news of the brave Admiral Vernon's taking Carthagena, the Bells in this city were rung, the Guns fired, at Night were Bonfires and Illuminations, and an uncommon face of Joy and Gladness appeared through the whole City. The Populace carried about 2 Men, one representing Admiral Vernon, whom they huzza'd all the Way; the other representing Don Blas, the Spanish Admiral, who looked very dejected and was houted.

Similar rejoicings took place at Wymondham, where it is added, "Trees were planted in the Streets like a Grove," and grand processions were made.

The following refers to a wonderful boat apparently exhibited in Norwich in the year 1722, and which was reported to give "much Satisfaction to all Beholders :"

> These are to inform all that are curious that here is arrived in Norwich, and is to be spoken with at the Lower Half Moon, the Author and Inventor of a wonderful and surprizing Machine or LEATHER BOAT, which he can fold up into a Handkerchief, and after it has been opened, by a Blast or Two of Wind, can enter therein, and Convey himself over or to any part of the River, be it ever so Large, at any Time, with Sailing and Rowing therein, which gives much Satisfaction to all Beholders. NOTE. Gentlemen, Ladies, and Others that have a Mind to be entertained with this Invention, being a strange Device, may send to the Place above mentioned, or may command him to any River or Water where they shall think Proper. The Master of this Machine stays in this Town but 14 Days.

RUNAWAY APPRENTICES, WIVES, &c.

Nothing is more common in the columns of the old newspapers than advertisements concerning runaway apprentices, very similar in their character to those which before the great war in America were so common in the newspapers of the United States. Here is one of these announcements and warnings, dated December 1, 1722 :

> Run Away on Sunday last from his Master, Mr. Geo. Kitson, Tayler, in Norwich, one PHINEAS SCOTT, his

Apprentice, a short thick Ladd about 19 Years old, in a Drab-coloured Coat with Bastard-Pearl Buttons on it, wears a Wigg, and sometimes a Furr'd Velvet Cap. Whoever can discover where he is Harboured shall have a Guinea paid by his said Master, and if Anyone entertains him they shall be prosecuted according to Law.

Sometimes the captors are requested to lodge the runaways in some one of His Majesty's gaols. The following chronicles the loss of a " stout sturdy Girl," who was a " little round-shouldered :"

Run Away from her Master, Mr. William Osborn of Lynn, one ANNE PEARSON, his Apprentice, who has Two Years to serve; she is a Stout Sturdy Girl about 19 Years of Age, Full-Faced, and a little Round-Shouldered; and had on when she went away a Purple and White coloured Gown : Whoever secures the said Anne Pearson and carries her to her Master aforesaid shall be well Rewarded and allowed reasonable Charges, but whoever harbours, entertains, or conceals her shall be prosecuted as the Law in such cases directs, by Me,

William Osborn.

The next of this class of advertisements which I have selected refers to a more serious delinquency than either of the two former. Here it is :

Whereas Sarah, the wife of William Rogers of Upton, in the county of Norfolk, Bricklayer, has lately eloped from her said Husband, and carry'd off with her divers Parcels of Goods and Sums of Money; this is to fore-warne all Persons from trusting her upon any account whatever, for her said Husband will pay no Debts that she shall contract : AND if any Person will stop and secure her and give notice of it to her said Husband, they shall have Half a Guinea Reward over and above their Charges. She is a Middle-Sized Woman of about 40, has a ruddy Complection, a Brown Eye, Long

Visaged, and has several Suits of Cloaths with her.
She is gon away with a tall thin Young Man of about
18 or 20 years old.

The following concerning a certain "thick-set quaddy
man," who in 1722 broke out of the Bethel, will be read
with interest by all who are acquainted with that noble institution, and the able and humane arrangements by which its
present management is characterised :

BROKE out of BETH-ELL [or BEDLAM] in
Norwich, on Thursday, the 9th of this instant August,
one George Bloodworth, a Distempered Man of about
35 Years of Age : He went away without either Hat or
Wigg, and is supposed to have on only a Wastecoat
and Breeches of a Dark Colour : He is a good thick-set
quaddy Man, pretty much Pock-broken, and of a
Swarthy Complection, the Hairs of his Face not cut
for Two Months Past, and his Shirt is marked with
G. B. Whoever secures the said George Bloodworth,
or will bring him to the Master of Bedlam aforesaid,
shall be fully satisfied for their Trouble.

MISCELLANIES.

I cannot close this sketch without bringing before the
attention of my readers a few other gleanings from the old
newspapers which I have been unable to include under any
of the above classes, but which I think will be acceptable
either from their quaintness or as illustrations of manners
and customs now grown obsolete. Among these latter I
have stumbled upon a number of advertisements showing
the manner in which the old word "pennyworth" was formerly used. It is not unusual to find a large estate announced
"to be sold a pennyworth," the phrase of course being equivalent to the modern formula, "to be sold a bargain." The
printer of the *Norwich Gazette* in 1722, "being determined
to take an apprentice," announces that "if he is a *lusty*

proper Ladd he will be accepted on more easie Terms," the word "lusty" in the sense intended by Mr. Crossgrove having long since disappeared from polite literature. Then there are advertisements showing the fearful character of small-pox among our forefathers in the eighteenth century. Here is one of them :—" Wanted a Journeyman Chandler having had the small pox, and being a good workman in the trade shall be kindly entertained by Robert Sadler, near the Red Well, Norwich." Here is the announcement of a marvel calculated to produce no small degree of alarm among the unlettered portion of the readers of Norwich newspapers in 1749 :—"Among the many Rationales that will be given with respect to the late trembling of the earth, it is said that Sir Isaac Newton Predicted that in the year 1750 the Planet Jupiter would in its passage be so near our Globe as possibly to brush it; if so, it would give Earth a great shake." Lest I should further disturb the gravity of my readers, and shake their faith in the sincerity of my transcriptions, I close these old volumes, and hope these gleanings may serve to wile away a half-hour, and give the modern student a useful glimpse of the nature of newspaper literature in the commencement of the eighteenth century.

II.

Old Ballads, Poetry &c.

Old Ballads.

BALLADS BY THOMAS DELONY.

Thomas Delony, of Norwich, was one of those minstrel bards that Bishop Percy in his *Reliques of Ancient Poetry* made known to our modern public. Mr. J. H. Dixon, who edited Delony's *Garland of Goodwill* for the Percy Society, says of the author:—"It would appear that the minstrel was a silk weaver, who made his poetical *debût* at Norwich about the year 1586. At any rate, the earliest metrical composition by him that is known to exist was printed in that year under the title of *A most joyfull Songe made in the Behalfe of all her Majesties faithful loving subjects*, which is a broadside of twenty-five four-line stanzas. *The Lamentation of Beccles*, another of his ballads, published after the great fire in that town, was also issued in 1586." Mr. Halliwell says:—"At a later period it is probable that hardly a month passed without the publication of some one or other of his efforts, but most of his productions have long since perished. They were for the most part of a humourous character, but he sometimes wrote in a serious, and even occasionally in a religious vein." He acquired great popularity before the close of the sixteenth century. Even the classic Drayton, in an allusion to his "rhyme," designates it "as full of state and pleasing;" and Tom Nash—that creature of genius, of famine, and despair —who from living at Lowestoft probably knew him personally, has in his *Have with you to Saffron Walden*, the following curious notice of him : – "Thomas Delony, the balleting silke-weaver, hath rime enough for all myracles, and wit to make a Garland of Goodwill more than the premisses, with an epistle of Momus and Zoylus; whereas his Muse, from the first peeping forth, hath stood at livery at an ale house whispe, never exceeding a penny quart, day nor night, and this deare yeare, together with the silencing of his looms, scarce that, he being constrained to betake him to carded ale, whence it proceede h that since Candlemas, or his jigge, John for the King, not one merrie dittie will come from him, but the Thunderbolt against Swearers—Repent, England, Repent—and the Strange Judgements of God." Mr. Dixon says :—" Delony's works exhibit the faults and excellencies of a self-taught man, whose life, there is too great reason to fear, was one continued struggle for existence, and who often wrote, not as fancy willed or the muse dictated, but because authorship was a worldly affair, an unpoetical matter of pounds shillings and pence. On no other hypothesis could the author of *The Banishment of the Two Dukes* be the author of *Shore's Wife*, or could the author of *The Spanish Lady* be the writer of disgusting ballads on the executions of the poor persecuted Catholics of his time."

Delony was a writer of romances as well as of ballads, and his *Jack of Newbury*, his *Thomas of Reading*, and his *History of the Gentle Craft* went through numerous editions.

In 1596 we find Delony mentioned by Stephen Slany, Lord Mayor of London, in a letter to Lord Burleigh (dated July 25th), as having published a " book for the silk weavers" which merited punishment. Stow tells us the nature of the offence when he says that in this book on the Dearth of Corn, Delony in a ballad " brought in the Queen speaking with her people dialogue wise in very fond and indecent sort." It is not known whether any proceedings were in consequence instituted against him, but he continued to write until the year 1600, when according to the evidence of Kempe, the actor (author of the *Nine Days' Wonder*), Delony was dead. Many of his historical ballads were collected soon after his decease, and published under the title of *Strange Histories*. An edition issued in 1607 is now so scarce that only two copies are known, and one of these is imperfect. From this I have selected some of the best publications of this Prince of Ballad Writers. The Three Old Ballads on the Overthrow of the Spanish Armada, are, however, reprinted from black-letter copies in the British Museum, supposed to be unique. They were written A.D. 1588.

The Queenes visiting of the Campe at Tilsburie, with her Entertainment there.

TO THE TUNE OF WILSON'S WILDE.

WITHIN the yeare of Christ our Lord
    a thousand and five hundreth full,
And eightie eight by just record,
    the which no man may disanull ;
And in the thirtieth yeare remaining
    of good Queene Elizabeth's reigning,
A mightie power there was prepared
    by Philip then the King of Spaine,
Against the maiden Queene of England
    which in peace before did reigne.

Her Ryall ships to sea she sent,
    to garde the coast on everie side :
And seeing how her foes were bent,
    her realme full well she did provide

With many thousands so prepared
    as like was never eist declared,
Of horsemen and of footemen plentie,
    whose good harts full well is seene
In the safegarde of their countrie
    and the service of our Queene.

In Essex faire, that fertill soile,
    upon the hill of Tilsburie :
To give our Spanish foes the foile,
    in gallant campe they now do lye,
Where good orders is ordained,
    and true justice eke maintained
For the punishment of persons
    that are lewde or badly bent ;
To see a sight so strange in England,
    'twas our gracious Queenes intent.

And on the eight of August she
    from faire Saint James tooke her way,
With many Lords of high degree
    in princely robes and rich aray,
And to bardge upon the water,
    being King Henryes royall daughter,
She did goe with trumpets sounding,
    and with dubbing drums apace,
Along the Thames, that famous river,
    for to view the campe a space.

When she as farre as Gravesend came,
    right over against that prettie towne :
Her royall grace with all her traine,
    was landed there with great renowne.
The Lordes and Captaines of her forces,
    mounted on their gallant horses,
Readie stood to entertaine her,
    like martiall men of courage bold :
Welcome to the campe dread soveraigne,
    thus they said both young and old.

The Bulworkes strong that stood thereby,
    well garded with sufficient men,
Then flags were spred couragiously,
    their cannons were discharged then.
Ech gunner did declare his cunning
    for joy conceived of her coming.
All the way her grace was riding,
    on each side stood armed men :
With muskets, pikes, and good caleevers,
    for her Graces safegarde then.

The Lord generall of the field
    had there his bloudie auncient borne ;
The Lord marshalls coulors eke,
    was carried there all rent and torne,
The which with bullets was so burned,
    when in Flaunders he sojourned.
Thus in warlike wise they martched,
    even as soft as foote could fall :
Because her Grace was fully minded
    perfectly to view them all.

Her faithfull souldiers great and small,
    as each one stood within his place,
Upon their knees began to fall
    desiring God to save her Grace.
For joy whereof her eyes was filled
    that the water downe distilled.
Lord blesse you all, my friendes, she said,
    but doe not kneele so much to me :
Then sent she warning to the rest,
    they should not let such reverence be.

Then casting up her Princely eyes,
    unto the hill with perfect sight :
The ground all covered she espyes,
    with feet of armed souldiers bright,
Whereat her royall hart so leaped,
    on her feet upright she stepped,

Tossing up her plume of feathers,
    to them all as they did stand :
Chearefully her body bending,
    waving of her royall hand.

Thus through the campe she passed quite
    in manner as I have declared :
At maister Riches for that night,
    her graces lodging was preparde.
The morrow after her abiding,
    on a princely paulfrey riding,
To the campe she cam to dinner,
    with her Lordes and Ladies all :
The Lord generall went to meete her,
    with his Guarde of yeomen tall.

The Sargeant trumpet with his mace,
    and nyne with trumpets after him,
Bare headed went before her grace,
    in coates of scarlet colour trim.
The king of Heralds tall and comely,
    was the next in order duely,
With the famous Armes of England,
    wrought with rich imbroidered gold,
On finest velvet, blue and crimson,
    that for silver can be sold.

With maces of cleane beaten gold,
    the Queenes two Sargeants then did ride,
Most comely men for to behold,
    in velvet coates and chaines beside.
The Lord generall then came riding,
    and Lord marshall hard beside him.
Richly were they both atired,
    in princelie garments of great price :
Bearing still their hats and fethers,
    in their handes in comely wise.

Then came the Queene on prauncing steede,
    atired like an Angell bright :

And eight brave footemen at her feete,
   whose jerkins were most rich in sight.
Her Ladies likewise of great honor,
   most sumpteously did waite upon her,
With pearles and diamonds brave adorned,
   and in costly cales of gold.
Her Guarde in scarlet then rid after,
   with bowes and arrowes stoute and bold.

The valiant Captaines of the field,
   meane space themselves in order set :
And each of them with speare and sheelde,
   to joyne in battaile did not let,
With such a warlike skill extended,
   as the same was much commended.
Such a battaile pitcht in England,
   many a day hath not beene seene :
Thus they stood in order waiting
   for the presence of our Queene.

At length her Grace most royally,
   received was and brought againe :
Where she might see most loyally
   this noble hoast and warlike traine.
How they came martching all together,
   like a wood in winter's weather.
With the strokes of drummers sounding,
   and with trampling horses than :
The earth and aire did sound like thunder,
   to the eares of everie man.

The warlike Armie then stood still,
   and drummers left their dubbing sound ;
Because it was our Princes will,
   to ride about the Armie round.
Her Ladies she did leave behind her,
   and her Guarde which still did minde her.
The Lord generall and Lord marshall,
   did conduct her to each place :

The pikes, the colours, and the lances,
    at her approch fell downe apace.

And then bespake our noble Queene :
    my loving friends and countrieman,
I hope this day the worst is seene,
    that in our wars ye shall sustaine.
But if our enimies doe assaile you
    never let your stomackes faile you.
For in the midst of all your troupe
    we ourselves will be in place :
To be your joy, your guide, and comfort,
    even before our enimies face.

This done the souldiers all at once,
    a mightie shout or crye did give :
Which forced from the assure skyes
    an Ecco loud from thence to drive.
Which fild her grace with joy and pleasure,
    and riding then from them by leasure,
With trumpets sound most loyally,
    along the court of guarde she went :
Who did conduct her Majestie
    unto the Lord chiefe generalls tent.

Where she was feasted royally,
    with dainties of most costly price :
And when that night approched nye,
    her Majestie with sage advice,
In gracious manner then returned,
    from the campe where she sojourned ;
And when that she was safelie sat,
    within her Barge, and past away,
Her farewell then the trumpets sounded,
    and the cannons fast did play.

Finis.   T. D.

*Imprinted at London by John Wolfe for
Edwarde White,* 1588.

*A Joyful new Ballad, declaring the happie obtaining of the
great Galleazzo, wherein Don Pietro de Valdez was the
chiefe, through the mightie power and providence of God,
being a speciall token of his gracious and fatherly goodness
towards us, to the great encouragement of all those that
willingly fight in the defence of his Gospel, and our good
Queene of England.*

TO THE TUNE OF MOUNSEURS ALMAIGNE.

O NOBLE England
  fall downe upon thy knee,
And praise thy God with thankfull hart
  which still maintaineth thee.
The forraine forces,
  that seekes thy utter spoile :
Shall then through his especiall grace
  be brought to shamefull foile.

With mightie power
  they come unto our coast :
To over runne our countrie quite,
  they make their brags and boast.
In strength of men
  they set their onely stay :
But we upon the Lord our God
  will put our trust alway.

Great is their number
  of ships upon the sea :
And their provision wonderfull,
  but Lord thou art our stay.
Their armed souldiers
  are many by account,
Their aiders eke in this attempt
  doe sundrie waies surmount.

The Pope of Rome
  with many blessed graines :
To sanctify their bad pretense
  bestowed both cost and paines.
But little land,
  be not dismaide at all ;
The Lord no doubt is on' our side,
  which soone will worke their fall.

In happie houre
  our foes we did discry .
And under saile with gallant wind
  as they cam passing by.
Which suddaine tidings
  to Plymouth being brought,
Full soone our Lord high Admirall,
  for to pursue them sought.
And to his traine
  coragiously he saide :
Now for the Lord and our good Queene
  to fight be not afraide.
Regard our cause,
  and play your partes like men :
The Lord no doubt will prosper us,
  in all our actions then.

This great Galleazzo,
  which was so huge and hye :
That like a bulwarke on the sea,
  did seeme to each mans eye.
There was it taken
  unto our great reliefe :
And divers Nobles in which traine
  Don Pietro was the chiefe.
Stronge was she stuft,
  with Cannons great and small :
And other instruments of warre,
  which we obtained all.

A certaine signe
  of good successe we trust:
That God will overthrow the rest,
  as he hath done the first.

Then did our Navie
  pursue the rest amaine :
With roaring noise of Cannons great,
  till they neare Callice came :
With manly courage,
  they followed them so fast :
Another mightie Gallion
  did seem to yeeld at last,
And in distresse
  for saveguard of their lives,
A flag of truce they did hang out
  with many mournfull cries :
Which when our men,
  did perfectly espie :
Some little barkes they sent to her
  to board her quietly.

But these false Spaniards,
  esteeming them but weake :
When they within their danger came,
  their malice forth did breake.
With charged cannons,
  they laide about them then :
For to destroy those proper barkes
  and all their valiant men.
Which when our men
  perceived so to be :
Like Lions fierce they forward went,
  to quite this injurie,
And bourding them
  with strong and mightie hand :
They kild the men untill their arke
  did sinke in Callice sand.

The chiefest Captaine
  Of this Gallion so hie :
Don Hugo de Moncaldo he,
  within this fight did die,
Who was the Generall
  of all the Gallions great :
But through his braines with pouders force
  a bullet strong did beat.
And manie more
  by sword did loose their breath :
And manie more within the sea
  did swimme and tooke their death.
There might you see
  the salt and foming flood :
Died and staind like scarlet red,
  with store of Spanish blood.

This mightie vessell
  was threescore yards in length :
Most wonderfull to each man's eie,
  for making and for strength.
In her was placed
  an hundreth Cannons great :
And mightily provided eke,
  with bread-corne, wine, and meat.
There was of oares,
  two hundreth I weene :
Threescore foote and twelve in length
  well measured to be scene.
And yet subdued,
  with manie others more :
And not a Ship of ours lost,
  the Lord be thankt therefore.

Our pleasant countrie,
  so fruitfull and so faire,
They doe intend by deadly warre,
  to make both poore and bare.

Our townes and cities,
　　to racke and sacke likewise :
To kill and murder man and wife
　　as malice doth arise.
And to deflower
　　our virgins in our sight :
And in the cradle cruelly
　　the tender babe to smite.
Gods holy truth
　　they meane for to cast downe :
And to deprive our noble Queene
　　Both of her life and crowne.

Our wealth and riches,
　　which we enjoyed long :
They doe appoint their pray and spoile,
　　by crueltie and wrong ;
To set our houses
　　a fier on our heades :
And cursedly to cut our throates,
　　as we lye in our beds.
Our children's braines,
　　to dash against the ground :
And from the earth our memorie
　　for ever to confound.
To change our joy
　　to griefe and mourning sad :
And never more to see the dayes
　　of pleasure we have had.

But God Almightie
　　be blessed evermore :
Who doth encourage Englishmen,
　　to beate them from our shoare.
With roaring Cannons,
　　their hastie steps to stay :
And with the force of thundering shot
　　to make them flye away.

Who made account
　before this time or day :
Against the walls of faire London
　their banners to display.
But their intent
　the Lord will bring to nought,
If faithfully we call and cry
　for succour as we ought.

And you deare bretheren
　which beareth armes this day,
For safegarde of your native soile,
　marke well what I shall say.
Regard your dueties,
　thinke on your countries good :
And feare not in defense thereof,
　to spend your dearest bloud.
Our gracious Queene
　doth greete you every one :
And saith she will among you be
　in every bitter storme.
Desiring you
　true English harts to beare :
To God, and her, and to the land
　wherein you nursed were.

Lord God Almightie,
　which hath the harts in hand :
Of everie person to dispose,
　defend this English land.
Blesse thou our Soveraigne
　with long and happie life :
Induc her Councel with thy grace
　and end this mortall strife.
Give to the rest
　of Commons more and lesse :
Loving harts, obedient minds,
　and perfect faithfullnesse.

That they and we,   *
and all with one accord :
On Sion hill may sing the praise
of our most mightie Lord.

Finis.   T. D.

LONDON :
Printed by John Wolfe, for Edward White,
1588.

---

*A new Ballet of the straunge and most cruell Whippes which
the Spanyards had prepared to Whippe and torment English
men and women : which were found and taken at the overthrow of certaine of the Spanishe shippes in July last
past, 1588.*

TO THE TUNE OF THE VALIANT SOLDIOUR.

A L you that list to looke and see
    what profite comes from Spayne,
And what the Pope and Spanyards both
    prepared for our gayne.
Then turne your eyes and bend your eares,
    and you shall heare and see
What courteous minds, what gentle harts,
    they beare to thee and mee.

They say they seeke for Englands good
    and wish the people well :
They say they are such holie men,
    all other they excell.
They bragge that they are Catholikes
    and Christes only Spouse :
And what so ere they take in hand
    the holie Pope allowes.

These holie men, these sacred Saints,
   and these that thinke no ill,
See how they sought against all right
   to murder, spoyle, and kill.
Our noble Queene and countrie first
   they did prepare to spoyle,
To ruinate our lives and lands
   with trouble and turmoyle.

And not content by fire and sword
   to take our right away :
But to torment most cruelly
   our bodies night and day.
Although they ment with murdring hands
   our guiltless bloud to spill :
Before our deathes they did devise
   to whip us first their fill.

And for that purpose had preparde
   of whips such wondrous store,
So straungely made, that sure the like
   was never scene before.
For never was there horse nor mule,
   nor dogge of currish kinde,
That ever had such whips devisde
   by any savadge minde.

One sorte of whips they had for men,
   so smarting, fierce and fell ;
As like could never be devisde
   by any devill in hell.
The strings whereof with wyerie knots,
   like rowels they did frame,
That every stroke might teare the flesh
   they layd on with the same.

And pluckt the spreading sinewes from
   the hardned bloudie bone,
To pricke and pearce each tender veine
   within the bodie knowne.

And not to leave one crooked ribbe,
  on any side unseene ;
Nor yet to leave a lumpe of flesh
  the head and foote betweene.

And for our seelie women eke,
  their hearts with griefe to clogge,
They made such whips wherewith no man
  would seeme to strike a dogge.
So strengthened eke with brasen tagges,
  and filde so rough and thin,
That they would force at every lash
  the bloud abroad to spinne.

Although their bodies sweet and fayre,
  their spoyle they ment to make ;
And on them first their filthie lust,
  and pleasure for to take.
Yet afterward such sower sauce
  they shoulde be sure to finde,
That they shoulde curse each springing braunch,
  that cometh of their kinde.

O Ladies fayre what spite were this,
  your gentle hearts to kill :
To see these devilish tyrants thus
  your childrens bloud to spill.
What griefe unto the husband deare
  his loving wife to see
Tormented so before his face
  with extreame villanie.

And thinke you not that they which had
  such dogged mindes to make
Such instruments of tyrannie,
  had not like hearts to take
The greatest vengeance that they might
  upon us every one :
Yes, yes, be sure, for godlie feare
  and mercie they have none.

Even as in India once they did
   against those people there,
With cruell curres in shamefull sorte
   the men both rent and teare.
And set the Ladies great with childe
   upright against a tree,
And shoot them through with pearcing darts,
   such would their practise bee.

Did not the Romans in this land
   sometime like practise use
Against the Brittaines bolde in heart
   and wonderously abuse
The valiant King whom they had caught
   before his Queene and wife,
And with most extreame tyrannie
   dispatcht him of his life?

The good Queene Voadicia,
   and eke her daughters three :
Did they not first abuse them all
   by lust and lecherie :
And after stript them naked all,
   and whipt them in such sorte :
That it would grieve each Christian hearte
   to heare that just reporte.

And if these ruffling mates of Rome
   did Princes thus torment :
Thinke you the Romish Spanyards now
   would not shewe their desent.
How did they late in Rome rejoyce,
   in Italie and Spayne :
What ringing and what bonfires,
   what masses sung amaine.

What printed bookes were sent about
   as filled their desire :
How England was by Spanyards wonne
   and London set on fire.

Be these the men that are so milde
  whom some so holie call :
The Lord defend our noble Queene
  and Countrie from them all.

             Finis.   T. D.

*Imprinted at London by Thomas Orwin
and Thomas Gubbin, and are to
be solde in Paternoster row
over against the blacke
Raven,* 1588.

WILLIAM THE CONQUEROR.

The copy of this ballad in *Strange Histories*, 1607, is entitled "The valiant courage and policy of the Kentishmen with long tails, whereby they kept their ancient laws and customs which William the Conqueror sought to take from them—to the tune of Rogero." Evans, who prints the ballad, has given the following account of the event which gave rise to it, taken from the *Lives of the Three Norman Kings of England*, by Sir John Hayward, 4to, 1613, p. 97 :—" Further, by the counsel of Stigand, Archbishop of Canterbury, and of Eglesine, Abbot of St. Augustine's (who at that time were the chief governors of Kent), as the King was riding towards Dover, at Swanscombe, two miles from Gravesend, the Kentishmen came towards him armed and bearing boughs as if it had been a moving wood ; they enclosed him upon the sudden, and with a firm countenance, but words well tempered with modesty and respect, they demanded of him the use of their ancient liberties and laws ; that in other matters they would yield obedience unto him ; that without this they desired not to live. The King was content to strike sail to the storm and to give them a vain satisfaction for the present ; knowing right well that the general customs and laws of the residue of the realm would in a short time overflow these particular places. So pledges being given on both sides, they conducted him to Rochester, and yielded up the Castle of Dover into his power."

The ballad as here given is from a unique copy of Delony's *Strange Histories*, dated 1607. It will be found to differ considerably from the version of it given in Percy's *Ballad Folio*, but it is, happily, a much better ballad, as well as an earlier printed one.

When William Duke of Normandy,
  With glittering spear and shield,
Had entered into fair England
  And foil'd his foes in field,

On Christmas Day, in solemn sort,
  Then was he crowned here,
By Albert Archbishop of York,
  With many a noble peer.

Which being done, he changed quite
  The customs of this land,
And punished such as daily sought
  His statutes to withstand :
And many cities he subdued,
  Fair London with the rest ;
But Kent did still withstand his force,
  And did his laws detest.

To Dover then he took his way,
  The Castle down to fling,
Which Arviragus builded there,
  The noble British King.
Which when the brave Archbishop bold
  Of Canterbury knew,
The Abbot of St. Augustine's eke,
  With all their gallant crew,

They set themselves in armour bright,
  These mischiefs to prevent,
With all the yeomen brave and bold
  That were in fruitful Kent.
At Canterbury they did meet
  Upon a certain day,
With sword and spear, with bill and bow,
  And stopp'd the Conqueror's way.

Let us not live like bondmen poor
  To Frenchmen in their pride,
But keep our ancient liberty,
  What chance so e'er betide.
And rather die in bloody field,
  In manly courage prest (ready),
Than to endure the servile yoke
  Which we so much detest.

Thus did the Kentish commons cry
  Unto their leaders still,
And so marched forth in warlike sort,
  And stand on Swanscombe hill :
Where in the woods they hid themselves,
  Under the shady green,
Thereby to get them vantage good
  Of all their foes unseen.

And for the Conqueror's coming there
  They privily laid wait,
And thereby suddenly appall'd
  His lofty high conceit ;
For when they spied his approach,
  In place as they did stand,
Then marched they to hem him in,
  Each one a bough in hand.

So that unto the Conqueror's sight,
  Amazed as he stood,
They seem'd to be a walking grove,
  Or else a moving wood.
The shape of men he could not see,
  The boughs did hide them so ;
And now his heart for fear did quake,
  To see a forest go.

Before, behind, and on each side,
  As he did cast his eye,
He spied those woods with sober pace
  Approach to him full nigh ;
But when the Kentishmen had thus
  Enclos'd the Conqueror round,
Most suddenly they drew their swords,
  And threw the boughs to ground.

Their banners they display'd in sight,
  Their trumpets sound a charge,
Their rattling drums strike up alarms,
  Their troops stretch out at large.

The Conqueror, with all his train,
  Were hereat sore aghast,
And most in peril when he thought
  All peril had been past.

Unto the Kentishmen he sent,
  The cause to understand,
For what intent, and for what cause,
  They took this war in hand?
To whom they made this short reply,
  For liberty we fight,
And to enjoy King Edward's laws,
  The which we hold our right.

Then said the dreadful Conqueror
  You shall have what you will,
Your ancient customs and your laws,
  So that you will be still;
And each thing else that you will crave
  With reason, at my hand,
So you will but acknowledge me
  Chief King of fair England.

The Kentishmen agreed thereon,
  And laid their arms aside,
And by this means King Edward's laws
  In Kent doth still abide;
And in no place in England else
  Those customs do remain,
Which they by manly policy
  Did of Duke William gain.

BANISHMENT OF THE DUKES OF NORFOLK AND HEREFORD BY RICHARD THE SECOND.

The subject of this ballad is the well-known quarrel between the Dukes of Norfolk and Hereford, which finally resulted in their banishment in 1398. Thomas Lord Mowbray, the first who held the Castle of Framling-ham, was the individual who caused the death of the Duke of Gloucester

It was for this and other services of a like nature that Richard created him "Duke of Norfolk." He was afterwards charged by the Duke of Hereford (who subsequently became Henry IV.) with speaking seditious words of his sovereign. No legal trial was entered upon, but the King consented to let the question be decided by private combat. The trumpet sounded for the shock of arms, when suddenly the King stopped the onset, and banished Norfolk for life and Hereford for ten years. Norfolk died at Venice about a year after he left England on his expiatory punishment.

Mr. J. W. Hales has remarked that the ballad account of the origin of the quarrel is not quite fair. Hereford accused Norfolk, not Norfolk Hereford, of treason. But the ballad goes with the winning side. *Vox populi* mostly shouts in favour of the successful.

Two noble dukes of great renown,
    That long had liv'd in fame,
Thro' hateful envy were cast down,
    And brought to sudden shame.

The Duke of Hereford was the one,
    A prudent prince and wise ;
'Gainst whom such malice there was shown,
    Which soon in sight did rise.

The Duke of Norfolk, most untrue,
    Declar'd unto the King,
The Duke of Hereford greatly grew
    In hatred of each thing,

Which by his grace was acted still
    Against both high and low ;
And how he had a trait'rous will
    His state to overthrow.

The Duke of Hereford then, in haste,
    Was sent for to the King ;
And, by the lords in order plac'd,
    Examin'd of each thing :

Who being guiltless of this crime,
    Which was against him laid,
The Duke of Norfolk at that time,
    These words unto him said :

How canst thou with a shameless face
  Deny a truth so stout ;
And here, before his royal grace,
  So falsely face it out ?

Did not these wicked treasons pass
  When we together were ;
How that the King unworthy was
  The royal crown to wear ?

Wherefore my gracious lord, quoth he,
  And you, his noble peers,
ᵓ whom I wish long life to be,
  .Vith many happy years :

I do pronounce before you all,
  This treacherous lord that's here,
A traitor to our noble King ;
  As time shall shew it clear.

The Duke of Hereford hearing that,
  In mind was grieved much ;
And did return this answer flat,
  Which did Duke Norfolk touch :

The term of traitor, truthless duke,
  In scorn and great disdain,
With flat defiance to thy face,
  I do return again ;

And, therefore, if it please your grace,
  To grant me leave (quoth he)
To combat with my deadly foe,
  That here accuseth me ;

I do not doubt but plainly prove,
  That like a perjured knight,
He hath most falsely sought my shame,
  Against all truth and right.

The King did grant this just request,
   And did therewith agree,
At Coventry in August next,
   This combat fought should be.

The dukes on sturdy steeds full stout,
   In coats of steel most bright,
With spears in rests, did enter lists,
   This combat fierce to fight.

The King then cast his warden down,
   Commanding them to stay ;
And with his lords he counsel took
   To stint that mortal fray.

·At length unto these noble dukes
   The king of heralds came,
And unto them, with lofty speech,
   This sentence did proclaim :

Sir Henry Bolingbroke, this day,
   The Duke of Hereford here,
And Thomas Mowbray, Norfolk Duke,
   Valiantly did appear ;

And having in honourable sort
   Repaired to this place ;
Our noble King, for special cause,
   Hath alter'd thus the case.

First, Henry, Duke of Hereford,
   Ere fifteen days be past,
Shall 'part the realm on pain of death,
   While ten years space doth last.

And Thomas, Duke of Norfolk, now,
   That hath begun this strife,
And, therefore, no good proof could bring ;
   I say, for term of life.

By judgment of our sovereign lord,
    Which now in place doth stand,
For evermore I banish thee
    Out of thy native land;

Charging thee, on pain of death,
    When fifteen days are past,
Thou never tread on English ground,
    So long as life doth last.

Thus they were sworn before the King,
    Ere they did further pass,
The one should never come in place
    Where as the other was.

Then both the dukes, with heavy hearts,
    Were parted presently,
Their uncouth streams of froward chance
    In foreign lands to try.

The Duke of Norfolk coming then
    Where he could shipping take,
The bitter tears fell down his cheeks,
    And thus his moan did make

Now let me sigh and sob my fill,
    Ere I from hence depart,
That inward pangs with speed may burst
    My sore afflicted heart.

Oh, cursed man! whose loathed life
    Is held so much in scorn;
Whose company is clean despis'd
    And left as one forlorn!

Now take thy leave and last adieu,
    Of this thy country dear,
Which never more thou must behold,
    Nor yet approach it near.

Now happy should I count myself,
   If death my heart had torn ;
That I might have my bones entomb'd,
   Where I was bred and born :

Or that by Neptune's wrathful rage
   I might be forc'd to die
While that sweet England's pleasant banks
   Did stand before mine eye :

How sweet a scent hath English ground
   Within my senses now !
How fair unto my outward sight
   Seems ev'ry branch and bough !

The fields and flow'rs, the streets and stones,
   Seem such unto my mind,
That in all other countries, sure,
   The like I ne'er shall find.

O, that the sun, with shining face,
   Would stay his steeds by strength ;
That this same day might stretched be
   To twenty years in length ;

And that the true performing tide
   Her hasty course would stay ;
That Æolus would never yield
   To bear me hence away !

That by the fountain of my eyes,
   The fields might water'd be ;
That I might grow my grievous plant
   Upon each springing tree.

But time, I see, with eagle's wings,
   So swift doth fly away ;
And dusty clouds begin to dim
   The brightness of the day.

The fatal hour draweth on,
    The winds and tides agree;
And now sweet England, over soon,
    I must depart from thee.

The mariners have hoisted sail,
    And call to catch me in;
And now, in woful heart, I feel,
    My torments to begin.

Therefore, farewell for evermore,
    Sweet England, unto thee;
And farewell, all my friends, which I
    Again shall never see.

O, England, here I kiss the ground
    Upon my bended knee?
Whereby to show to all the world
    How dearly I love thee.

This being said, away he went,
    As fortune did him guide,
And at the length, thro' grief of heart,
    In Venice there he died.

The noble duke, in doleful sort,
    Did leave his life in France,
And at the last, the mighty Lord
    Did him full high advance.

The Lords of England afterwards
    Did send for him again,
While that King Richard at the wars
    In Ireland did remain;

Who, by the vile and great abuse
    Which thro' his deeds did spring,
Deposed was, and then the Duke
    Was truly crowned King.

A TRUE RELATION OF THE LIFE AND DEATH
OF SIR ANDREW BARTON, A PYRATE & ROVER ON THE SEAS.

TUNE—"COME FOLLOW MY LOVE," ETC.

The father of Andrew Barton was a Scotchman, and he having suffered by
sea from the Portuguese, obtained from the King of Scotland letters of
marque for his two sons to make reprisals. But complaints were soon
made to the Government of England, that under pretence of searching
for Portuguese goods Barton, who was called Sir Andrew Barton,
interrupted the English trade. The complaints were numerous, but
Henry [A.D. 1511] was reluctant to provoke a quarrel with Scotland, till
the Earl of Surrey (afterwards Duke of Norfolk) indignant at the
interruptions, declared before the Council Board that while he had an
estate capable of furnishing a ship, or a son able to command it, the
narrow seas should not be infested by a rover. The King accepted the
offer of Surrey, and two ships were immediately fitted out under the
Earl's sons, Sir Thomas (called Lord Howard by old historians, created
Earl of Surrey in his father's lifetime, and the father of the poet
Earl), and Sir Edward. Barton had the reputation of being one of the
ablest sea officers of the time, but after an obstinate engagement he was
defeated. He died encouraging his men with his whistle to hold out to
the last. His ships with their freights and crews were carried into the
Thames. The battle of Flodden, in which James IV lost his life, is said to
have been caused by this capture.

The present text of the following ballad is taken from an original black
letter copy preserved in the British Museum, and edited by Mr. J. O.
Halliwell for the Percy Society. The ballad is principally known by the
version published by Bishop Percy in his *Reliques*, but on comparison that
will be found to differ very materially from the one here given.

When Flora with her fragrant flowers
　　Bedeckt the earth so trim and gay,
And Neptune with his dainty showers
　　Came to present the month of May,
King Henry would a hunting ride,
　　Over the river Thames passed he,
Unto a mountain-top also
　　Did walk, some pleasure for to see:

Where forty merchants he espy'd,
　　With fifty sail came towards him,
Who then no sooner were arriv'd,
　　But on their knees did thus complain:

"An't please your grace, we cannot sail
  To France no voyage to be sure,
But Sir Andrew Barton makes us quail,
  And robs us of our marchant ware."

Vext was the King, and turning him,
  Said to the Lords of high degree,
"Have I ne'er a Lord within my realm
  Dare fetch that traytor unto me?"
To him reply'd, Charles Lord Howard,
  "I will, my liege, with heart and hand,
If it will please you grant me leave," he said,
  "I will perform what you command."

To him then spoke King Henry,
  "I fear, my Lord, you are too young."
"No whit at all, my Liege," quoth he;
  "I hope to prove in valour strong:
The Scotch Knight I vow to seek
  In what place soever he be,
And bring ashore with all his might,
  Or into Scotland he shall carry me."

"A hundred men," the King then said,
  "Out of my realm shall chosen be,
Besides sailors and ship-boys,
  To guide a great ship on the sea:
Bow-men and gunners of good skill
  Shall for this service chosen be,
And they at thy command and will
  In all affairs shall wait on thee."

Lord Howard call'd a gunner then,
  Who was the best in all the realm,
His age was three score years and ten,
  And Peter Simon was his name.
My Lord call'd then a bow-man rare,
  Whose active hands had gain'd fame,
A gentleman born in Yorkshire,
  And William Horsley was his name.

"Horsley," quoth he, "I must to sea
    To seek a traytor, with good speed ;
Of a hundred bow-men brave," quoth he,
    "I have chosen thee to be the head."
"If you, my Lord, have chosen me
    Of a hundred men to be the head,
Upon the main mast I'll hanged be
    If twelve score I miss one shilling's breadth."

Lord Howard then of courage bold,
    Went to the sea with pleasant cheer,
Not curb'd with winter's piercing cold,
    Tho' it was the stormy time of year ;
Not long had he been on sea,
    More in days than number three,
But one Henry Hunt there he espy'd,
    A merchant of New-castle was he ;

To him Lord Howard call'd out amain,
    And strictly charged him to stand,
Demanding then from whence he came,
    Or where he did intend to land :
The merchant then made answer soon,
    With heavy heart and careful mind,
"My Lord, my ship it doth belong
    Unto New-castle-upon-Tine."

"Canst thou shew me," the Lord did say,
    "As thou didst sail by day and night,
A Scottish rover on the sea,
    His name is Andrew Barton, knight ?"
Then the merchant sigh'd, and said
    With grieved mind, and well away,
"But over well I know that wight
    I was his prisoner yesterday :

As I, my lord, did sail from France
    A Burdeave voyage to take so far,
I met with Sir Andrew Barton thence,
    Who rob'd me of my merchant ware :

And mickle debts God knows I owe,
  And every man doth crave his own ;
And I am bound to London now,
  Of our gracious King to beg a boon."

"Show me him," said Lord Howard then,
  "Let me once the villain see,
And ev'ry penny he hath from thee ta'en
  I'll double the same with shillings three."
"Now God forbid," the merchant said,
  "I fear your aim that you will miss :
God bless you from his tyranny,
  For little you think what man he is.

He is brass within and steel without,
  His ship most huge and mighty strong,
With eighteen pieces of ordnance
  He carrieth on each side along :
With beams for his top-castle
  As also being huge and high,
That neither English nor Portugal
  Can Sir Andrew Barton pass by."

"Hard news thou shew'st," then said the lord,
  "To welcome stranger to the sea :
But as I said I'll bring him aboard,
  Or unto Scotland he shall carry me."
The merchant said, "If you will do so,
  Take councel then, I pray, withal,
Let no man to his top-castle go,
  Nor strive to let his beams downfall."

"Lend me seven pieces of ordnance then
  Of each side of my ship," said he,
"And to morrow, my Lord,
  Again I will your honour see.
A glass I set as may be seen,
  Whether you sail by day or night,
And to morrow be sure before seven,
  You shall see Sir Andrew Barton, knight."

The merchant set my Lord a glass,
　So well apparent in his sight,
That on the morrow, as his promise was,
　He saw Sir Andrew Barton, knight;
The lord then swore a mighty oath,
　"Now by the heavens that be of might,
By faith, believe me, and by troth,
　I think he is a worthy knight."

Sir Andrew Barton seeing him
　Thus scornfully to pass by,
As tho' he cared not a pin
　For him and his company;
Then called he his men amain,
　"Fetch back yon pedlar now," quoth he,
"And ere this way he comes again,
　I'll teach him well his courtesie."

"Fetch me my lyon out of hand,"
　Saith the lord, " with rose and streamer high;
Set up withal a willow-wand,
　That merchant like I may pass by."
Thus bravely did Lord Howard pass,
　And on anchor rise so high;
No top-sail at last he cast,
　But as a foe did him defie.

A piece of ordnance soon was shot
　By this proud pirate fiercely then,
Into Lord Howard's middle deck,
　Which cruel shot killed fourteen men,
He called then Peter Simon, he,
　"Look how thy word do stand instead,
For thou shalt be hanged on main-mast
　If thou miss twelve score one penny breadth."

Then Peter Simon gave a shot,
　Which did Sir Andrew mickle scare,
In at his deck it came so hot,
　Kill'd fifteen of his men of war;

"Alas," then said the Pirate stout,
 "I am in danger now I see ;
This is some lord I greatly fear,
 That is set on to conquer me."

Then Henry Hunt, with rigour hot,
 Came bravely on the other side,
Who likewise shot in at his deck,
 And killed fitty of his men beside :
Then, "Out, alas," Sir Andrew cry'd,
 "What may a man now think or say,
Yon merchant-thief that pierceth me,
 He was my prisoner yesterday."

Then did he on Gordion call,
 Unto the top castle for to go,
And bid his beams he should let fall,
 For he greatly fear'd an overthrow.
The lord call'd Horsley, now in haste,
 "Look that thy word stand instead,
For thou shalt be hanged on main-mast,
 If thou miss twelve score a shilling's breadth."

Then up mast-tree swerved he,
 This stout and mighty Gordion ;
But Horsley, he most happily
 Shot him under his collar-bone :
Then call'd he on his nephew then,
 Said, "Sister's sons I have no mo,
Three hundred pound I will give thee,
 If thou wilt to top-castle go."

Then stoutly he began to climb,
 From off the mast scorn'd to depart :
But Horsley soon prevented him,
 And deadly pierc'd him to the heart.
His men being slain, then up amain
 Did this proud pirate climb with speed,
For armour of proof he had put on,
 And did not dint of arrows dread :

"Come hither, Horsley," said the Lord,
 " See thou thy arrows aim aright ;
Great means to thee I will afford,
 And if thou speedst, I'll make thee knight."
Sir Andrew did climb up the tree,
 With right good will and all his main ;
Then upon the breast hit Horsley he,
 Till the arrow did return again ;

Then Horsley 'spied a private place
 With a perfect eye in a secret part
His arm swiftly flew apace
 And Smote Sir Andrew to the heart :
" Fight on, fight on, my merry men all,
 A little I am hurt, yet not slain ;
I'll but lie down and bleed awhile,
 And come and fight with you again.

And do not," said he, " fear English rogues,
 And of your foes stand not in awe,
But stand fast by St Andrew's crosse
 Until you hear my whistle blow."
They never heard his whistle blow,
 Which made them all full sore afraid.
Then Horsley said, " My Lord aboard ,
 For now Sir Andrew Barton's dead."

Thus boarded they this gallant ship,
 With right goodwill and all their main,
Eighteen score Scots alive in it,
 Besides as many more was slain.
The Lord went where Sir Andrew lay
 And quickly thence cut off his head.
" I should forsake England many a day
 If thou were alive as thou art dead. "

Thus from the wars Lord Howard came,
 With mickle joy and triumphing ;
The pirate's head he brought along
 For to present unto our King,

Who briefly unto him did say,
　Before he knew well what was done,
" Where is the knight, and pirate gay,
　That I myself may give the doom ?"

" You may thank God," then said the lord,
　" And four men in the ship," quoth he,
" That we are safely come ashore,
　Sith you never had such an enemy :
That is, Henry Hunt, and Peter Simon,
　William Horsley, and Peter's son ;
Therefore reward them for their pains,
　For they did service at their turn."

To the merchant therefore the King he said,
　" In lieu of what he hath from thee tane,
I give thee a noble a-day,
　Sir Andrew's whistle and his chain ;
To Peter Simon a crown a-day ;
　And half-a-crown a-day to Peter's son,
And that was for a shot so gay,
　Which bravely brought Sir Andrew down ;

Horsley, I will make thee a knight,
　And in Yorkshire thou shalt dwell ;
Lord Howard shall Earl Bury hight,
　For this act he deserveth well ;
Ninety pound to our English men,
　Who in this fight did stoutly stand ;
And twelve pence a-day to the Scots till they
　Come to my brother King's high land."

AN EXCELLENT SONG ON THE WINNING OF CALES
BY THE ENGLISH.

The fate of the Armada did not quench the fury of Philip II, who prepared a fleet for a second invasion of England, but Elizabeth anticipated
the attack, by a descent on the Spanish coast, and the victory celebrated
in the following very spirited sea song commemorates that event. The
expedition sailed from Plymouth under the command of Admiral Lord

Howard, with the Earl of Essex as General of the Army, on the 1st of June, 1596, and reached Cadiz on the 20th of that month. The armament was intended to destroy the Spanish fleet in Cadiz, and was equipped with such great celerity, that it arrived off that city before any news of its preparation had reached Spain. The smallest of the ships, commanded by the Admiral, entered the harbor the day after their arrival, and the soldiers under the Earl of Essex attacked the town, and would have put the garrison to the sword, had it not been ransomed by the payment of about 600,000 ducats. The Spaniards offered two millions of ducats as a ransom for their fleet lying in Puerto Real, but this was refused by the Lord High Admiral, who sent Sir Walter Raleigh and Lord Thomas Howard to destroy it. A large number of vessels, freighted for the West Indies, two rich galleons with 100 trap guns, a number of ships of war, and 1200 pieces of ordnance, were taken or sunk. The Spaniards fought well, but in the end were completely defeated, and their loss was estimated at twenty millions of ducats. Cadiz was plundered, all the forts demolished, and a great part of the town laid in ashes.

Percy says that the Earl of Essex knighted on this occasion not fewer than sixty persons, which gave rise to the following sarcasm :—

> "A gentleman of Wales, a knight of Cales,
>   And a laird of the north country ;
> But a yeoman of Kent, with his yearly rent,
>   Will buy them out all three."

The ballad is re-printed from Delony's "Garland of Good Will," and will be found to contain many variations from that which Percy printed.

> Long had the proud Spaniards
>   Advanced to conquer us,
> Threatening our country
>   With fire and sword ;
> Often preparing
>   Their navy most sumptuous,
> With all the provision
>   That Spain could afford.
>   Dub, a-dub, dub,
>   Thus strike the drums,
>   Tan-ta-ra, ta-ra-ra,
>   The Englishman comes.
>
> To the seas presently
>   Went our lord admiral,
> With knights couragious,
>   And captains full good ;

The Earl of Essex,
  A prosperous general,
With him prepared
  To pass the salt flood,
    Dub a-dub, &c.

At Plymouth speedily
  Took they ships valiantly ;
Braver ships never
  Were seen under sail ;
With their fair colours spread,
  And streamers o'er their head ;
Now, bragging Spaniards
  Take heed of your tail.
    Dub-a-dub, &c.

Unto Cales cunningly
  Came we most happily,
Where the King's navy
  Did secretly ride ;
Being upon their backs,
  Piercing their butts of sack,
Ere that the Spaniards
  Our coming descry'd.
    Tan-ta-ra, ta-ra-ra,
      The English man comes ;
    Bounce-a-bounce, bounce-a-bounce,
    Off went the guns.

Great was the crying,
  Running and riding,
Which at that season
  Was made at that place ;
Then beacons were fir'd,
  As need was required ;
To hide their great treasure
  They had little space.
    Alas ! they cry'd,
      English man comes, &c.

There you might see the ships,
　　How they were fired fast,*
And how the men drown'd
　　Themselves in the sea ;
There you may hear them cry,
　　Wail and weep piteously,
When as they saw no shift
　　Te escape thence away.
　　　　Dub-a-dub, &c.

The great *Saint Philip*,
　　The pride of the Spaniards,
Was burnt to the bottom,
　　And sunk in the sea ;
But the *Saint Andrew*,
　　And eke the *Saint Matthew*,
We took in fight manfully
　　And brought them away.
　　　　Dub-a-dub, &c.

The Earl of Essex,
　　Most valiant and hardy,
With horsemen and footmen
　　March'd towards the town ;
The enemies which saw them,
　　Full greatly affrighted,
Did fly for their safeguard,
　　And durst not come down.
　　　　Dub-a-dub, &c.

Now, quoth the noble earl,
　　Courage, my soldiers all !
Fight, and be valiant,
　　And spoil you shall have ;
And well rewarded all,
　　From the great to the small ;

---

* The Duke of Medina, the Spanish Admiral, set fire to the ships in
order to prevent their falling into the hands of the English.

But look that the women
And children you save.
Dub-a-dub, &c.

The Spaniards at that sight,
Saw 'twas in vain to fight,
Hung up their flags of truce,
Yielding the town ;
We march'd in presently,
Decking the walls on high
With our English colours,
Which purchas'd renown.
Dub-a-dub, &c.

Ent'ring the houses then,
And of the richest men,
For gold and treasure
We searchĕd each day ;
In some places we did find
Pye baking in the oven,
Meat at the fire roasting,
And men run away.
Dub-a-dub, &c.

Full of rich merchandize,
Every shop we did see,
Damask and sattins,
And velvet full fair,
Which soldiers measure out
By the length of their swords ;
Of all commodities,
Each one hath share.
Dub-a-dub, &c.

Thus Cales was taken,
And our brave general
March'd to the market place,
There he did stand ;

There many prisoners
  Of good account were took;
Many crav'd mercy,
  And mercy they found.
    Dub-a-dub, &c.

When as our general
  Saw they delayèd time,
And would not ransom
  The town as they said,
With their fair wainscots,
  Their presses and bedsteads,
Their joint-stools and tables,
  A fire we made.
And when the town burnt in a flame,
  With tan-ta-ra, tan-ta-ra-rara,
    From thence we came.

THE SPANISH LADY'S LOVE TO AN ENGLISH MAN.

This beautiful old ballad, says Percy, most probably took its rise from one of those descents made on the Spanish coasts in the time of Elizabeth. In the West of England there was a tradition that the gentleman was a member of the Popham family, by whom the lady's picture, and the chain and bracelets mentioned in the ballad, were said to have been preserved. Another tradition identifies the hero in Sir Richard Levison, of Trentham, in Staffordshire, who distinguished himself in the Spanish expeditions towards the close of Elizabeth's reign. The story, modified by different circumstances but agreeing in the main incidents, is common to many ballads, of which this is probably the earliest, and certainly best worthy of preservation. It is pervaded by a sweetness and gentleness of spirit that greatly heightens the pathos of the narrative. The subject was dramatized by Thomas Hull in a musical entertainment produced at Covent Garden in 1765. The following ballad is taken from Deloney's " Garland of Good Will," published by the " Percy Society."

Will you hear a Spanish lady,
  How she woo'd an English man?
Garments gay, as rich as may be,
  Deck'd with jewels, had she on.

Of a comely countenance and grace was she ;
And by birth and parentage of high degree.

As his prisoner there he kept her,
    In his hands her life did lie ;
Cupid's bands did tie her faster,
    By the liking of her eye ;
In his courteous company was all her joy ,
To favour him in anything she was not coy.

At the last there came commandment
    For to set the ladies free ;
With their jewels still adornéd,
    None to do them injury.
Alas ! then said this lady gay, full woe is me :
O ! let me still sustain this kind captivity.

O ! gallant captain, show some pity
    To a lady in distress ;
Leave me not within the city,
    For to die in heaviness.
Thou hast set this present day my body free,
But my heart in prison strong remains with thee.

How should'st thou, fair lady, love me,
    Whom thou know'st thy country's foe ?
Thy fair words make me suspect thee,
    Serpents are where flowers grow.
All the evil I think to thee, most gracious knight,
God grant unto myself the same may fully light.

Blessed be the time and season
    That you came on Spanish ground :
If you may our foes be terméd,
    Gentle foes we have you found.
With our cities, you have won our hearts each one ;
Then to your country, bear away that is your own.

Rest you still, most gallant lady,
    Rest you still, and weep no more ;

Of fair lovers there are plenty,
    Spain doth yield a wondrous store.
Spaniards fraught with jealousie we often find,
But English men throughout the world are counted kind.

    Leave me not unto a Spaniard,
        You alone enjoy my heart;
    I am lovely, young, and tender,
        And so love is my desert;
Still to serve thee day and night my mind is prest;
The wife of every English man is counted blest.

    It would be a shame, fair lady,
        For to bear a woman hence;
    English soldiers never carry
        Any such without offence.
I will quickly change myself, if it be so,
And like a page I'll follow thee where'er thou go.

    I have neither gold nor silver
        To maintain thee in this case;
    And to travel 'tis great charges,
        As you know, in every place.
My chains and jewels every one shall be thine own,
And eke ten thousand pounds in gold, that lies unknown.

    On the seas are many dangers,
        Many storms do there arise,
    Which will be to ladies dreadful,
        And force tears from wat'ry eyes.
Well, in worth, I could endure extremity,
For I could find in heart to lose my life for thee.

    Courteous lady, be contented,
        Here comes all that breeds the strife;
    I, in England, have already
        A sweet woman to my wife.
I will not falsifie my vow for gold or gain,
Nor yet for all the fairest dames that live in Spain.

Oh ! how happy is that woman
 That enjoys so true a friend ;
Many days of joy God send you !
 Of my suit I'll make an end :
Upon my knees I pardon crave for this offence,
Which love and true affection did first commence.

Commend me to thy loving lady,
 Bear to her this chain of gold,
And these bracelets for a token,
 Grieving that I was so bold ;
All my jewels, in like sort, bear thou with thee,
For these are fitting for thy wife, and not for me.

I will spend my days in prayer,
 Love and all her laws defie ;
In a nunnery will I shroud me,
 Far from other company ;
But ere my prayers have end, be sure of this,
For thee and for thy love I will not miss.

Thus farewel ! most gentle captain,
 And farewel my heart's content ;
Count not Spanish ladies wanton,
 Though to thee my love was bent ;
Joy and true prosperity go still with thee.
The like fall ever to thy share, most fair lady.

THE REBELLION OF WATT TYLER AND JACKE STRAW WITH OTHERS AGAINST K. RICHARD THE SECOND.

TO THE TUNE OF "THE MILLER WOULD A-WOOING RIDE."

Watt Tyler is from Darford gan,
And with him many a proper man,
And he a captaine is become,
Marching in field with phife and drumme.

Jacke Straw, an other in like case,
From Essex flockes a mighty pace.
Hob Carter with his stragling traine,
Jacke Shepheard comes with him amaine ;
So doth Tom Miller, in like sort
As if he meant to take some fort.
With bowes and bils, with speare and shield,
On Black-heath have they pitcht their field :
An hundred thousand men in all,
Whose force is not accounted small ;
And for King Richard did they send,
Much evil to him they did intend,
For the taxe the which our King
Upon his commons then did bring.
And now because his royall Grace
Denyed to come within their chase,
They spoyled Southwark round about,
And took the Marshals prisoners out.
All those that in the Kings-bench lay,
At libertie they set that day ;
And then they marcht with one consent
Through London with a lewd intent.
And for to fit their lewd desire,
They set the Savoy all on fire ;
And for the hate that they did beare
Unto the Duke of Lankasteare,
Therefore his house they burned quite,
Through envy, malice, and despight.
Then to the Temple did they turne,
The lawyers bookes there did they burne,
And spoyld their lodgings one by one,
And all they could lay hand upon.
Then into Smithfield did they hie,
To Saint Jones place that stands thereby,
And set the same on fier flat,
Which burned seven days after that.
Unto the Tower of London then
Fast trooped these rebellious men,

And having entered soone the same,
With hidious cryes and mickle shame,
The grave Lord Chauncelor then they tooke,
Amazde, with fearefull pittious looke ;
The Lord High Treasurer likewise they
Took from that place that present day ;
And with their hooting lowd and shrill
Stroke off their heads on Tower Hill.
Into the cittie came they then,
Like rude disordered franticke men.
They robd the churches every where,
And put the priestes in deadly feare.
Into the Counters then they get,
Where men in prison lay for debt ;
They broke the doores and let them out,
And threw the Counter bookes about,
Tearing and spoyling them each one,
And records all they light upon.
The doores of Newgate broke they downe,
That prisoners ran about the towne,
Forcing all the smiths they meete
To knocke the irons from their feete ;
And then, like villaines voyde of awe,
Followed Watt Tyler and Jacke Strawe.
And though this outrage was not small,
The King gave pardon to them all,
So they would part home quietly ;
But they his pardon did defie.
And being all in Smithfield then,
Even threescore thousand fighting men,
Which there Watt Tyler then did bring,
Of purpose for to meete our King.
And therewithall his royall grace
Sent Sir John Newton to that place,
Unto Watt Tyler, willing him
To come and speake with our young King.
But the proud rebell, in despight,
Did picke a quarrell with the knight.

The Mayor of London being by,
When he beheld this villainie,
Unto Wat Tyler rode he then,
Being in midst of all his men,
Saying, traitor, yield, 'tis best;
In the King's name I thee arrest:
And therewith to his dagger start,
And thrust the rebell to the hart;
Who falling dead unto the ground,
The same did all the host confound,
And downe they threw their weapons all,
And humbly they for pardon call.
Thus did that proud rebellion cease,
And after followed a joyfull peace.

THE MAIDEN'S SONG.

It was a knight in Scotland borne,
   Follow my love, come over the strand,
Was taken prisoner and left forlorne,
   Even by the good Earle of Northumberland.

Then he was cast in prison strong,
   Follow my love, leape over the strand,
Where he could not walke nor lie along,
   Even by the good Earle of Northumberland.

And as in sorrow thus he lay,
   Follow my love, come over the strand,
The earle's sweete daughter walkt that way,
   And she the faire flower of Northumberland.

And passing by, like an angell bright,
   Follow my love, come over the strand,
This prisoner had of her a sight,
   And she the faire flower of Northumberland.

And loud to her this knight did crie,
   Follow my love, come over the strand,
The salt teares standing in his eye,
   And she the faire flower of Northumberland.

Faire lady, he said, take pity on me,
   Follow my love, come over the strand,
And let me not in prison dye,
   And you the faire flower of Northumberland.

Faire sir, how should I take pity on thee,
   Follow my love, come over the strand,
Thou being a foe to our countrey,
   And I the faire flower of Northumberland?

Faire lady, I am no foe, he said,
   Follow my love, come over the strand,
Through thy sweete love heere was I stay'd,
   For thee, the faire flower of Northumberland.

Why shouldst thou come heere for love of me,
   Follow my love, come over the strand,
Having wife and children in the countrie,
   And I the faire flower of Northumberland?

I swear, by the Blessed Trinitie,
   Follow my love, come over the strand,
I have no wife, nor children I,
   Nor dwelling at home in merrie Scotland.

If curteously you will set me free,
   Follow my love, come over the strand,
I vow that I will marrie thee
   So soon as I come in faire Scotland.

Thou shalt be a lady of castles and towers,
   Follow my love, come over the strand,
And sit like a queene in princely bowers,
   When I am at home in faire Scotland.

Then parted hence this lady gay,
Follow my love, come over the strand.
And got her father's ring away,
To helpe this sad knight into faire Scotland.

Likewise much gold she got by sleight,
Follow my love, come over the strand,
And all to helpe this forlorne knight
To wend from her father to faire Scotland.

Two gallant steedes both good and able,
Follow my love, come over the strand,
She likewise took out of the stable,
To ride with this knight into faire Scotland.

And to the jaylor she sent this ring,
Follow my love, come over the strand,
The knight from prison forth to bring,
To wend with her into faire Scotland.

This token set the prisoner free,
Follow my love, come over the strand,
Who straight went to this faire lady,
To wend with her into faire Scotland.

A gallant steed he did bestride,
Follow my love, come over the strand,
And with the lady away did ride,
And she the faire flower of Northumberland.

They rode till they came to a water cleare,
Follow my love, come over the strand,
Good sir, how should I follow you here,
And I the faire flower of Northumberland?

The water is rough and wonderfull deepe,
Follow my love, come over the strand,
And on my saddle I shall not keepe,
And I the faire flower of Northumberland.

Feare not the foorde, faire lady, quoth he,
   Follow my love, come over the strand,
For long I cannot stay for thee,
   And thou the faire flower of Northumberland.

The lady prickt her wanton steed,
   Follow my love, come over the strand,
And over the river swom with speede,
   And she the faire flower of Northumberland.

From top to toe all wet was shee,
   Follow my love, come over the strand ;
This have I done for love of thee,
   And I the faire flower of Northumberland.

Thus rode she all one winter's night,
   Follow my love, come over the strand,
Till Edinborow they saw in sight,
   The chiefest towne in all Scotland.

Now chuse, quoth he, thou wanton flower,
   Follow my love, come over the strand,
Where thou wilt be my paramour,
   Or get thee home to Northumberland.

For I have wife and children five,
   Follow my love, come over the strand,
In Edinborow they be alive,
   Then get thee home to faire England.

This favour shalt thou have to boote,
   Follow my love, come over the strand,
I'll have thy horse, go thou on foote,
   Go, get thee home to Northumberland.

O, false and faithless knight, quoth she,
   Follow my love, come over the strand,
And canst thou deale so bad with me,
   And I the faire flower of Northumberland ?

Dishonour not a ladies name,
　Follow my love, come over the strand,
But draw thy sword and end my shame,
　And I the faire flower of Northumberland.

He tooke her from her stately steed,
　Follow my love, come over the strand,
And left her there in extreme need,
　And she the faire flower of Northumberland.

Then sate she downe full heavily,
　Follow my love, come over the strand,
At length two knights came riding by,
　Two gallant knights of faire England.

She fell downe humbly on her knee,
　Follow my love, come over the strand,
Saying, courteous knights, take pittie on me,
　And I the faire flower of Northumberland.

I have offended my father deere,
　Follow my love, come over the strand,
And by a false knight that brought me heere,
　From the good Earle of Northumberland.

They took her up behind them then,
　Follow my love, come over the strand,
And brought her to her father's again,
　And he the good Earle of Northumberland.

All you faire maidens be warned by me,
　Follow my love, come over the strand,
Scots were never true, nor never will be,
　To lord, nor lady, nor faire England.

JEALOUSY.

A maiden faire I dare not wed,
For feare to have Acteon's head ;

A maiden blacke is often proud,
A maiden little will be loud ,
A maiden that is high of growth
They say is subject unto sloath.
Thus faire or foule, yea, little or tall,
Some faults remaine among them all.
But of all the faults that be,
None is so bad as jealousie.
For jealousie is fierce and fell,
And burnes as hot as fire in hell.
It breeds suspicion without cause,
And breakes the bonds of reason's lawes.
To none it is a greater foo
Than unto those where it doth grow.
And God keepe me both day and night
From that fell, fond, and ugly spright;
For why of all the plagues that be,
The secret plague is jealousie.
Therefore I wish all women kind,
Never to beare a jealous minde.

THE WEAVER'S SONG.

When Hercules did use to spin,
  And Pallas wrought upon the loome,
Our trade to flourish did begin,
  While conscience went not selling broome.
Then love and friendship did agree
To keepe the band of amitie.

When princes sonnes kept sheep in field,
  And queenes made cakes of wheaten flower,
Then men to lucre did not yield,
  Which brought good cheere in everie bower.
Then love and friendship did agree
To hold the bands of amitie.

But when that giants, huge and hie,
   Did fight with speares like weavers beames,
Then they in iron beds did lie,
   And brought poore men to hard extreames.
Yet love and friendship did agree
To hold the bands of amitie.

Then David tooke his sling and stone,
   Not fearing great Goliahs strength,
He pearc't his braines and broke the bone,
   Though he were fiftie foote of length.
For love and friendship, &c.

But while the Greekes besieged Troy,
   Penelope apace did spin,
And weavers wrought with mickle joy,
   Though little gaines were coming in.
For love and friendship, &c.

Had Helen then sate carding wooll,
   (Whose beauteous face did breed such strife)
Shee had not been Sir Paris trull,
   Nor caus'd so many lose their life.
Yet we by love did still agree, &c.

Or had King Priams wanton sonne
   Beene making quils with sweet content,
He had not then his friends undone
   When he to Greece a gadding went.
For love and friendship did agree, &c.

The cedar trees indure more stormes
   Than little shrubbs that sprout on hie,
The weavers live more voyd of harmes
   Than princes of great dignitie.
While love and friendship doth agree, &c.

The shepheard sitting in the field
   Doth tune his pipe with hearts delight ;

When princes watch with speare and shield,
    The poore man soundly sleepes all night.
While love and friendship doth agree, &c.

Yet this by proofe is daily tride,
    For God's good gifts we are ingrate,
And no man through the world so wide
    Lives well contented with his state.
No love and friendship we can see
To hold the bands of amitie.

FLODDEN FIELD.

King Jamie hath made a vow,
    Keepe it well if he may,
That he will be at lovely London
    Upon Saint James his day.

Upon Saint James his day at noone
    At faire London will I be,
And all the lords in merrie Scotland
    They shall dine there with me.

Then he spake good Queene Margaret,
    The teares fell from her eye :
Leave off these warres, most noble King,
    Keepe your fidelitie ;

The water runs swift and wondrous deepe
    From bottome unto the brimme,
My brother Henry hath men good enough,
    England is hard to winne.

Away (quoth he) with this silly foole,
    In prison fast let her lie,
For she is come of the English bloud,
    And for these words she shall dye.

With that bespake Lord Thomas Howard,
    The Queenes Chamberlaine that day :

Q

If that you put Queene Margaret to death,
  Scotland shall rue it alway.

Then in a rage King Jamie did say,
  Away with this foolish mome,
He shall be hanged, and the other be burned,
  As soon as I come home.

At Flodden Field the Scots came in,
  Which made our English men faine,
At Bramstone Greene this battaile was seene,
  There was King Jamie slaine.

Then presently the Scots did flie.
  Their cannons they left behind,
Their ensignes gay were won all away,
  Our souldiers did beate them blinde.

To tell you plaine, twelve thousand were slaine
  That to the fight did stand ;
And many prisoners tooke that day,
  The best in all Scotland.

That day made many fatherlesse child,
  And many a widow poore,
And many a Scottish gay lady
  Sate weeping in her bower.

Jacke with a feather was lapt all in leather,
  His boastings were all in vaine,
He had such a chance with a new morrice dance,
  He never went home again.

THE WOOLLEN MANUFACTORY.

The following graphic description, from the pen of Delony, of a woollen manufactory at the end of the sixteenth century, is of peculiar interest at the present day, as he, in consequence of having been a weaver, was well acquainted with all the details of such an establishment.

Within one roome, being large and long,
  There stood two hundred loomes full strong.

Two hundred men, the truth is so,
Wrought in these loomes all in a row.
By every one a prettie boy
Sate making quils with mickle joy;
And in another place hard by,
An hundred women merrily
Were carding hard with joyfull cheere,
Who singing sat with voyces cleere.
And in a chamber close beside,
Two hundred maydens did abide.
In peticoats of stammel red,
And milke-white kerchers on their head;
Their smocke sleeves like to winter snow
That on the western mountaines flow,
And each sleeve with a silken band
Was featly tied at the hand;
These pretty maids did never lin,
But in that place all day did spin;
And spinning so with voyces meet,
Like nightingales they sung full sweet.
Then to another loome came they,
Where children were in poore array,
And every one sat picking woll,
The finest from the course to cull.
The number was seven score and ten,
The children of poore silly men.
And these, their labours to requite,
Had every one a penny at night,
Beside their meate and drink all day,
Which was to them a wondrous stay.
Within another place likewise,
Full fiftie proper men he spies;
And these were shearemen every one,
Whose skill and cunning there was showne.
And hard by them there did remaine
Full four score rowers taking paine.
A dye-house likewise had he then,
Wherein he kept full fortie men;

And likewise in his fulling mill,
Full twenty persons kept he still.
Each weeke ten good fat oxen he
Spent in his house for certaintie,
Beside good butter, cheese, and fish,
And many another holesome dish.
He kept a butcher all the yeere,
A brewer eke for ale and beere.
A baker for to bake her bread,
Which stood his household in good stead.
Five cookes within his kitchen great
Were all the yeere to dresse his meat.
Sixe scullion boyes unto their hands
To make clean dishes, pots, and pans.
Beside poore children that did stay
To turn the broaches every day.
　　The old man that did see this sight
Was much amaz'd, as well he might.
This was a gallant cloathier sure,
Whose fame for ever shall endure.

AS I CAME FROM WALSINGHAM.

The scene of this ballad is the same as "Gentle herdsman, tell to me," and was probably written not long after the dissolution of the monasteries, while the remembrance of them was fresh in the minds of the people. Bishop Percy, in his *Reliques*, calls it "As ye came from the Holy Land," and his copy of the ballad was communicated to him by Mr. Shenstone, as corrected by that gentleman from an ancient copy, and supplied with a concluding stanza. This is, to say the least, very singular, as the Bishop's old folio MS. was found to contain this ballad, and the last stanza is so good that it certainly needed no such substitute as the Bishop printed. I have taken the ballad from Delony's "Garland of Goodwill," as privately printed for the members of the Percy Society.

The pilgrimage to Walsingham suggested the plan of many popular pieces. In the Pepys' Collection, vol. i., p. 226, there is a kind of interlude, the first stanza of which is—

As I went to Walsingham
　To the shrine with speede,
Met I with a jolly palmer
　In a pilgrimes weede.

Now God you save, you jolly palmer!
Welcome, lady gay,
Oft have I sued to thee for love,
Oft have I said you nay.

The following ballad was once very popular; it is quoted in Fletcher's "Knight of the Burning Pestle," Act 2, and in another old play called "Hans' Beer-pot: his Invisible Comedy," &c., 4to, 1618. The tune "Walsingham," to which it was sung, is mentioned by Mr. Chappell as in Queen Elizabeth's and Lady Neville's Virginal Books, and other old tune books.

In "The Weakest Goes to the Wall," 1600, the scene being laid in Burgundy, the following lines are given:—

King Richard's gone to Walsingham, to the holy-land,
To kill Turk and Saracen, that the truth do withstand;
Christ his cross be his good speed, Christ his foes to quell,
Send him help in time of need, and to come home well.

Among other superstitions belonging to the place, says a writer in *Chambers's Book of Days*, was one that the Milky Way pointed directly to the home of the Virgin, in order to guide pilgrims directly on their road, hence it is called the Walsingham Way, which had its counterpart on earth in the broad way which led through Norfolk. At every town that it passed through a cross was erected pointing out the path to the holy spot.

As you came from the holy-land
Of Walsingham,
Met you not with my true love
By the way as you came?

How should I know your true love,
That have met many a one
As I came from the holy-land,
That have come, that have gone?

She is neither white nor brown,
But as the heavens fair;
There is none hath a form so divine
On the earth, in the air.

Such a one did I meet (good sir)
With angel-like face;
Who like a queen did appear
In her gait, in her grace.

She hath left me here all alone,
　　All alone and unknown,
Who sometime lov'd me as her life,
　　And call'd me her own.

What's the cause she hath left thee alone,
　　And a new way doth take,
That sometime did love thee as her life,
　　And her joy did thee make?

I loved her all my youth
　　But now am old, as you see;
Love liketh not the fallen fruit,
　　Nor the withered tree?

For love is a careless child,
　　And forgets promise past;
He is blind, he is deaf, when he list,
　　And in faith never fast.

For love is a great delight,
　　And yet a trustless joy;
He is won with a word of despair,
　　And is lost with a toy.

Such is the love of womankind,
　　Or the word (love) abus'd
Under which many childish desires
　　And conceits are excus'd.

But love is a durable fire,
　　In the mind ever burning;
Never sick, never dead, never cold,
　　From itself never turning.

BALLADS BY VARIOUS AUTHORS.

OLD ROBIN, OF PORTINGALE.

The following tragical old Ballad is taken from "Bishop Percy's Reliques." The Bishop acknowledges that the copy of "Old Robin" in his Folio MS. required in his opinion considerable corrections, and that he had made alterations and improvements before publishing the ballad. As " Percy's " celebrated Ballad Folio has recently been printed entire for private circulation, we give a copy of a few verses of this ballad to show clearly the corrections which the Bishop made :—

> God! let never soe old a man
> Marry soe yonge a wiffe
> as did old Robin of portingale
> he may rue all the dayes of his liffe.

> ffor the Maiors daughter of Lin, god wott
> he chose her to his wife,
> & thought to have lived in quietnesse
> with her all the dayes of his liffe.

> they had not in their wed bed laid
> scarcely were both on sleepe
> but vpp she rose & forth shee goes
> to Sir Gyles & fast can weepe
> saies " Sleepe you, wake you, faire Sir Gyles,
> or be not you within ?"

Compare this ballad also with Little Musgrave and Lady Barnard.

> Let never again soe old a man
> Marrye soe yonge a wife,
> As did old Robin of Portingale
> Who may rue all the days of his life.

> For the Mayor's daughter of Lin, God wott,
> He chose her to his wife,
> And thought with her to have lived in love,
> But they fell to hate and strife.

> They scarce were in their wed-bed laid,
> And scarce was hee asleepe,
> But upp shee rose, and forth shee goes
> To the steward, and gan to weepe.

Sleepe you, wake you, faire Sir Gyles?
　　Or be you not within?
Sleepe you, wake you, faire Sir Gyles,
　　Arise, and let me inn.

O I am waking, sweete, he said,
　　Sweete ladye, what is your will?
I have unbethought me of awhile
　　How my wed-lord weell spill.

Twenty-four good knights, shee sayes,
　　That dwell about this towne,
Even twenty-four of my next cozens
　　Will helpe to dinge him downe.

All that beheard his litle footepage
　　As he watered his master's steed,
And for his master's sad perille
　　His verry heart did bleed.

He mourned still, and wept full sore;
　　I sweare by the holy roode,
The teares he for his master wept
　　Were blent water and bloude.

And that beheard his deare master
　　As he stood at his garden pale;
Sayes, ever alacke, my litle footepage,
　　What causes thee to wail?

Hath any one done to thee wronge,
　　Any of thy fellowes here?
Or is any one of thy good friends dead,
　　That thou shedst manye a teare?

Or, if it be my head bookes-man,
　　Aggrieved he shal bee,
For no man here within my howse
　　Shall do wrong unto thee.

O, it is not your head bookes-man,
　　Nor nonĕ of his degree :
But on tŏ-morrow ere it be noone
　　All deemed to die are yee.

And of that bethank your head steward,
　　And thank your gay ladie.
If this be true, my litle footepage,
　　The heyre of my land thoust bee.

If it be not true, my dear master,
　　No good death let me die.
If it be not true, thou litle footepage,
　　A dead corse thou shalt lie.

O call now downe my faire ladye,
　　O call her downe to mee ;
And tell my ladye gay how sicke
　　And like to die I bee.

Downe then came his ladye faire,
　　All clad in purple and pall ;
The rings that were on her fingers
　　Cast light thorrow the hall.

What is your will, my owne wed-lord ?
　　What is your will with me ?
O see, my ladye deere, how sicke
　　And like to die I bee.

And thou be sicke, my own wed-lord,
　　Soe sore it grieveth me ;
But my live maydens and myselfe
　　Will ' watch thy ' bedde for thee.

And at the waking of your first sleepe,
　　We will a hott drinke make ;
And at the waking of your ' next ' sleepe,
　　Your sorrows we will slake.

He put a silk cote on his backe,
　　And mail of manye a fold ;
And hee putt a steele cap on his head,
　　Was gilt with good red gold.

He layd a bright browne sword by his side,
　　And another at his feete ;
" And twenty good knights he placed at hand
　　To watch him in his sleepe."

And about the middle time of the night
　　Came twentye-four traitrous inn ;
Sir Giles he was the foremost man,
　　The leader of that ginn.

Old Robin with his bright browne sword
　　Sir Gyles' head soon did win ;
And scant of all those twenty-four
　　Went out one quick agenn.

None, save only a little footepage,
　　Crept forth at a window of stone :
And he had two armes when he came in,
　　And he went back with one.

Upp then came that ladie gaye,
　　With torches burning bright :
She thought to have brought Sir Gyles a drinke,
　　But shee found her owne wedd knight.

The first thinge that she stumbled on
　　It was Sir Gyles his foote :
Sayes, Ever alacke, and woe is mee !
　　Here lyes my sweete hart-roote.

The next thinge that she stumbled on
　　It was Sir Gyles his heade :
Sayes, Ever alacke, and woe is me !
　　Here lyes my true love deade.

He cutt the pappes beside her brest,
   And did her body spille ;
He cutt the eares beside her heade,
   And bade her love her fille.

He called then up his little foot-page,
   And made him there his heyre ;
And sayd, henceforth my worldlye goodes
   And countrye I forsweare.

He shope the crosse on his right shoulder
   Of the white 'clothe' and the redde,*
And went into the holy land,
   Whereas Christ was quicke and dead.

In the foregoing piece, *Giles*, steward to a rich old merchant trading to Portugal, is qualified with the title of *Sir*, not as being a knight, but rather, Bishop Percy thinks, as having reached an inferior order of priesthood.

GENTLE HERDSMAN, TELL TO ME.

DIALOGUE BETWEEN A PILGRIM AND HERDSMAN.

Bishop Percy says the scene of this beautiful old ballad is laid near Walsingham, in Norfolk, where was anciently an image of the Virgin Mary, famous over all Europe for the numerous pilgrimages made to it and the great riches it possessed. Erasmus has given a very exact and humorous description of the superstitions practised there in his time. He tells us, the rich offerings in silver, gold, and precious stones that were there shown him were incredible, there being scarce a person of any note in England but that some time or other paid a visit or sent a present to "Our Lady of Walsingham." At the dissolution of the monasteries in 1538 this splendid image, with another from Ipswich, was carried to Chelsea, and there burnt in the presence of Commissioners. This poem is printed by Bishop Percy from a copy in manuscript, which he says had greatly suffered by the hand of time. Vestiges of several of the lines remaining, the Bishop ackowledges that some

---

* Every person who went on a crusade to the Holy Land usually wore a cross on his upper garment, on the right shoulder, as a badge of his profession. Different nations were distinguished by crosses of different colors. The English wore white ; the French, red, &c. This circumstance seems to be confounded in the ballad.

conjectural supplements were made by him, which for greater exactness he distinguished by italics.

One of the editors of the *Ballad* folio, speaking of this ballad, says a lady who has killed her lover with her caprice and boldness determines to retire to some secret place and fast and pray till she dies. The picture here given of the forlorn figure—young of years, fair of face, green of thoughts—begging her way to Walsingham, remorseful, aye, and hopeless, is prettily drawn. Goldsmith has borrowed from her speech in the charming ballad recited by Mr. Burchell in the *Vicar of Wakefield*, and the reader will have pleasure in comparing his paraphrase with the original. The stranger, standing " confessed a maid in all her charms," tells how she had trifled with the affections of her Edwin :—

" The dew, the blossom on the tree
With charms inconstant shine ;
Their charms were his, but woe to me,
Their constancy was mine,

" For still I try'd each fickle art,
Importunate and vain ;
And while his passion touch'd my heart
I triumph'd in his pain.

'· Till quite dejected with my scorn
He left me to my pride ;
And sought a solitude forlorn
In secret, where he died.

" But mine the sorrow, mine the fault,
And well my life shall pay ;
I'll seek the solitude he sought,
And stretch me where he lay.

" And there, forlorn, despairing, hid,
I'll lay me down and die ;
'Twas so for me that Edwin did,
And so for him will I."

There the likeness ends. The eighteenth-century poet could not bear to let the poor thing pass away from the scene still dejected and unhoping. The sentimental bosom of his time could not abide such dismal endings. The poet in this case, as his contemporaries in many another, gives it relief and comfort at the expense of probability.

" Forbid it, Heaven ! " the Hermit cry'd
And clasp'd her to his breast,
The wondering fair one turned to chide—
'Twas Edwin's self that press'd.

" Turn, Angelina, ever dear,
My charmer, turn to see
Thy own, thy long-lost Edwin here
Restored to love and thee.

"Thus let me hold thee to my heart,
　　And every care resign :
And shall we never never part,
　　My life—my all that's mine ?

" No, never from this hour to part,
　　We'll live and love so true ;
The sigh that rends thy constant heart,
　　Shall break thy Edwin's too."

Contrast this gushing finale with the concluding stanzas of the older ballad, in which the contrite pilgrim moves slowly away towards her appointed goal.

Gentle heardsman, tell to me,
　　Of curtesy I thee pray,
Unto the towne of Walsingham
　　Which is the right and ready way.

" Unto the towne of Walsingham
　　The way is hard for to be gon,
And very crooked are those pathes
　　For you to find out all alone."

Weere the miles doubled thrice,
　　And the way never soe ill,
Itt were not enough for mine offence ;
　　Itt is so grievous and soe ill.

" Thy yeeares are young, thy face is faire,
　　Thy witts are weake, thy thoughts are greene ;
Time hath not given thee leave, as yett,
　　For to committ so great a sinne."

Yes, heardsman, yes, soe woldest thou say,
　　If thou knewest soe much as I ;
My witts, and thoughts, and all the rest,
　　Have well deserved for to dye.

I am not what I seeme to bee,
　　My clothes and sexe doe differ farr.
I am a woman, woe is me !
　　Born to greefe and irksome care.

For my beloved, and well-beloved,
  My wayward cruelty could kill :
And though my teares will nought avail,
  Most dearely I bewail him still.

He was the flower of noble wights,
  None ever more sincere colde bee ;
Of comely mien and shape hee was,
  And tenderlye hee loved mee.

*When thus I saw he lo*ved me well,
  *I grewe so proud his pa*ine to see,
That I, who did not know myselfe,
  Thought scorne of such a youth as he.

And grew soe coy and nice to please,
  As women's lookes are often soe,
He might not kisse, nor hand forsooth,
  Unlesse I willed him soe to do.

Thus being wearied with delayes
  To see I pittyed not his grieffe,
He got him to a secrett place,
  And there he dyed without releefe.

And for his sake these weedes I weare,
  And sacriffice my tender age ;
And every day Ile begg my bread,
  To undergo this pilgrimage.

Thus every day I fast and pray,
  And ever will doe till I dye ;
And gett me to some secrett place,
  For soe did hee, and soe will I.

Now, gentle heardsman, aske no more,
  But keepe my secretts I thee pray :
Unto the towne of Walsingham
  Show me the right and readye way.

" Now, goe thy wayes, and God before !
For He must ever guide thee still :
Turne downe that dale, the right hand path,
And soe faire pilgrim, fare thee well ?"

To show what constant tribute was paid to " Our Lady of Walsingham,"
the Bishop gives a few extracts as under from the Household Book of
Henry Algernon Percy, fifth Earl of Northumberland :

ITEM. My Lorde usith yerly to send afor Michaelmas for his Lordschip's
offerynge to our Lady of Walsingham—iiijd.

ITEM. My Lorde usith ande accustamyth to sende yerely for the
upholdynge of the light of wax, which his Lordship fyndith birnynge
yerly befor our Lady of Walsyngham, continynge xjlb of wax in it after
vijd ob, for the fyndynge of every lb. redy wrought by a covenant maid
with the Channon by great, for the hole yere, for the fyndinge of the said
lyght byrnning—vis viiijd.

ITEM. My Lorde usith, and accustomith to syende yerely to the Channon
that Kepith the Light before our Lady of Walsingham, for his reward for
the hole yere, for Kepynge of the said Light, lyghtynge of it at all service
tymes dayly thorowt the yere—xijd.

ITEM.—My Lord usith and accustomyth yerely to send to the Prest that
Kepith the Light, lyghtynge of it at all service tymes daily thorowt the
yere—iijs iiijd.

A LAMENT FOR WALSINGHAM.

The following ballad on Walsingham, is in a small quarto volume, in the
Bodleian Library, apparently, says Mr. Chappell, in the handwriting of
Philip, Earl of Arundel (eldest son of the Duke of Norfolk), who suffered
in the reign of Elizabeth.

In the wrackes of Walsingam
    whom should I chuse
But the Queen of Walsingam
    to be guide to my muse ?
Then thou Prince of Walsingam
    grannt me to frame
Bitter plaints to rewe thy wronge,
    bitter woe for thy name.

Bitter was it, oh ! to see
    The seely sheepe
Murdered by the raveninge wolves
    while the sheephardes did sleep !
Bitter was it, oh ! to vewe
    the sacred vyne,
Whiles the gardiners placed all close,
    rooted vp by the swine.

Bitter, bitter, oh ! to behould
    the grape to growe
Where the walls of Walsingam
    so statly did sheue.
Such were the workes of Walsingam
    while she did stand !
Such are the wrackes as now do shewe
    of that holy-land !
Levell, levell, with the ground
    the towres doe lie,

Which with their golden glittering tops
    pearsed once to the skye !
Wher weare gates, no gates ar now ;
    the waies vnknowen,
Wher the presse of peares did passe,
    while her fame far was blowen,
Oules do scrike wher the sweetest himnes
    lately wer songe ;
Toades and serpentes hold their dennes
    where the Palmer's did thronge.

Weepe, weepe, O Walsingam,
    whose dayes are nightes,
Blessinge turned to blasphemies,
    hold deeds to despitee !
Sinne is wher our ladie sate
    heaven turned is to hell ;
Sathan sittes wher our Lord did swaye !
    Walsingam, oh ! farewell !

THE BAILIFF'S DAUGHTER OF ISLINGTON.

Islington in Norfolk is stated by Bishop Percy to be the supposed locale of this ballad, and Mr. I. O. Halliwell has adopted the idea by inserting the ballad in his "Norfolk Anthology." The full title is "True Love Requited; or the Bailiff's Daughter of Islington." It was printed by Percy from a black-letter copy in the Pepys collection.

There was a youthe, and a well-beloved youthe,
　　And he was a squire's son ·
He loved the bailiffes daughter deare,
　　That lived in Islington.

Yet she was coye, and would not believe
　　That he did love her soe,
Noe, nor at any time would she
　　Any countenance to him showe.

But when his friends did understand
　　His fond and foolish minde,
They sent him up to fair London
　　An apprentice for to binde.

And when he had been seven long yeares,
　　And never his love could see :
Many a tear have I shed for her sake,
　　When she little thought of mee.

Then all the maids of Islington
　　Went forth to sport and playe,
All but the bailiffes daughter deare ;
　　She secretly stole awaye.

She pulled off her gowne of greene,
　　And put on ragged attire,
And to fair London she would go
　　Her true love to enquire.

And as she went along the high road
　　The weather being hot and drye
She sat her downe upon a green bank
　　And her true love came riding bye.

R

She started up with a colour so redd
    Catching hold of his bridle reine ;
One penny, one penny, kind sir, she sayd,
    Will ease me of much paine.

Before I give you one penny sweetheart,
    Pray tell me where you were .borne.
At Islington, kind sir, sayd shee,
    Where I have had many a scorne.

I prythee, sweetheart, then tell to mee,
    O tell me whether you knowe
The bailiffes daughter of Islington ;
    She is dead, sir, long agoe.

If she be dead, then take my horse
    My saddle and bridle also ;
For I will into some farr countrye
    Where noe man shall me knowe.

O staye, O staye, thou goodlye youthe,
    She standeth by thy side ;
She is here alive, she is not dead,
    And readye to be thy bride.

O farewell griefe, and welcome joye,
    Ten thousand times therefore ;
For now I have found mine own true love
    Whom I thought I should never see more.

THE WHITE FALCON.

From *Verses and Ditties made at the Coronation of Queen Anne Boleyn,*
which were devised and made by John Leland and Nicholas Udall. The
last-named is celebrated as the author of the first English comedy, *Ralph
Roister Doister,* and as Master of Eton has been held up to notoriety by
Roger Ascham for his severity to his scholars, who says that divers of the
scholars of Eton ran away from thence for fear of him. Thomas Tusser,

who was one of his pupils, thus alludes to the usage he received at his hands:

> From Paules I went, to Eaton sent,
> To learne streightwaies, the Latin pàraies,
> Where fiftie-three stripes given to me,
>   at once I had :
> For fault but small, or none at all,
> It came to pass thus beat I was.
> See, Udall, see, the mercie of thee
>   to me poore lad.

"This song of 'The White Falcon' was sung at the end of a pageant got up by the Lord Mayor of London to celebrate the coronation of Anne Boleyn. It represented Saint Anne (the Queen's patron saint) and Mary Cleophas with her four children. One of these made a goodly oration to the Queen of the fruitfulnesse of Saint Anne and her generation, trusting that the like fruit should come of her."—Hall's *Chronicle*. This spoken, a cloud opened and let down a white falcon, in the descending of which was pronounced by another child as followeth:

> Behold and see the Falcon white,
> How she beginneth hir wings to spread
> And for our comforte to take hir flight,
> But where woll she sease as you doo red ?
> A rare sight and yet to be joyed,
> On the rose, chief flower that ever was,
> This bird to light that all birds dothe pass.*

The speech being delivered and the Queen about to depart, the following ballad was sung :

> This white Falcon, rare and gaison,
>   This bird shineth so bright,
> Of all that are, no bird compare,
>   May with this Falcon whight.

---

* The white falcon was the badge of Anne Boleyn (see Williment's *Regal Heraldry*, where it is engraved), the rose upon which the falcon lights being Henry VIII., who bore the flattering legend on his coins of "Rosa sine spine," and a ballad on his expedition to France in 1513 has the words :

> " The rose will into Frawnse spring,
> Almythy God bym thyder bring,
> And save this flowr which is our kyng,
> Thys rose, thys rose, this Kyull Rose."

The virtues all, no man mortal
  Of this bird may write
No man earthly, enough truly
  Can praise this Falcon whight.

Who will express great gentleness
  To be in any wight,
He will not miss, but call him this,
  The gentle Falcon whight;

This gentle bird, as white as curd,
  Shineth both day and night;
Nor far nor near, is any pere
  Unto this Falcon whight.

Of body small, of power regal
  She is and sharp of sight
Of courage hault, no manner fault
  Is in this Falcon whight.

In chastity exceedeth she
  Most like a virgin bright
And worthy is to live in bliss
  Always this Falcon whight.

But how to take and use her make
  Is time, as truth is plight,
That she may bringe fruit according
  For such a Falcon whight.

And where by wrong she hath fleen long
  Uncertain where to light
Her self repose, upon the rose
  Now may this Falcon whight.

Whereon to rest, and build her nest,
  God grant her most of might
That England may, rejoice alway
  In this same Falcon whight.

SONG IN PRAISE OF ANNE BOLEYN.

This ballad, by Nicholas Udall, was sung upon the same occasion as the last ("The White Falcon"), and came at the end of the pageant called "The Judgment of Paris," which is thus described in the MS. :

"At the little counduite in Chepe sid was exhibited The Jugement of Paris, in maner and fourme following:

Mercurie.	Juppiter this aple unto the hath sent,
	Commanding in this cause to geve true jugement.
Paris.	Juppiter a straunge office hath geven me,
	To juge whiche is fairest of these ladies three.
Juno.	All riches and kingdomes bee at my behest :
	Give me the aple, and thou shalt have the best.
Pallas.	Adjuge it to me, and for a kingdome
	I shall geve the incomparable wisdome.
Venus.	Preferre me, and I shall rewarde the, Paris.
	With the fairest ladie that on the erthe is.
Paris.	I should breke Juppiter's high commandement,
	If I should for mede or rewarde geve jugement.
	Therefore, ladie Venus before both these twain,
	Your beautie moche exceeding, by my sentence
	Shall win and have this aple. Yet to be plain,
	Here is the fouerthe ladie, now in presence,
	Most worthie to have it of due congruence,
	As pereles in riches, wit, and beautee,
	Which are but sundrie qualities in you three.
	But for hir worthynes this aple of gold
	Is to symple a rewarde a thousand fold.

Hall tells us, in the account of this day's proceedings, that Mercury presented to the Queen a ball of gold, divided; signifying the three gifts which the goddesses gave her—wisdom, riches, and felicity; but Fairbolt says, from the last verse of this ballad, Venus appears to have received the ball, and the Queen was consoled by a very high-flown compliment.

Queene Anne so gent,
Of high descent,
Anne excellent
    In noblenesss ;
Of ladies all
Now principal,
Should win this ball
    Of worthiness.

Passing beauty
And chastity,
With high degree
    And great riches ;

So coupled be
In unity,
That chief are ye
   In worthiness.

When Jupiter
His messager
Sent down hither,
   He knew certes,
That you victrice
Of all ladies,
Should have the price
   Of worthiness.

And wise Paris,
Made judge in this,
Anon I wys,
   Most high Princess,
Well understood
Your virtues good,
Your noble blood,
   And worthiness.

Your dignity
When he gan see,
The ladies three,
   Queen Anne peerless,
He bead gave place
Unto your grace,
As meet it was
   In worthiness.

The golden ball,
Of price but small,
Have Venus shall,
   The fair goddess ;
Because it was
Too low and bace
For your good grace
   And worthiness.

ANNE BOLEYN.

Translation from the Metrical *Histoire D'Anne Boleyn.*

S'elle estoit belle et de taille élégante,
Estoit des yeuex encore plus attirante,
Lesquelz sçavoit bien conduyre à propos
En les tenant quelquefoys en repos ;
Aucunefoys envoyant en message
Porter du cueur le secret tesmoignage.

Much as her form seduc'd the sight
  Her eyes could even more surely woo ;
And when and how to shoot their light
  Into men's hearts full well she knew.
For sometimes, in repose, she hid
Their rays beneath a downcast lid ;
And then again, with wakening air,
  Would send their sunny glances out,
Like heralds of delight, to bear
  Her heart's sweet messages about.

O DEATH ! ROCK ME ASLEEP.

The family of Boleyne was of ancient date in Norfolk. Sir Geoffrey, a mercer, and Lord Mayor of London in 1458, married the daughter of Lord Hoo and Hastings. This appears to have been the spring of their fortunes. His son Sir William died in 1505, and was succeeded by Sir Thomas, who enjoyed high place and power under Henry VIII., was made governor of Norwich Castle, jointly with Sir Henry Wyatt, master of the King's Jewel Room, and afterwards sole constable of the castle. After an embassy to Spain, he was raised to the peerage in 1525 as Viscount Rochfort. He subscribed the articles against Wolsey in 1529, and was advanced to the Earldom of Wiltshire and Ormond. In the next year he was made Privy Seal. His connection with the Howards arose from his marriage with Elizabeth, the daughter of the Duke of Norfolk. When his daughter Anne, through whose increasing influence at Court he ascended these heights of prosperity, was about to be married to Henry VIII, her brother George was deputed to announce the event to the King of France, and with him greatness grew as rapidly as with his father so long as his sister was able to preserve her power over the King.

In the Second Part of Shakespeare's *King Henry IV.*, act ii., scene 4, Pistol, snatching up his sword, exclaims:

> What! shall we have incision? shall we imbrue?
> Then death rock me asleep, abridge my doleful days.

This is in allusion to the following song, which is supposed to have been written by Anne Boleyn. The words were first printed by Sir John Hawkins in his *History of Music,* having been communicated to him by a udicious antiquary then deceased, whose opinion was that they were written either by or in the person of Anne Boleyn. But as George, Viscount Rocbfort, brother to the above lady, and who suffered on her account, has the fame of being the author of several songs and sonnets, Ritson is inclined to attribute the authorship of this poem to him.

> O death! O death! rock me asleep!
> Bring me to quiet rest:
> Let pass my weary, guiltless life
> Out of my careful breast.
> Toll on the passing bell,
> Ring out my doleful knell,
> Let thy sound my death tell.
> Death doth draw near me,
> There is no remedy, no remedy,
> There is no remedy.
>
> My pains who can express?
> Alas! they are so strong;
> My dolour will not suffer strength
> My life for to prolong.
> Toll on, &c.
>
> Alone in prison strong,
> I wail my destiny;
> Woe worth this cruel hap that I
> Should taste this misery.
> Toll on, &c.
>
> Farewell my pleasures past,
> Welcome my present pain;
> I feel my torments so increase,
> That life cannot remain.

Cease now the passing bell,
Rung is my doleful knell,
For the sound my death doth tell.
Death doth draw nigh,
Sound my end dolefully,
For now I die.

THE LEGEND OF THE HEADLESS HORSES.

Sir John Fastolfe, K G., is said to have built his castle at Caister, near
Great Yarmouth, with the ransom obtained for the Duke d'Alençon, whom
he had taken prisoner at the Battle of Verneuil.

Queen Anne Boleyn was born at Blickling, near Aylsham, in Norfolk,
and ever after her tragic fate the Spectre of the Headless Horses has
been, it is asserted, frequently seen in the neighbourhood of Blickling and
Caister.

Sir John he was a valiant knight,
He kept his sword—and honor bright;
He bloody battles fought in France,
And at Verneuil he broke a lance.

Some noble prisoners there he won,
Their chief—the French Duke d'Alençon;
And with his ransom—paid in gold,
He built a castle—we are told—

At Caister—where he liv'd in state,
And din'd off gold and silver plate.
Of worldly goods he had great store;
Belov'd he was by rich and poor.

Manors he had, in number twenty,
Which for a knight was surely plenty!
And one he sold, without much stickling,
To Jeffery Boleyn, Lord of Blickling.

Fair Anne, the daughter of this knight,
King Henry's love gain'd at first sight,
But he, by jealousy misled,
On Tower Hill cut off her head.

Lord Rochfort, too, her brother dear,
Fell victim to the tyrant's fear ;
When this sad news to Blickling sped,
Each honest heart with anguish bled.

That very time, at dead of night,
Four headless horses took their flight,
Dragging behind them, as they ran,
The SPECTRE of a headless man !

Beneath his arm a head he bore,
Its tangled hair all wet with gore !
Pursued he was by demons foul,
With piercing shriek and dismal howl !

O'er hedge, o'er ditch, o'er fence, o'er gate,
They gallop on, at heedless rate ;
Over twelve bridges they must bound,
Ere morn shall stop their horrid round.

Sometimes by Fastolfe's ruin'd tower,
They through the neighbouring country scour,
Their snortings loud (without their heads !)
Make people tremble in their beds !

One winter's night, now long since past,
Giles Scroggins, shelter'd from the blast,
Sat drinking by the alehouse fire,
And cared for neither priest nor squire.

But joys like these are soonest fled,
Giles must go forth, to home and bed ;
The clock struck twelve, poor Scroggins started,
He seiz'd his hat, and then departed.

Trembling in darkness, first he stood,
Then trudg'd away for Caister wood,
But ere he reach'd that favour'd spot,
To see THE SPECTRE 'twas his lot.

He heard the hoofs behind him clattering,
(Poor Giles' teeth with fear were chattering!)
And scarcely could he shelter find,
Before IT pass'd him like the wind?

When all was still from earth to sky,
Giles look'd, but nothing could descry;
At last he reach'd his cottage door,
And straightway fell upon the floor!

His anxious wife, who watch'd that night,
Had heard the tempest with affright;
Drink was, she knew, in Giles' head,
So quickly bundled him to bed.

DESCRIPTION OF TWO MONSTROUS CHILDREN.

In the superstition of the days of Elizabeth every unknown or unusual natural phenomenon was looked upon as a warning from heaven of social and political disaster, and was, therefore, watched with the most intense interest. Among these signs none created greater apprehension than monstrous births, which we find continually recorded even by the historians and more serious writers of the day. The year 1562, the fourth of Elizabeth's reign, is recorded by Holinshed and Stowe as especially fertile in "monsters." Numerous broadsides were published about this period descriptive of these prodigies, generally accompanied with a picture. In the collection of ballads formerly in the library of the late George Daniel, Esq., from which the following ballad is selected, there are no less than five belonging to 1562, the year just mentioned. First we have a " true reporte" of a child born at Great Horkesley, near Colchester, having neither legs nor arms. The description of the child is prefaced by verses setting forth the mysterious design of these monsters. The next gives an account of a monstrous pig with a dolphin's head, born at Charing Cross, accompanied with verses moralising upon the phenomenon. A monstrous child born at Freshwater, in the Isle of Wight, is described or explained

in a moral or religious light in a ballad by John Barker, and dated 1564.
And in the case of a monstrous child born at Maidstone, in Kent, having
"first the mouth slitted on the right side, like a libarde's (leopard's)
mouth, terrible to beholde," which the author of the ballad explains as a
rebuke to the kingdom for its wickedness, and as a sign of God's displeasure:

> This monstrous shape to thee, England,
>   Playn shewes thy monstrous vice,
> If thou ech part wylt vnderstand,
>   And take thereby aduice.

The following ballad written by John Mellys, of Norwich, is an example
of the moral or religious light in which such things were viewed, and well
illustrates the superstition of those days.

*The true discription of two monsterous children laufully
begotten betwene George Stevens and Margerie his wyfe,
and borne in the parish of Swanburne, in Buckyngham-
shyre, the iiij. of Aprill, Anno Domini 1566; the two children having both their belies fast joyned together, and
embracyng one another with their armes : which children
wer both alyve by the space of half-an-hower, and wer bap-
tized and named the one John and the other Joan.*

> I read how Affrique land was fraught,
>   For their most filthy life,
> With monstreus shapes confuzedly,
>   That therin wer full rife.

> But England now pursues their vyle
>   And detestable path,
> Embracyng eke all mischeefs great,
>   That moves God's mightie wrath.

> As these onnaturall shapes and formes,
>   Thus brought forth in our dayes,
> Are tokens true and manifest
>   How God by dyuers wayes

Doth styrre vs to amendment of
   Our vyle and cankred lyfe,
Which to, to much abused is
   In man, in chylde, in wyfe.

We wallow so in filthie sin,
   And naught at all regarde,
Nor wyll not feare the threats of God
   Tyll we, for just rewarde,

Be ouerwhelmed with mischeefs great,
   Which, ready bent for vs,
Full long ago decreed wer,
   As Scriptures doth discus.

Both tender babes and eke brute beastes,
   In shape disfourmed bee ;
Full manie wayes he plagues the earth,
   As dayly we may see.

Thus mightie loue, to pearce our harts,
   These tokens straunge doth send,
To call vs from our filthie lyfe,
   Our wicked wayes t'amend.

And thus by these two children here,
   Forewarnes both man and wyfe,
How both estates ought to bewayle
   Their vyle and wretched lyfe.

For sure we all may be agast
   To see these shapes vnkynd,
And tremblyng feare may pearce our harts,
   Our God to haue in myud.

For yf we printed in our brest
   These signes and tokens straunge,
Wold make vs from our sinnes to shrinke,
   Our liues anew to chaunge.

But some proude boastyng Pharisie,
   The parents wyll detect,
And judge with heapes of vglie vice
   Their liues to be infect.

No, no, but lessons for vs all,
   Which dayly doe offend ;
Yea, more, perhaps, then hath the freends
   Whom God this birth did lend.

For yf you will, with single eye,
   Note vell and view the text,
Ann marke our Sauiours aunswer eke
   That thereto is annext.

Where his disciples asked him,
   To know therein his mynd,
Yf greatter wer the parents sinnes,
   Or his that was borne blynd.

To whom Christ answered in a breef,
   That neither hee nor they
Deserued had that crooked fate,
   Although they sin each day ;

But to the ende Gods glorie great,
   And miracles diuine,
Might on the earth apparaunt be,
   His works for to define.

Such like examples moued me
   In these forgetfull dayes,
To rue our state, that vs among
   Vice beares such swings and swayes ;

Wherein the goodnesse great of God
   We way and set so light ;
By such examples callyng vs
   From sin both day and night.

Where we doe runne at random wyde,
    Ourselves flatteryng styll,
And blazyng others faults and crimes,
    Yet we ourselues most yll.

But if we doe consider right,
    And in even balaunce way
The ruine great of hartic loue
    Among us at this day;

And well behyld, with inward eyes,
    Th' embracyng of these twinnes,
That God by them vpbraides vs for
    Our false discemblyng sinnes;

We would with Niniuie repent
    Our former passed yeares,
Bewaylyng eke our secret sinnes
    In sackecloth and in teares.

Therefore in time amend your state,
    And call to God for grace,
Bewayle your former lyfe and sinnes,
    While you have time and space.

FINIS.   QUOD JOHN MELLYS, NOR.

*Imprinted at London by Alexander Lacy, for William Lewes, dwellyng in Cow
Lane, above Holborne Cundit, ouer against the signe of the Plough.*

THE DEATH OF JOHN LEWES,
WHO WAS BURNED AT NORWICH AS A HERETIC,
ON THE 18th OF SEPTEMBER, 1583.

The broadside from which the following ballad is copied is in the library
of the Society of Antiquaries. Its title in full is " A declaration of the
death of John Lewes, a most detestable and obstinate heretick burned at
Norwich the 18th daye of September, 1583, about three of the clocke in
the after noone. Imprinted at London by Richard Jones, dwelling neere

Holburne Bridge, October 8th." The ballad is in black letter, except the words which I have printed in italics : these are modern. It has a wood-cut at the top representing a man at the stake.

Among the city archives preserved in the Guildhall, Norwich, there is a folio manuscript volume on vellum containing a series of chronological memoranda relating to Norwich. In this volume is the following note :— "1583. This year, the xviij day of September, before these new Sheriffs (Henry Pye and Edward Johnson) were sworne, one Abydall Lewis, an heretic, for denying the divinity of Christ was burnt in the Castle ditch, where Doctr. Gardener, Deane of Xt Church, preached, and the said Lewes died most obstinately without repentance or any speech."

TO THE TUNE OF "JOHN CARELESSE."

Shall silence shroude such sin
   As Satan seems to showe,
E'en in his imps, in these our dayes
   That all men might it prove.

No, no, it cannot be
   But such as love the Lorde,
With heart and voice will him confesse
   And to his word accord.

And do not as this Devil did,
   Though shape of man he bare,
Denying Christ did silence keepe
   At death, devoide of care.

Yet did this wretch most wickedly
   John Lewis, who to name,
Full boldly speake and brutishly,
   Gods glory to defame.

In presence of those persons which
   Were learned, wise, and grave,
That wish't in heart with weeping teares
   Repentance he would crave.

But he despising reverence
   To *Prince* or any state,
Not them regardes but used terms
   As each had been his mate.

For he did then each wight, the which
  With him had any talke;
Thus did his tongue most devilishly
  With defamy still walke.

But when that no persuasion might
  Procure him to relent,
Then *Judgment* did by *Justice* right
  Unto his death consent.

That he should burned be to death
  This *Justice* did awarde,
Now marke what after did ensue
  And thereto have regarde.

The time then of his death being come,
  Which was the eighteenth daye
Of *September* in eighty-three,
  This wretch wrought his decay.

For when he to the place was brought
  Where he his life should ende,
He forced was a time to stay
  A sermon to perpende.

The which was preached by the *Deane*
  Of *Norwich*, in such wise,
Which well might move each sinful soule
  From seat of sin to rise.

He like a tender Father did
  Give documents most pure
Unto this wretch, as to his childe
  From ill, him to procure.

But all in vaine, this varlet wilde
  His doctrine did detest:
For when he spake of Christ Gods Son
  He made thereat a jest.

And smilingly his face would turne
    From Preachers present there,
Which argued that he never stood
    Of God or man in feare.

When that the sermon drew to ende
    Then did the *Deane* desire
Him that he would fall on his knees—
    And Gods mercy require.

But, still he stood as any stone
    Not liftinge hand or eye
Unto the Heavens, which showed his heart
    To God was nothing nigh.

The *Sheriff* strikes him on the breast,
    Wishing him to returne,
Yea Gentlewomen, two or three
    Before he went to burne

Would seeme to pull him on his knees,
    His sins for to confesse ;
But he full stoutly stood therein,
    Not meaning nothing lesse.

From preaching place unto the stake
    They straight did him conveye,
Where preachers two or three him wyld
    Unto the Lord to pray.

And Christ our Saviour to confesse
    Both God and man to be :
That soule and body by true faith
    In him might be set free.

From Satan who had him in holde,
    But he not this regarde ;
As countenance his did show full plaine.
    For why, no worde was heard

That he did speake : but like a dog
  Did end his days with shame :
Nor bending knee, hand, heart, or tongue
  To glorifye God's name.

For though that divers Preachers then
  Both Godly, grave, and wise
Did hope (in heart) to win this man
  Yet all would not suffice ;

For not one worde that they could get
  What so they did or said :
Till one that was right earnest set
  By these words him assayed :

If that thou dost not Jesus Christ
  God's only Sonne confesse
Both God and Man ; and hope in him
  For thy salvation doutlesse ;

As sure as now thou shalt be burnt
  Before us here at stake ;
So sure in Hell thou shalt be burnt
  In that infernal lake.

Quoth he, thou liest, and no more words
  At all this Captive said :
Nor no repentant sign would show,
  Which made us all dismayed.

And when the fire did compasse him
  About on every side,
The people look't he then would speake,
  And therefore loud they cryed :

Now call on Christ to save thy soule :
  Now trust in Christ his death ;
But all in vain, no words he spake
  But thus yields up his breath.

Oh wofull state, oh danger deepe
That he was drowned in :
Oh grant us God, for Christ his sake,
We fall not in such sin.

And we that think we stand in faith
So firm Lorde let it be
To thee thy Sonne and Holy Ghoste,
One God in Persons three.

FINIS.   H. GILBERT.

Ane morta non fa mele.

THE CHILDREN IN THE WOOD.

" Wayland Wood," near Watton, Norfolk, vulgarly called *Wailing* Wood,
from a tradition that two infants were basely murdered in it by their uncle,
is said to have been the scene of this beautifully pathetic story.

Addison, in the *Spectator*, says, " The old ballad of ' Two Children in the
Wood' is one of the darling songs of the common people, and has been
the delight of most Englishmen in some part of their age. The song is a
plain and simple copy of nature, destitute of all the helps and ornaments
of art. The tale of it is a pretty tragical story, and pleases for no other
reason but because it is a copy of nature. There is even a despicable
simplicity in the verse ; and yet because the sentiments appear genuine
and unaffected, they are able to move the mind of the most polite reader
with inward meltings of humanity and compassion."

Bishop Percy says the subject of this very popular ballad seems to be
taken from an old ballad entitled, " Two Lamentable Tragedies ; the one
of the Murder of Maister Beech, a chandler in Thames Street, &c., the
other of a young child murthered in a wood by two ruffians with the
consent of his uncle," by Robert Yarrington, 1601, 4to. The Bishop says
also that " whoever compares the play with the ballad, will have no doubt
but the former is the original ; the language is far more obsolete, and
such a vein of simplicity runs through the whole performance that had
the ballad been written first, there is no doubt but every circumstance of
it would have been received into the drama."

The play upon which Percy thinks the ballad is founded is dated 1601.
But in the Registers of the Stationers' Company, under the date of
October 15th, 1595, we find : " Thomas Millington entred for his copie
under t'handes of bothe the wardens, a ballad intituled, ' The Norfolk
Gentleman, his Will and Testament, and howe he commytted the keeping
of his children to his owne brother, who delte most wickedly with them,

and how God plagued him for it.'" This entry, as Mr. Chappell remarks, agrees almost verbatim with the title of the ballad in the Pepy's collection (1, 518), but which is of later date. This is the copy which Percy refers to in his introduction to the ballad. There is a copy of this ballad in the Roxburghe Collection in the British Museum, and two copies may be seen in the Halliwell Collection of Ballads and Broadsheets, Cheetham Library, Manchester; one copy is printed in "Aldermanbury Churchyard, London," but the printer's name is not given. The other has on it, "Printed and sold by Lane & Walker, St. Andrew's, Norwich, a true story, 1665."

Sharon Turner, in his *History of England*, says, "I have sometimes fancied that the popular ballad of *The Children in the Wood* may have been written at this time on Richard [3] and his nephew before it was quite safe to stigmatise him more openly." This theory has been ably advocated by Miss Halsted, in the appendix to her Richard III., as Duke of Gloucester and King of England. Her argument is based chiefly upon internal evidence, there being no direct proof that the ballad is older than the date of the entry at Stationers' Hall.*

Mr. I. O. Halliwell, in his Descriptive Notices of Popular English Histories, printed for the Percy Society in 1848, gives the following as the title of one of the tracts in his collection:—

"The History of the two Children in the Wood Reviv'd, or Murder Reveng'd, containing the sad and lamentable Story of the Deaths of two Children of a Gentlemen, who, after the Decease of their Parents, were delivered, by their uncle, to two ruffians, to be murdered for the estates, but in the end they were left in an unfrequented wood, and there starved to Death, and covered over by a Robin Redbreast: Together with the sad relation of the heavy judgments which befel their unnatural uncle, who died miserable in prison, and how it came to be discovered by one of the ruffians upon his being condemned for a notorious robbery. With many other passages and circumstances at large. 12 mo. Licensed and entered according to order, n. d."

The full title of the ballad is "The Children in the Wood, or the Norfolk Gentleman's last Will and Testament," to the tune of "Rogero," &c.

> Now ponder well, you parents deare,
>   These wordes which I shall write;
> A doleful story you shall heare,
>   In time brought forth to light.
> A gentleman of good account
>   In Norfolk dwelt of late,
> Who did in honor far surmount
>   Most men of his estate.

---

* Chappell's Popular Music of the Olden Time, page 200.

Sore sicke he was, and like to dye,
   No helpe his life could save ;
His wife by him as sicke did lye,
   And both possest one grave.
No love between these two was lost,
   Each was to other kinde,
In love they liv'd, in love they dyed,
   And left too babes behind :

The one a fine and pretty boy,
   Not passing three years olde ;
The other a girl more young than he,
   And fram'd in beautyes molde.
The father left his little son,
   As plainlye doth appeare,
When he to perfect age should come,
   Three hundred pounds a yeare.

And to his little daughter Jane
   Five hundred pounds in gold,
To be paid down on marriage-day,
   Which might not be controll'd :
But if the children chance to dye,
   Ere they to age should come,
Their uncle should possesse their wealth ;
   For so the wille did run.

Now, brother, said the dying man,
   Look to my children deare ;
Be good unto my boy and girl,
   No friends else have they here :
To God and you I recommend
   My children deare this daye ;
A little while be sure we have
   Within this world to staye.

You must be father and mother both,
   And uncle all in one ;
God knows what will become of them,
   When I am dead and gone :

With thát bespoke their mother deare,
　O brother kinde, quoth shee,
You are the man must bring our babes
　To wealth or miserie !

And if you keep them carefully,
　Then God will you reward ;
But if you otherwise should deal,
　God will your deedes regard,
With lips as cold as any stone,
　They kist their children small :
God bless you both, my children deare ;
　With that the teares did fall.

These speeches then their brother spake
　To this sicke couple there,
The keeping of your little ones
　Sweet sister do not fear :
God never prosper me nor mine,
　Nor aught else that I have,
If I do wrong your children neare,
　When you are layd in grave.

The parents being dead and gone,
　The children home he takes,
And bringes them straite into his house,
　Where much of them he makes.
He had not kept these pretty babes
　A twelvemonth and a daye,
But for their wealth he did devise
　To make them both awaye.

He bargain'd with two ruffians strong,
　Which were of furious mood,
That they should take these children young,
　And slaye them in a wood.
He told his wife an artful tale,
　He would the children send
To be brought up in faire London,
　With one that was his friend.

Away then went those pretty babes,
  Rejoicing at that tide,
Rejoicing with a merry minde,
  They should on cock horse ride.
They prate and prattle pleasantly,
  As they rode on the waye,
To those that should their butchers be,
  And work their lives decaye :

To that the pretty speeche they had,
  Made Murder's heart relent :
And they that undertooke the deed,
  Full sore did now repent.
Yet one of them more hard of heart,
  Did vowe to do his charge,
Because the wretch that hired him,
  Had paid him very large.

The other won't agree thereto,
  So here they fall to strife ;
With one another they did fight,
  About the children's life :
And he that was of mildest mood,
  Did slaye the other there,
Within an unfrequented wood ;
  The babes did quake for feare !

He took the children by the hand,
  Tears standing in their eye,
And bad them straightwaye follow him,
  And look they did not crye :
And two long miles he ledd them on,
  While they for food complaine.
Staye here, quoth he, I'll bring you bread,
  When I come back again.

These pretty babes, with hand in hand,
  Went wandering up and downe ;
And never more could see the man
  Approaching from the town :

Their prettye lippes with black-berries,
　Were all besmear'd and dyed,
And when they sawe the darksome night,
　They sat them downe and cryed.

Thus wandered these poor innocents,
　Till death did end their grief,
In one another's armes they dyed,
　As wanting due relief:
No burial 'this' pretty 'pair'
　Of any man receives
Till Robin-redbreast piously
　Did cover them with leaves.

And now the heavy wrathe of God
　Upon their uncle fell;
Yea, fearful fiends did haunt his house,
　His conscience felt an hell:
His barnes were fir'd, his goodes consum'd,
　His landes were barren made,
His cattle dyed within the field,
　And nothing with him stay'd.

And in a voyage to Portugal
　Two of his sonnes did dye;
And to conclude, himself was brought
　To want and miserye:
He pawn'd and mortgaged all his land
　Ere seven years came about,
And now at length this wicked act
　Did by this means come out:

The fellowe, that did take in hand
　These children for to kill,
Was for a robbery judg'd to dye,
　Such was God's blessed will:
Who did confess the very truth,
　As here hath been display'd:
Their uncle having dyed in gaol
　Where he for debt was layd.

You that executors be made,
And overseers eke
Of children that be fatherless,
And infants mild and meek ;
Take you example by this thing,
And yield to each his right,
Lest God with such like miserye
Your wicked minds requite.

NANCY AND JEMMY OF YARMOUTH,
OR THE
CONSTANT LOVERS' GARLAND.

IN FOUR PARTS.

PART 1. Showing how beautiful Nancy of Yarmouth fell in love with young Jemmy the Sailor.

PART 2. How the Father conveyed a letter to destroy young Jemmy, his daughter's sweetheart.

PART 3. Showing how the Ghost of young Jemmy the Sailor appeared to beautiful Nancy of Yarmouth.

PART 4. How the Ghosts of these two unfortunate lovers appeared to the Boatswain, and he, having his trial, was hanged at the yard's arm.

TUNE, THE YARMOUTH TRAGEDY.

PART I.

Lovers, I pray, lend an ear to my story,
Take an example by this constant pair ;
How love a young virgin did blast in her glory,
Beautiful Nancy of Yarmouth we hear.

She was a merchant's only daughter,
Heir unto fifteen hundred a year ;
A young man courted her who called her his jewel,
The son of a gentleman who lived near.

Many long years the maid he admired ;
When they were infants in love they agreed ;
And when at age this young couple arrived
Cupid an arrow between them displayed.

Their tender hearts were linked together,
But when her parents the same did hear,
They to their charming young beautiful daughter
Acted a part that was hard and severe.

Daughter, they said, give over your proceedings;
If that against our consent you do wed,
For ever more we resolve to disown you
If you wed with one that is mean bred.

Her mother said, You are a great fortune,
Besides, you are beautiful charming and young;
You are a match, dear child, that is fitting
For any Lord that is in Christendom.

Then did reply the young beautiful virgin,
Riches and honour I do defy;
If that I am denied of my dearest lover
Then farewell world which is vanity.

Jemmy's the man that I do admire,
He is the riches that I do adore,
For to be great I never desire,
My heart is fixed never to love more.

Then said her father, 'Tis my resolution,
Although I have no more daughters but thee,
If that with him you resolve for to marry
Banished for ever from me thou shalt be.

Well, cruel father, but this I desire,
Grant me that Jemmy once more I may see,
Though you do us part I still will be loyal,
For none in the world I admire but he.

For the young man he sent in passion,
Saying, For ever, sir, take your leave;
I have a match more fit for my daughter,
Therefore it is but folly to grieve.

Honour'd father, then said the young lady,
Promised we are by the powers above ;
Why of all comforts will you bereave me ?
Our love is fixed never to be removed.

Then said her father, A trip to the ocean
You first shall go in a ship of my own,
And I'll consent you shall have my daughter
When to Yarmouth again you return.

Honour'd sir, then said the two lovers,
Since 'tis your will we are bound to obey ;
Our constant hearts can never be parted,
But our eager desires no longer can stay.

Then said Nancy, Behold, dearest Jemmy,
Here take this ring, the pledge of our vow,
With it my heart keep it safe in your bosom,
Carry it with you wherever you go.

Then in his arms he closely did infold her,
While crystal tears like a fountain did flow,
Crying, My heart in return I do give you,
And you shall be present wherever I go.

When on the ocean, my-dear, I am sailing,
The thoughts of my jewel the compass shall steer ;
These tedious long days speedy time will devour
And bring me home safe again to my dear.

Therefore be constant, my dear lovely jewel,
For by the heavens if you are untrue,
My troubled ghost shall torment you for ever,
Dead or alive I will have none but you.

Her lovely arms round his neck she twined,
And saying, My dear, when you are on the sea,
If the fates unto us should prove cruel
That we each other no more ever see,

No man alive shall ever enjoy me ;
Soon as the tidings of death reach my ear,
Then like a poor unfortunate lover
Down to the grave I will go to my dear.

Then with a sorrowful sigh he departed ;
The winds next morning blew a pleasant gale ;
All things being ready the famed Mac Calley
Then for Barbadoes she straightway set sail.

PART II.

Jemmy was floating upon the wide ocean,
And her cruel parents were plotting the while,
How that the heart of their beautiful daughter
With cursed gold should strive to beguile.

Many a lord of fame, birth, and breeding,
Came to court this young beautiful maid ;
But their rich presents and proffers she slighted,
Constant I'll be to my jewel, she said.

Now for awhile we leave this fair maiden
And tell how things with her did go ;
In fair Barbadoes the ship fairly arrived,
But now observe this lover's overthrow.

Young Jemmy, comely in every feature,
A Barbadoes love whose fortune was great,
So fixed her eyes that she cried, If I have not
This brave English sailor I'll die for his sake.

She drest herself in a gallant attire,
With costly diamonds she plaited her hair,
A hundred slaves drest to attend her,
She sent for this young man to come to her.

Come noble sailor, she cried, can you fancy
A lady whose riches are very great ?
A hundred slaves you shall have to attend you,
Music to charm you in your silent sleep.

In robes of ·gold, my dear, I'll deck you,
Pearls and rich jewels I'll lay at your feet,
In a chariot of gold you shall ride for your pleasure ;
If you can fancy me, answer me straight.

Amazed with wonder awhile he stood gazing,
Forbear, noble lady, at length he reply'd,
In flourishing England I've vow'd to a lady,
At my return to make her my bride.

She is a charming young beautiful creature,
She has my heart, I can love no more ;
I bear in my eyes her sweet lovely feature,
No other creature on earth I adore.

Hearing of this she did rave in distraction,
Crying, Unfortunate maid thus to love
One that does basely slight all my glory
And of my person he will not approve.

Lords of renown I their favour slighted,
Now I must die for a sailor so bold ;
I must not blame him because he is constant,
True love is far better than gold.

A costly jewel she instantly gave him,
Then in her trembling hand took a knife,
One fatal stroke, before they could save her,
Quickly did put an end to her life.

Great lamentation was made for this lady,
Jemmy on board the ship he did steer,
And then to England they homeward came sailing
With a longing desire to meet with his dear.

But when her father found he was returning,
A letter he wrote to the boatswain his friend,
Saying a handsome reward I will give you
If you the life of young Jemmy will end.

Void of all grace and for the sake of the money,
The cruel boatswain the same to complete,
As they on the deck were lovingly walking
He suddenly tumbled him into the deep.

PART III.

In dead of the night, when all were asleep,
His troubled ghost to his love did appear,
Crying, Arise, you beautiful Nancy,
Perform the vows you made to your dear.

You are my own, therefore tarry no longer;
Seven long years for your sake did I stay;
Hymen does wait for to crown us with pleasure,
The bride guests are ready, then come away.

She cried, Who is there under my window,
Surely it is the voice of my dear;
Lifting her head off her downy pillows
Straight to the casement she then did repair.

By the light of the moon, which brightly was shining,
She espied her lover, who to her did say,
Your parents are sleeping; before they awake,
Stir my dear creature and come away.

O Jemmy, she cried, if my father should hear thee,
We shall be ruined; therefore pray prepare,
At the sea side I will instantly meet you,
With my two maids I'll come to you there.

Her nightgown embroidered with gold and silver
Carelessly round her body she throws,
With the two maids who did attend her
To meet her true love she instantly goes.

Close in his arms the spirit did infold her,
Jemmy, she said, you are colder than clay,
Sure you can never be the man I admire,
Paler than death you appear unto me.

Yes, fairest creature, I'm your true lover,
Dead or alive you know you are mine ;
I come for my vow; my dear, you must follow
My body now to a wat'ry tomb.

I for your sake refused gold and silver,
Beauty and riches for you I despised ;
A charming young lady did for me expire ;
For thinking of you I was deaf to her cries.

Your cruel parents have been my undoing,
And I do sleep in a wat'ry tomb ;
Now for your promise, my dear, I am suing ;
Dead or alive, love, you are my own.

PART IV.

The trembling lady was sorely affrighted ;
Amazed, she stood near the brink of the sea ;
With eyes lift up to heaven she cried, Cruel parents,
Heaven requite you for your cruelty.

Indeed, I promised, my dearest creature,
Dead or alive I would then be his own ;
Now to perform my solemn vow I'm ready,
And to follow him to his wat'ry tomb.

The maids they heard the sad lamentation,
But the apparition indeed could not see ;
Thinking the lady was fallen into distraction,
They strove to persuade her contented to be.

But still she cried, My dear, I am coming,
And in thy bosom I'll soon fall asleep ;
When she had spoken, this unfortunate lady
Suddenly plunged herself into the deep.

But when to her father the maids told the matter
He wrung his hands, crying, What have I done ?
Oh ! dearest child, it was thy cruel father
That did provide thee a wat'ry tomb.

Two or three days being expired,
These two unfortunate lovers were seen,
In each other arms they were floating
By the side of the ship on the wat'ry main.

The cruel boatswain was struck with horror,
Straight did confess the sad deed he had done,
Shewing the letter that came from her father
Which was the cause of these lovers' doom.

On board of the ship he was tried for the murder,
At the yard's arm was hanged for the same ;
Her father he soon broke his heart for his daughter
Before the ship into the harbour then came.

The cursed gold has caused destruction ;
Why should the rich court after gain ?
I hope this story it will be a warning
That cruel parents may ne'er do the same.

True love is better than jewels and treasure   ,
Riches can never buy true love I know ;
But this young couple they liv'd without measure
Love was the occasion of their overthrow.

A WARNING-PIECE FOR INGROOSERS OF CORNE ;

BEING

A true Relation how the *Divell* met with one Goodman *Inglebred* of
Bowlon, within six miles of *Holgay* in *Norfolk* ; as he was comming from
Linn Market, and Bargain'd for a great quantity of Barly for eight
shillings a Bushell and gave earnest; and when he came to fetch it
brought Carts and Horses (to their thinking), and while 'twas measuring
the *Divell* vanished, and tore the Barne in pieces, and scattered all the
Corne with such Windes and Tempest, which hath done such great harme
both by Sea and Land, the like was never heard of before; the Farmer
now* lycing destracted.

Sent in a Letter to be Printed by *Christopher Emmerson, George Dixon,*
and *George Higgins*.   .

* "new " in original.

Good People all pray lend an eare
 to this my Song, that's strange and true,
Wherein I breifly shall Declare,
 the full Relation here to you.

If any Misers you do know,
 that hoards up Corne, to starve *the* Poore,
If that these Lines you to them show
 'twill make them sure bring out their Store.

In *Norfolk* did this chance befall,
 at *Bowton* where this Man did dwell,
And Goodman *Inglebred* they do him call,
 who had great store of Corne to sell.

But he as many thousands more,
 without any remorse or pitty,
Was fully resolv'd to keep his Store,
 to bring a Dearth in Town and City.

He being at Market on a day,
 at *Linn*, a plaace that's known full well :
And Riding home upon the way,
 He had a Customer from Hell.

The Divell did him over take,
 in Habbit being very brave,
Who did a bargaine with him make,
 and Halfe-a-crowne in earnest gave.

The price was very great they made,
 and Barly that must be the Graine,
Eight shillings a bushell must be paid,
 being well contented with such gaine.

And thus the Divell and he agreed,
 likewise the time to fetch the same ;
The Miser hy'd him home with speed,
 for to provide against he came.

When he came home he was full glad,
  and to his Wife he did unfold
What bargin, and what price he had,
  likewise what quantity he sold.

With that his Wife made this reply,
  as by his Servants it was told,
None but the Divell would give so high
  a price (quoth she) as you have sold.

THE SECOND PART, TO THE SAME TUNE.

To Thrashing straight he set his Men,
  to make it ready against the day,
And the Divell was as ready then,
  against the time to fetch't away.

The day being come, the Divell brought
  his Furniture, to take these stores,
With Horse *and* Carts, as to their thought,
  the Man he straight threw 'ope *the* doores.

To measuring straight his Barly out,
  this Man begun with all his spéed ;
With that the Divell made a Rout,
  and of his Bargain soone was fréed.

The Divel vanish'd straight away,
  such Storms and Winds, nere heard before,
No People thereabouts durst stay ;
  the Barns in péeces all he tore.

His Barns and Corne it was all spoil'd,
  and all the Country round likewise,
Had all their Houses then Vntyl'd,
  such Winds they nere saw from *the* Skys.

This Farmer fell distracted straight,
  he cannot take no Rest nor Sléep,
And cryes the Divil doth for him waight,
  his Bargaine must with him kéep.

All you that hoard, and buy up Corne,
    and kéepe it up, to make it déere,
Although you long have béen forborne,
    there's Rods in piklec for you I beare.

Your Villainy now is brought about,
    and pay for't deare you will ere long,
Your Stores you will be made bring out,
    you shall not doe the Poore such wrong.

The Lord I hope will heare the cryes,
    of thousands which are in distresse,
Of gallant Hearts, that daily lýes
    still hoping, yet have no redresse.

The Lord preserve our King, and blesse
    him from the trecherous hands of those
That are his Enemies, yet professe
    they love him, yet prove secret Foes.

The Quéen God send her safe to land,
    and all the Progeny preserve;
Likewise for those that faithfull stand
    and from him yet did never swerve.

My prayers shall daily be for those,
    with many thousands more beside.
But such I take his cheifest Foes,
    that's given to Covetuousness and Pride.

For you that deale in Corne and Graine,
    to whom these Lines in cheif belong,
Beware of such unlawfull gain,
    where none but Poore doth bear the wrong.

So to conclude and make an end,
    for Peace and Plenty, let us pray,
That God may stand the poore-mans freind,
    for the Poore are now the rich-mans pray.

London, printed for *William Gilbertson,* at the Bible in *Giltspur-street.*

THE NORFOLK FARMER'S JOURNEY TO LONDON.

This curious ballad was written by Edward Ford, probably early in the seventeenth century. The original is entitled "A merry discourse betweene Norfolke Thomas and Sisly Standtoo't, his wife: together with their thanklesse journey from Norfolke to London, onely to see their friends, and how they doe respect and entertaine 'um for their love and labour."

To London is mad Thomas come
With Sisly, here, his wife alone,
To see some friends, I hear are gone
    To Heaven awhile ago :
But I do hope it is a lye,
As I shall find it by and by,
Or else poore Tom and Sisse should cry
    Till Doomes-day.

THOMAS.

For though they be none of the best,
I should be loath, I do protest,
To hear that they are gone to rest
    And never take their leave :
For I do love 'um all so well,
A little thing would make me dwell
Within the sounding of Bow-bell,
    At London.

SISLY.

Nay, husband, do not you say so ;
Our cottage poore wee'l not forego
For the best house that stands aroo
    'Twixt Cheap and Charing Crosse ;
For though our house be thatch't with straw,
We do not live, as some, in awe,
For 'tis our own by common law,
    In Norfolke.

Besides, we live at heart's content ;
We take no care to pay our rent,
For that is done incontinent,
    In twinkling of an eye.
When here at London, as they say,
They brawle and brabble every day,
And few or none but finds a way
    To Hogdsdon.

THOMAS.

Mum, Sisly ; keep your clapper still ;
There's them can hear at Highgate Hill ;
There's rats has been in Peggie's mill,
    Or else she lies herselfe.
What if the world be vilde and bad,
Shall I be such a foolish lad
To blaze and noyse it all abroad ?
    I scorn it.

Although, indeed, I must confesse
Thou speakest but truth, my honest Sisse,
Yet ever while you live marke this,
    And take it for a rule,
That every chimney must not smoake,
Nor every beggar weare a cloake,
Nor every truth must not be spoke
    In sadnesse.

But hang that cobler and his ends,
That lives too well, and never minds :
Would they were whipt that nere offends !
    Peace, chuck, I meane not thee.
But thou wilt scold sometime, I know,
The more is Thomas Standtoo't's wo ;
But, hang it, come let's trip and go
    To Fleet Street.

And thus they trudg'd along the street,
With many a jostle they did meet,
Which put poore Thomas in a sweat,
    And something angry, too ;
Which made him thinke they told a lye,
That said there did so many dye,
When as he could not go hardly
    For people.

SISLY.

At length, quoth she, good husband, stay,
And tell me what this place is, pray,
Where things are carried as they may ?
    I never saw the like.
For yonder's one doth ride in state,
And here's a beggar at a gate,
And there's a woman that will prate
    For nothing.

See, here is one that soundly beats,
And thumps his hemp until he sweats ;
And here's another greedy eats :
    I fear hee'l choke himselfe.
And yonder goes a gallant bilk,
And there's a woman winding silk,
And here's another fetching milk,
    At Hackney.

And here's the prettiest sight of all,
A woman that is mighty tall,
And yet her spouse a little squall :
    I wonder how they met.
And here's a man in armour stands,
And has it seemes lost both his hands ;
'Tis pitty that he has no lands
    To keep him.

Now you must by this time suppose them about the Exchange.

And here's a world of people fine,
That do in silks and satins shine :
I would that suite and cloak were mine,
     I hope I wish no harme.
And here hangs pictures two or three,
The best that ever I did see :
I thinke one looks full butt at me,
     And laughs too.

And here's a man hath many a rat,
Both in his hand and on his hat ;
Me thinks he keeps 'um very fat,
     O, strange what tailes they have.
And here's a gentlewoman, too,
That hides her face from me and you :
I wonder what she means to do
     In summer.

And here's an empty church, I see,
Great pity 'tis, most certainly,
It should indeed no fuller be,
     And all these people here.
And there's an old man carries wood,
And here's a young man doth no good ;
And here's a woman wears a hood ;
     Hey dazie !

THOMAS.

Come, Sisly, let us go along,
And not stand gaping here among
A sort of people that do throng ;
     I never saw the like.
But let us to our brother go,
That will us welcome well, I know,
For he himselfe did tell me so
     At Norfolke.

Soft ! let us knock, for here's the doore ;
But if because our clothes are poore,
They should not let us in therefore,
  'Two'd make a dog to laugh ;
For I have heard my mother say
That if a man fall to decay
There's few or none will bid him stay,
  Y'are welcome.

But silence ! not a word but mum ;
For see, our brother now doth come,
Methinks he looks as he were dum ;
  What makes him not to speake ?
Good brother, we our loves unfold,
For though my Sisse and I are old,
Yet we have made a little bold
  To see you.

BROTHER.

And truly I do thank you for 't ;
Ye'r welcome both with all my heart :
We'll drink a cup before we part ;
  An't please you but to stay.
For I have friends within, truly,
That if they should a stranger see,
They straight would very fearefull be
  Of danger.

THOMAS.

Why, brother, we no sicknesse have,
Nor are we started from our grave ;
Your love is all that we do crave :
  What need you then to feare ?
We do not come to eat your roast,
Nor yet to put you unto cost,
But now, I see, our labour's lost,
  Poore Sisly !

BROTHER.

Pray do not think the fault is mine,
For if you'l drink a pint of wine,
I'll give it you, and nere repine.
      Hang money ! what care I ?
And had I not so many ghease,
Indeed I seriously professe,
Your welcome should be more, or lesse,
      Good brother.

THOMAS.

No, thank you, brother ; e'ene farewell,
A blind man now with ease may smell,
That all things are not carried well :
      What love, pray, call you this ?
Come now, unto thy sister we
Will go with all celerity ;
No doubt that she shall kinder be
      Unto us.

They condescend and were content,
And to their sister straight they went ;
But all in vain their time was spent,
      For when they hither came,
Their sister did her maid compell
And bid her thus much to them tell,
Indeed she was not very well
      At that time.

From thence they to their couzen go,
Being much desirous for to know
Whether that she would serve 'um so,
      Or use 'um in that kind.
But being there, this newes was brought
That she a smock had newly bought,
And she was gone to have it wrought
      With woosted.

Well now, says Thomas to his dear,
What sayst thou, Sisly, to this gear?
We have gone far, yet nere the near
    We thank our kindred for't.
But if that brothers be so kind,
What favour shall a stranger find?
Protest, it troubles much my mind
    To think on't.

SISLY.

Nay husband, let us not do so ;
The best is, we can homewards go,
And yet not trouble friend nor foe ;
    What need we then to care?
For now each one, I'll tell you true,
Will only ask you, How do you?
I am glad to see you well, Sir Hugh,
    Good morrow.

THOMAS.

Why then, old Sisly thou and I
Will back again to Norfolke hie,
And bid a fig for company ;
    Our dog is sport enough.
But when we come to London next,
Our friends shall have a better text,
I swear and vow I am soundly vext ;
    Who cares for't?

UPON THE NORFOLK LARGESS.

We have a custom, no where else is known,
For here we reap, where nothing ere was sown,
Our harvestmen shall run ye, cap and leg,
And leave their work at any time to beg :

They make a harvest of each passenger,
And therefore have they a lord treasurer.
Here ye must pence, as well as pray'rs bestow,
'Tis not enough to say, God speed the plow.
These ask as men that meant to make ye stand,
For they petition with their arms in hand;
And till ye give, or some good sign appears,
They listen to ye with their harvest-eares.
If nothing drops into the gaping purse,
Ye carry with ye, to be sure, a curse;
But if a largess come, they shout ye deaf,
Had you as many eares as a wheat-sheaf.
Sometimes the hollow greater is by odds,
As when 'tis answered from the ivye tods.
Here all unite, and each his accent bears,
That were but now together by the eares.
And, which a contradiction doth imply,
Because they get a largess they must cry;
Cry with . . . . . whoever of it hears,
May wish their tankard had no other teares;
    Thus in a word our reapers now-a-days
    Reap in the field and glean in the highways.

PROSPERITY TO HOUGHTON.

Nunc est bibendum—Hor.

TO THE TUNE OF AN APE, A LION, A FOX, AND AN ASS, &c.

I.

Some bards of old times, much delighted with sack,
Have wrote in its praise, and extoll'd the sweet smack;
Ding a ding D'urfey (peace rest with his soul)
Has rendered immortal the strong beer of Knowl:
Some there are smote too with love of mild ale,
And others stand up when they're able for stale;
Yet the Hogen of Houghton remains still unsung,
Tho' such excellent liquor was ne'er tip't o'er tongue.

II.

Had the Trojans drank Hogen, those blades of renown,
They'd ne'er suffer'd the Greeks t'have demolish'd their town,
But have fought all like furies ; inspired with this
Paris long kept his life and his favourite Miss :
Who takes but his dose on't, was ne'er known to sneak,
And 'tis the only thing extant to make a cat speak ;
So says Dr. Turner, and he sure can tell,
At least till he gets himself rocky with Nell.

III.

The old ballads write Homer delighted with nectar,
And make a great fuss with the tall boy called Hector ;
But had fortune thrown him on Norfolk's fair coast,
He'd have only prais'd Hogen and sung Col. Hoste :
Amongst all his heroes not one can be found
Could tip up four bottles and then stand his ground ;
And for Bully Achilles, who did swagger and damn,
With this Hogen the doctor had soon made a lamb.

IV.

Your foreign Monsieurs with Champagne make a rout,
And dull English skulls love Nump Parson's stout ;
Tokay's too much guzzled by paltry Poles,
But its Hogen agrees best with true British souls ;
The doctor's perswaded Sir Robert's one glass
Is the occasion things now are at so good a pass ;
And swears if Sir Joseph's as wise as some think,
He should part with his Rolls for a draught of such drink.

V.

Come, a health to Sir Robert. Sure none can refuse.
And he that won't pledge, may he die in a noose ;
Small return for his cares. May he still be adored,
And let's take one more to my lady and lord ;
May Houghton long flourish to give us delight,
May its masters be all great and good as the Knight ;
May a race long succeed, like the place without faults,
That may tread in his paths, and keep full the vaults.

VI.

But hold, one cup more I must take if I die,
You may guess what I mean, here's Miss Hammond's soft eye ;
She's so lovely, so lively, as the blooming bud fresh,
She all language can utter, or painting express.
'Tis well judged of Venus to stay in the sky,
She'd make a poor figure when t'other is by ;
And while poupets of drawing-room beauties make boast,
I'll defy them to match me the liquor or toast.

HOUGHTON HARE HUNTING.

This and the preceding ballad are copied from the collection in the Cheetham Library, formed by Mr. Halliwell. They are both of them from the celebrated press of Horace Walpole at Strawberry Hill.

TUNE, " AND A BEGGING WE WILL GO."

I.

Come all ye gallant Knights and squires,
Tell why poor Puss's fall
Has ne'er been sung nor thought on by
One sportsman of you all ?
   When to Houghton we do go, &c.

II.

Young complimented fox-hunting,
· And on it wrote a song ;
No matter if 'twas true or not,
At least you'll grant 'twas long.
   When to Houghton we do go, &c.

III.

To Hogen next, Floyd gave its due,
And sung Miss Hammond's eye,
And why poor Bun is quite forgot,
I cannot tell, not I.
   When to Houghton we do go, &c.

IV.

But since none else will venture it,
The merits I will sing
(If you'll all join in chorus) of
Both Tows-hill and of Fring.
  When a hunting we do go, &c.

V.

How both of them, each in his turn,
Have brought good nags to shame ;
And sure I hope their riders were
Not in the least to blame.
  When a hunting we did go, &c.

VI.

Lord Lifford, one of Euston's suit,
With blood saw cover'd o'er,
Grey horse e'er got on Tows-hill top,
Both sides so whip so spore.
  When a hunting we did go, &c.

VII.

Mount Edgcomb too, who ne'er was wont
To make his court down wind,
To Fring Hills made poor Cloudy yield,
And fairly staid behind.
  When a hunting we did go, &c.

VIII.

Since then a hare shews sport enough,
To make fox-hunters sob,
Why should she not be sung by them,
And with them bear a Bob.
  When a hunting we do go, &c.

O NOBLE FESTUS.

DR. CORBET, BISHOP OF NORWICH, 1582-1635.

Bishop Percy in his *Reliques* says this was written about the beginning of
the seventeenth century by Dr. Corbet, the witty Bishop of Norwich, and

the copy he printed was from a third edition of his poems, 12mo, 1672, compared with a more ancient copy in the editor's folio M.S. The editors of this celebrated folio have given some interesting notes to this poem, the pith of which we extract.

Fuller, in his *History of the University of Cambridge*, says that when Sir Walter Mildmay appeared at Court after he had founded Emmanuel College, "the queen told him 'Sir Walter, I hear you have erected a Puritan foundation.' 'No, Madam,' saith he, 'far be it from me to countenance anything contrary to your established laws; but I have set an acorn, which, when it becomes an oak, God alone knows what will be the fruit thereof.' " John Gifford, Ezekiel Culverwell, Jeremiah Burroughes, Stephen Marshall, Thomas Shepherd, Nathaniel Ward, Samuel Crooke, John Cotton, Thomas Hooker, John Nates, John Stoughton, all well-known Puritan divines, were members of Mildmay's College.

Richard Greenham referred to in the poem was born 1531, educated at and fellow of Pembroke Hall, Cambridge. He became pastor of the congregation at Drayton near Cambridge. Bishop Hall says he excelled in experimental divinity, that he knew how to stay a weak conscience, how to raise a fallen, and how to strike a remorseless one. Brook, in his *Lives of the Puritans*, says he took such uncommon pains, and was so remarkably ardent in his preaching, that at the conclusion of the service his perspiration was so great that his shirt was usually as wet as if it had been drenched in water; was a most exact and conscientious Nonconformist, choosing on all occasions to suffer rather than sacrifice a good conscience; died a most comfortable and happy death in the year 1591. With regard to the "cure" the reading of his writings is said in the following piece to have effected, Brook says: "In addition to his public ministerial labours, he had a remarkable talent for comforting afflicted consciences, and in this department the Lord greatly blessed his endeavours. Having himself waded through the deep waters, and laboured under many painful conflicts, he was eminently qualified for relieving others. The fame of his usefulness in resolving the doubts of inquiring souls having spread through the country, multitudes from all quarters flocked to him as to a wise physician, and by the blessing of God obtained the desired comfort. Numerous persons, who to his own knowledge had laboured under the most racking terrors of conscience, were restored to joy and peace in believing. When any complained of blasphemous thoughts, his advice was 'do not *fear* them but *abhor* them.' " William Perkins (1558—1602), who is also referred to, was of Cambridge, a fellow of Christ's College, and afterwards preacher at St. Andrew's Church. He was both a Boanerges and a Barnabas, according to Brook. "Mr. Perkins' sermons were all law and all gospel. He used to apply the terrors of the law so directly to the consciences of his hearers, that their hearts would often sink under the convictions; and he used to pronounce the word 'damn' with so peculiar an emphasis that it left a doleful echo in their ears a long time after." "As for his books," says Fuller, "it is a miracle almost to conceive how thick they lye, and yet how far they overspread all over Christendom."

His popularity is attested by numerous editions of his works being issued during his life. The reference in the following piece is, no doubt, to his " Golden chaine, or the description of Theologie, containing the order of the causes of Salvation and Damnation, according to God's Word, a view whereof is to be seen in the table annexed." See Vol. 1 of the 1612 edition of his works. This table, a side note on it informs us, "may be instead of an ocular catechisme to them which cannot reade; for by the pointing of the finger they may sensibly perceive the chiefe points of religion, and the order of them." The reader is instructed that "the white line sheweth the order of the causes of salvation from the first to the last. The blacke line sheweth the order of the causes of damnation." Some of these latter causes are " the decree of reprobation," "a calling not effectual," " no calling," "ignorance and vanitie of mind," " the hardening of the heart," " a reprobate sense," " greediness in sinne," " fulnes of sinne." A bold analysis of perdition this; an audacious piece of theological presumption. The black line has a fearful look, as of some dark, deadly flood moving across the page. No wonder

> Those crooked veins
> Long stuck in my brains,
> That I feared my reprobation.

Am I mad, O noble Ffestus,
   when zeal and godly knowledge
put me in hope to deale with the Pope,
   as well as the best in the colledge ?
Boldlye I preacht, " War & cross, war a surplus,
   Mitres, copes, and rochetts !
Come heare me pray 9 times a day,
   & ffill your head with crotchetts."

In the house of pure Emanuell,
   I had my educatyon,
till my ffriends did surmise I dazed my eyes
   with the light of reuelation.
      Boldlye I preacht, &c.

They bound me like (a) bedlam,
   & lash(t) my 4 poore quarters.
while this does endure, ffaith makes me sure
   to be one of Ffox his Martyrs.
      Boldlye I preacht, &c.

These iniuryes I sufferd
  with Antich(r)ist's perswasion,
lett loose my chaine ! neither Roome nor Spaine
  can withstand my strong inuasyon.
        Boldlye I preacht, &c.

I assailed the seuen-hill cittye,
    where I mett the great rede dragon ;
I kept him alooffe with the armor prooffe,
    thoughe now I have neuer a ragg on.
        Boldlye I preacht, &c.

with a ffiery sword and targett,
    twice ffought I with this monster;
but the sonnes of pryde my zeale doe deryde,
    & all my deeds misconstrer.
        Boldlye I preacht, &c.

I vnhorst the hore of Babell,
    with the launce of Inspiration ;
I made her stinke, and spill the drinke
    in the cupp of abbominatyon.
        Boldlye I preacht, &c.

ffrom the beast with 10 herns, Lord bless vs,
    I have plucked of 3 allreadye ;
if they'll lett me alone I'll leaue him none,
    but they say I am to headye.
        Boldlye I preacht, &c.

    I saw 2 in the visyon,
        with a fflying booke betweene them,
    I have beene in despaire 5 times in a yeere,
        & beene cured by reading Greenham.
            Boldlye I preacht, &c.

I haue read in Perkins table*
the blacke line of damnatyon ;
these crooked vaines long stucke in my braines,
that I ffeared my reprobacion.
Boldlye I preacht, &c.

In the holy tounge of Canaan
I placed my chiefest tresure,
till I hurt my ffoote with an Hebrew roote,
that I bled beyond all measure.
Boldlye I preacht, &c.

I was before the Archbishoppe,†
& all the hie commissyon ;
I gave him no grace, but told him to his fface
that he ffauored superstition.
Boldlye I preacht, &c.

TO THE LADYES OF THE NEW DRESSE, THAT WEARE THEIR GORGETS AND RAYLES DOWN TO THEIR WAISTES.

BY DR. CORBET, BISHOP OF NORWICH—1582-1635.

The fondness of the English for adopting new fashions, and the absur-
dity of some of those adopted, caused many satirical songs of much point
and merit to be written during the last century, some of which were sung
at places of amusement. *The Universal Magazine* and *The London Magazine*
contain several of this class, both spirited and humorous. The short-
waisted gowns were fertile sources of satire, and the spencers worn by
both sexes came also in for a fair share of ridicule. A caricature was published, representing a group of dogs wearing spencers, looking at some
dancing dogs similarly dressed, the master of whom exclaims:—

> " Don't think my puppies stand alone ;
> If you will make the search, sir,
> Puppies at the bar you'll find,
> And puppies in the church, sir !

---

* Lowndes says the works of this Puritan are distinguished for
their piety, learning, extensive knowledge of the Scriptures, and strong
Calvinistic argumentation.
† Archbishop Laud.

Half-coat pups and booted pups.
And pups without their hair, sir,
Puppies deck'd in square-cut coats,
And puppies light as air, sir."

Sometimes the author gave striking pictures of the simplicity of ladies in the "good old times," contrasting it with the extravagance and affectation of those in his own day. These were published that all those who would venture on the voyage of matrimony might see what equipments modern luxury had then made necessary.

Then, as now, the virulence of satire, the ridicule of song, like the preaching of the moralists, were vanquished by the fickle goddess Fashion. The votaries of Fashion have been faithful, although, like their mistress, "ever changing, ever new."

Ladyes that weare black cipress veiles,*
Turn'd lately to white linnen rayles,†
And to your girdle weare your bands, ‡
And shew your armes instead of hands.
What can you doe in Lent so meet,
As, fittest dress, to weare a sheet?
'Twas once a band, 'tis now a cloake,
An acorne one day proves an oake ;
Weare but your linnen to your feet,
And then your band will prove a sheet.
By which devise, and wise excesse,
You'll doe your penance in a dresse,
And none shall know by what they see,
Which lady's censur'd, and which free.

THE LADIES' ANSWER.

(Harl. MS., No. 6396.)

BY DR. CORBET, BISHOP OF NORWICH.

Blacke cipress veiles are shroudes on night,
White linnen rayles are raies of light,

---

* Cipress was a fine kind of crape or gauze.
† The rayle was the neckerchief. The gorget was so very similar, that the terms are nearly synonymous.
‡ Alluding to the great length of the falling band, which was allowed to hang down upon the shoulders, and was not supported by any under-props.

Which though we to the girdles weare,
We've hands to keep your hands off there.
A fitten dresse we have in Lent,
To shew us truly penitent.
Who makes the band to be a cloke;
Makes John-a-style of John-an-oake.
We weare our garments to the feet,
Yet need not make our bandes a sheet;
The clergie weare as long as we,
Yet that implies conformity.
Be wise; recant what you have writte,
Least you do penance for your witte;
Love's charm hath power to weare a stringe,
To tye you as you tied your ringe;*
There by love's sharpe but just decree,
You may be censured, we go free.

UPON HIS MAJESTIES PROGRESS INTO NORFOLK.

September 28, 1671.

Yarmouth had first (O more than happy port)
The honour to receive the King and Court,

---

* In a ludicrous ballad, describing James the First's visit to Oxford and Woodstock, in 1621, when Corbet, in his office of chaplain, preached before the King, he is thus spoken of :—

> The reverend dean,
> With his band starched clean,
> Did preach before the king;
> A ringe was his pride,
> To his band-strings tied,
> Was not this a pretty thing?

> The ring, without doubt,
> Was the thing put him out,
> And made him forget what was next;
> For every one there
> Will say, I dare swear,
> That he handled it more than his text.

And entertain, season providing dishes,
The King of England with the king of fishes.
A royal mess, what herring pray were they?
Not red, nor white -pickel'd, nor bloat they say;
No milcb, but all hard rows, strange kind of meat!
Herrings you might digest, but could not eat.
Whose eyes were rubies, and whose scales were gold :
Herrings that never stinck, though ne'er so old.
The senate of the shoal, whose golden chain
Argues 'um the triumvirate of the main;
A glittering trine, but by the way, me thinks,
'Twas no good supper-meat, herrings and links.
Yet, for all all that, it was good fish when caught,
Wou'd I'd a swill of such at twelve a groat.
Should Norwich put such herrings in their pies,
Their charters wou'd be heavier than excise.
Oysters may of their pearls high value set,
But these are herrings for a royal net.
To which add all that art or nature cou'd,
Nothing cou'd be too dear, nothing too good :
The treat was what or wit or wealth cou'd give,
The cates being like the guests, superlative.
Whose superabundance did contribute more
Than some can feast their Kings with to the poor.
Next to his Majesty, at the Town-hall,
His Royal Highness, Lord High Admiral,
Vouchsaf'd his princely presence (save the crown)
The highest honour ever deign'd the town.
The Duke of Buckingham and Monmouth's graces,
In the next sphear took their illustrious places,
With other lords of principal account,
Whose grandieurs my poor heraldry surmount.
When the town sparkel'd with such cavaliers,
Yarmouth was sure nobly supply'd with peers.
Had you the gold that flew about, there seen,
You wou'd have thought you had in Guiny been.
Pieces did answer pieces shot for shot,
As if that gold the art of guns had got.

Sure Cæsar's beams and sun-like equipage
Gilded the town and made this golden age.
No Bristoll milk out of their conduits spun
Though not the conduits, yet the pipes did run.
Goblets and gold, they shovel out their wealth,
And think their wine too little for his health.
Souldiers and servants with the court come down,
Might at the Feathers, gratis, be high-flown.
They say his Majesty there knighted four,
I only wonder he did knight no more ;
For who observes how they set all to rights,
Wou'd think they acted more like lords than knights.
To those he added, but he gave no names,
But answer'd for a ship, and called it James.
All pleased the King, and the King all did please,
Never was day more full of happiness.
The general joy to see his Majesty,
Their acclamations witness to the sky.
Twelve hundred shot, add yet a thousand more,
From shoar to sea, and from the sea to shoar,
With such salutes did one another greet,
You wou'd have feared that heaven and earth wou'd meet.
Salutes are thunder'd all abroad the main,
Which Neptune answers to his lord again.
For while the earth did eccho with their joyes,
The sea cou'd not forbear to make a noise,
The very waves in tumults fret and fome
For madness, that they cou'd no nearer come.
Thus was the King, whilst mount to mount roar out,
Besieg'd with salutations round about.
The smoak rose up in clouds and made a night,
And lynstocks were the candles gave us light.
The priming powder at the touch-holes flash,
And every mount a mountain Ætna was.
Thus earth and water carol to their King,
And as in consort Iopœan sing ;
Farewell fair Yarmouth, and agen farewell,
Where noble hearts in noble houses dwell.

The King has judg'd thy great, thy generous town,
A jewel worthy of a monarch's crown.
Next, Norwich ward great Cæsar sets his face,
Like sunshine to a long-benighted place.
The mounted magistrates to meet him rid ;
And their formalities his wellcome bid,
Whose persons though confined to city ground,
Their love and loyalty yet know no bound.
First the recorder did the whole present,
And gave the King a solemn complement ;
Not empty words, but truth in such a dress,
A man might through it see her nakedness.
'Twas pat and pithy, not a formal story,
And he's as well now as Sir Francis Corye.
Next, they surrender on their loyal knees,
The cup, the sword, the maces and the keyes,
Ensigns of power ; and Cæsar takes 'um too,
And what does Cæsar take but Cæsar's due ?
Whilst he whom our election did prefer
To be the major, is made the sword-bearer.
This was September right, the senat's fall,
But royal Rayes rais'd 'um agen withall ;
And redeliver'd into hands so just
The ensigns of authority and trust.
Next, Aaron with his sons observe their course,
My lord with all the lord's embassadours,
As th' holy priesthood in procession rod,
To invite the King unto the house of God ;
As once a part of the Levitick stem
Met Alexander from Hierusalem.
Then high-born Howard waits the King's approaches,
With's prancing horses and his princely coaches,
And with all grace attends his sovereign home,
And does a landlord to his lord become.
Receives his Majesties at the Duke's place,
Which at that time a royal palace was.
A city rather, and so throng'd about,
As Norwich city seem'd a suburb to 't.

But that the King filled both, for people run
To royal beams, as atomes to the sun.
Next flockt the gentry, who as numerous were
As twinckles in the star-be-dappled sphear.
Fame filled the streets, there was no room to pass ;
Sure Norwich then a populous city was.
The King may thank Sir Peter Glean that day,
For but for him, the King had no highway ;
He clear'd him a free pass where he might ride,
And pal'd it in with pikes on either side ;
And musquets in close order, all in new
Red coats, and all alike lyn'd with true blew ;
Thus representing to his Majesty
Their unity and uniformity.
Nor may I here that gorgeous troop forget,
Hundreds of florid citizens that met
Their sovereign equipt in black and white,
An object both of wonder and delight ;
With scarlet ribons in their hats, to show
Their blood was likewise at his service too.
Argus had there met objects with his eyes,
But twice as many wou'd not half suffice ;
Windows and walls were nothing else you'd think,
Yet deemed disloyal to themselves to wink,
But had you heard the tempest of their lungs,
You wou'd have thought them nothing else but tongues.
Their vocal vollies deafened every ear,
And drums and trumpets no loud music were.
They rent the skies, and tore the very ground,
Muskets and canons in the vogue were drown'd,
And bells, that with such sweat and pains were rear'd,
Might have rung backward for owt they were heard.
'Twas such a clamour so transcending measure,
That bells themselves could not appeal to Cæsar.
But face about, here's more yet to be seen,
Two wonders in a day, the King and Queen,
With such a crowd of beauties might out-dare
Bold Saladine, and crown a holy warre.

Now, Norwich, say to grace thy hemisphear,
The sun, and moon, and stars at once shone there.
Thus the pair royal are together met,
And the Duke's place more graced than ever yet.
Where they conducted are into a room
Hung all with arras fresh come off the loom ;
Adorned with all magnificence, and quite
Set round with flambeux, made a day of night.
For supper, there I beg to hold my peace ;
Think what the eye, the ear, the tast wou'd please,
All that they had, nothing did want that night,
(Except by too too much) an appetite.
In summe the bill of fare let him pronounce,
Knows what it is to treat two courts at once.
Paston and Hobart did bring in the meat,
Who the next day at their own houses treat.
Paston to Oxney did his sovereign bring,
And, like Arraunoh, offer'd as a King.
Blecklyn two monarchs and two Queens has seen,
One King fetcht thence, another brought a Queen.
Great Townsend of the treats brought up the rear,
And doubly was my Lord Lieutenant there.
And now with Norwich, for whose sake I writ,
Let me conclude. Norwich did what was fit,
Or what with them was possible, at least ;
That city does enuff that does its best.
There the King knighted the so famous Brown,
Whose worth and learning to the world are known.
They offer'd to the King at the new Hall,
Banquets and guynies, and their hearts withall ;
For Norwich, true, others may treat more high,
But to her power, none more heartily.
S'has long a widow been, and 'tis but right
T' accept a widow for a widow's mite.
Norwich strain'd all that Norwich could extend,
Nor cou'd she more, should Jove himself descend.

THE NORFOLK FREEHOLDERS—A NEW BALLAD.

This ballad is taken from "The Court Parrot. A new miscellany of prose and verse, London printed. Sold by J. Dormer & S. Slow, price one shilling, 1734, 48 pages, 8vo." The title page contains the list of contents, which says that the "Norfolk Freeholders," an excellent ballad, was printed on purpose to send down after a certain projector who vainly opposes the interest of Sir Edmund Bacon and William Woodhouse, Esq.

TO THE TUNE OF "HOGAN OF HOUGHTON."

Ye Norfolk Freeholders, whose generous hearts
Are proof against bribes, and the Courtier's mean arts,
Of your Freedom and Power, express a true sense,
And bravely stand up in your country's defence.
Let no insignificant censures affright,
Nor deter you from acting what's honest and right ;
For wise men agree (and 'tis sure the same thing)
That serving our country is serving our king.

If wisdom and prudence direct now your choice,
A Bacon and Woodhouse lay claim to your voice.
We know by experience one patriot is just,
And for gold ne'er betray'd, nor abus'd his great trust.
To so worthy a member let Woodhouse be join'd,
Whose judgment, whose courage, whose greatness of mind,
Contemns those designs that are sordid and base,
And can ne'er be corrupted by pension or place.

Your foreign Monsieurs may their liberty loose,
And be doom'd all their lives to wear wooden shoes ;
Hard restraints may be laid upon Russians and Poles,
But it's liberty suits best with true English souls :
Let's agree, and abandon then each servile knave,
Who for honour or gain would his country enslave,
For ever oppose, boys, such narrow soul'd elves,
And choose men as free and as brave as yourselves.

Come, an health to *Sir Edmund*, and round let it pass,
May he be excis'd that refuses his glass ;
What curse more severe can befal the fond fool,
Who tamely submits to become a court tool?

Sir Edmund the noble, the generous, and wise,
Detests from his heart that damn'd scheme of *excise :*
Our trade he'll defend as the source of all wealth,
Let us vote in *his* interest, and drink to *his* health,

The casty may gull, and deceive the unwise,
And with gravity propagate marvellous lies ;
But all who have common discretion and sense,
Discern their design and laugh at their pretence.
Thus we know that the tale about the Tithe Bill
Is the pure invention of politic skill ;
These are methods oft practis'd, so says Dr. Swift,
When a bad cause is sinking, and at the last shift.

But, hold—one more glass we will drink, tho' we die,
'Tis an health to a Woodhouse—sure none can deny ;
May he with Sir Edmund meet equal success,
May Heaven, indulgent, their enterprize bless ;
And may ev'ry country now meet with such friends,
Who like Bacon and Woodhouse have no private ends ;
Then, then shall fair liberty splendid appear,
And the plow with our trade shall enrich us each year.

CRY OF THE RADISH BOYS AT GREAT YARMOUTH.

This ballad was printed in 1842, and the editor appended the following remarks :—" This singular poetical cry strictly and only belongs to Great Yarmouth ; it is older than the memory of the oldest inhabitant now living. Every enquiry to ascertain who was the author, and the period when it was written, has left the origin of it in mystery. An unsuccessful attempt was made at the early part of the present century to introduce a more refined poem as the radish cry, but it was soon forgotten. The following is the first verse :—

"The radishes are red, the tops are green,
These are the finest radishes that ever was seen."

There are about one hundred and fifty boys employed every season to retail these vegetables. Their shrill voices are heard daily about eight or ten hours proclaiming this eccentric ditty to the amusement of every stranger, and to secure a small income.

Moredosher,* Moredosh ;†
    Come here, yew-raw,
Spring redosh,
    Come two bunch, ee yow-who.

Come you that got money,
    Whilst I a' got none,
Buy all my spring radishes,
    And let me go home.

Come all yo' pretty maids,
    That used to buy any,
For here's your spring radishes,
    Two bunches a penny.

Come all yo' old women,
    Be joyful and sing,
For here's your old radish boy
    Now come agin.

Here I am,
    Both weary and tired ;
For here's my last pennuth,
    And I don't care who buy it.

THE YARMOUTH WATER FROLIC.

The following poem was penned by Dr. Glover, of the East Essex Regiment of Militia, which in 1779 was encamped on Hopton Common, near Yarmouth, under the command of Colonel Bullock. The procession which the poet has so humorously described, instituted for the purpose of proclaiming the bounds of the town, was formerly conducted with much parade, and attended by many gentlemen of the neighbourhood. In the year just-named, William Fisher, Esq. was Mayor of Yarmouth, and he invited the officers of the East Essex Regiment to join the party and partake of his hospitality. Glover *(bon rivant)* being one of the party, produced, a few days after, the verses which I here print.

---

  * Supposed to be corrupted from "More radish here" into "More redosh here," and lastly contracted into "Moredosher."
  † Corrupted from more radish.

In seventeen hundred and seventy nine,
The first day the dog-star appear'd as a sign,
At Yarmouth the fam'd water frolic began,
An annual custom 'fore memory of man.
By the quay-side a squadron of pleasure boats rode,
Their holds with choice wines and provisions well stow'd,
Sails, awnings, and colours were gaily display'd,
And they dauc'd on the white waves with pleasing parade.

At nine in the morn, his good worship the Mayor,
With his corporate train to the bridge did repair;
The marshal-men clearing his way to the barge,
While the fifes sweetly played, and the drums beat a charge.
In great state he marched, and the multitude round
Made the skies with their loud accclamations resound;
So Venice's Doge on a grand gala day,
Issues out with his senate to marry the sea.

The Muse would be thrown in a fit of despair.
Should she strive to describe half the characters there—
Field officers, clergymen, lawyers, physicians,
And gay macaronies, and grave politicians,
Cits's, sailors, foxhunters—nay, fine ladies too,
All with one accord join in this jovial crew;
Which cover'd the quay in such crowds to embark,
That it seemed Noah's family ent'ring the ark.

No sooner they weigh'd, and were sail getting under,
But Jove three salutes gave of his terrible thunder;
This compliment pass'd, from lightnings keen,
A grand *feu-de-joye* in the heaven was seen.
The kind Pleiades then, to do all in their power,
Politely pour'd down a most plenteous shower;
Thus, like fishes, thro' Breydon* they merrily drove,
With water not only below, but above.

* An extensive water leading in the direction from Yarmouth river (the Yare) to Norwich river.

At the Cross* they refreshed, and at fam'd Garianonum,†
His Worship uncorked a fine old magnum bonum ;
Norwich river they entered, Burgh Castle they passed,
And near Reedham their anchors this brilliant fleet cast.
Here the gentry debark'd and their compliments paid,
While the servants adroitly the table cloths laid,
When such feasting began as few folks could remember,
Who ne'er din'd at Guildhall on the ninth of November.

During this entertainment, concertos most grand
Were delightfully played by the East Essex band,
When the cattle on shore were so pleas'd with the sound,
That, like Orpheus's brutes, they came dancing around.
Nay, stranger, 'tis said the old river god Yare
Popp'd his head above water to look at the Mayor ;
While two tritons rose from their pearly resort,
And swam off with a flaggon of Warmington's port.‡

The dinner being ended, and chaplain said grace,
The toast in a regular routine took place ;
No skylights, no heeltaps, the chairman allowed,
And mirth, wit, and humour spontaneously flow'd.
Each guest did his utmost endeavour to please,
With songs, stories, *bon mots*, and catches and glees ;
At some of the jokes e'en the priests cried encore,
And the table was constantly kept in a roar.

Among the mad mortals who were at this show,
Was the half-gaitered doctor§ and Captain Jacko ;
The first a strange genius much given to foolery,
And the other replete with good nature and drollery.

* One of the direction posts in the form of a cross, in the channel of Breydon.
† Now called Burgh Castle, on the Yare, four miles from Yarmouth, a strong fortress during the Roman Empire.
‡ Put into the water to cool, and stolen by the pirates alongside.
§ Glover.

There was Major O Fatoo, a fine honest fellow,
Alert, and in spirits both sober and mellow ;
These with many more jolly dogs joined in the sport,
Which instead of the Mayor's, made it Comus's court.

Shades of evening descending, the gallies unmoor,
And pass'd by the places we've mention'd before,
When the people on land as the boats came in view,
Their tokens of joy with fresh vigour renew.
When the music's loud clangour, and the cannons dread rattle,
Made some wise ones suppose it the heat of a battle ;
Who, long apprehensive from foreign armadas,
Declar'd they at last had arrived to invade us.

Now arriv'd at the quay from this watery roam,
It was midnight ere most of the parties got home,
For when at the bridge they began to depart,
Each good fellow found himself heavy at heart.
So tost off a glass to drive sorrow away,
And repeated with pleasure what pass'd on that day,
The frolicks of which, howe'er Cynics may scorn,
Shall be lisped out in praises by children unborn.

THE NORFOLK DROLLERY.

This is a rare little work by Matthew Stevenson, printed at London in
1673, under the title of " Norfolk Drollery, or a compleat collection of the
newest Songs, Jovial Poems, and Catches," printed for R. Reynolds, 12mo.
The work was printed in the same year under another title, "Poems,
or a Miscellany of Sonnets, Satyrs, Drollery, Panegyricks, Elegies, etc.,"
and in 1685, the same book was published under another title. The "Drollery " is not often met with, and Mr. Halliwell says it fetches from £3 to
£4 at London sales. There are two dedications, one "To the most vir-
tuous and ingenious Madam Mary Hunt, of Sharington Hall in Norfolk ; "
the other " To the worshipful my very noble friend, Thomas Brown, Esq.,
of Elsing Hall in Norfolk." After the dedication, follow these lines by
Arthur Tichborne, "To the accomplished and his ingenious friend, Mr.
Matthew Stevenson, on his facetious Poems " :—

Tell me no more of Laureated Ben,
Shakesphear and Fletcher, once the wiser men.

Their acts ('tis true) were sublime ; yet I see
They'r all revisedly compos'd in thee.
Here the swoln critick, ideot, and huff,
Shall bite their fingers, swear they have enough ;
Whilst that the learned and sagacious wit
Shall speak thy worth, 'tis excellent well writ.
So that thy poems, justly styled, runs,
Not defunct Johns, but living Stevensons.

Mr. Halliwell, in his " Norfolk Anthology," has selected from this volume " every poem," he says, " of the slightest interest connected with the county." I cannot be so prodigal with my space, but I will select those that have the greatest claim upon the attention of Norfolk readers.

TO THE FAIR MADAM M. H,. AT SHARRINGTON HALL IN NORFOLK.

Inspire me now or never (Muse),
My theam is higher than it use ;
And yet unless her self inspire,
My muse and I are ne're the higher.
Fancy, sublime thy self, and raise
Some rapture, 'tis an angel's praise !
I can a due to great ones give,
But she is a superlative ;
What's writ of her must be exprest
Above my self a sphear at least;
Others (and that too may suffice),
I serve with single sacrifice :
But to her altar he that comes,
Can bring no less than hecatombs.
Ten thousand hearts may sacrifice,
And burn themselves in her bright eyes,
Her face is a perpetual May,
And fairer than Jove's milky way.
Something there's in't does ravish me,
But I can't tell what 'tis I see,
For if I could define the bliss,
Alas ! it were not what it is.
Her soul does through her body shine,
And make the whole, wholly divine.
Her ingenuity is such,
Impossible to praise too much ;

x

Nor had my language been so free,
But here's no fear of flattery :
For when I have done, I've said no more
Than all that knew her knew before.
Go number all the stars of heaven ;
Her praises and those stars are even.
I might her trophies higher rear,
And truly too, but I forbear,
Lest if her fame be further hurl'd,
I make a bonfire of the world :
Some happier pen, his own and virtue's friend,
Come and begin her praises where I end.

UPON MADAM E. B. OF BLAKENEY IN NORFOLK—A BEAUTIFUL CHILD.

Sweet pretty blossom, bloomy thing,
The pride and glory of the spring.
Come, painters, come improve your arts,
In due proportions ; see her parts,
So equal, so harmonious be,
As nature's choicest symmetrie.
Apelles need not wandring go
For scatter'd features, to and fro,
For did he hither but repaire,
In her they all collective are.
The sparkling planets of her eyes
Are rivals to the spangled skies ;
The liquid rubies of her lips
The orient pearls within eclipse ;
Her cheeks are made up of delighte,
Like roses damaskt red and white,
With a sweet dimple in her chin,
For Cupid to inhabit in.
Her nose, the gnomon of her face,
As it were, points to every grace :
Over which paradise of bliss,
Stands a diviner frontis piece.

Two myrtle groves her ey-brows are,
If groves might with them compare.
The hair that on her shoulder lies,
Is but the shadow of her eyes ;
Whilst the pale drooping lily stands
Asham'd to see her wither'd hands.
What then may we expect, when time
Has ripened her into her prime ?
—— *inest sua gratia parvis.*

UPON A COUNTRY PARSON AND HIS MAN, AND A PARISHIONER WHOSE NAME WAS IVORIE.

The parson sued him 'cause he called him knave,
For which poor Ivory 7 and sixpence gave ;
And so at six and sevens they both drank on,
That ere they went away, they were quite gone.
The seven and sixpence so had Ivory stir'd,
He could not give the parson a good word.
Nay, such a dose he to his temples gave,
That if he wou'd, he cou'd not call him knave ;
And (what I cou'd have wish't had not been true),
The liberal dose silenced the parson too.
This hap, alas ! had never come to pass,
Had but the priest concluded with his glass ;
But cupper cupt so much, the sack ran down
All the neglected preface of his gown.
To ale be-buttered too, as if (alack),
The priest had in his stomach mulled the sack.
His man too drunk, which made him much the bolder,
Yet got no sack, save one upon his shoulder.
He reeled about, and run at every shelf,
And neither knew his master nor himself.
Ivory asleep, fell down, and in the close,
Did, for an Ivory, get a scarlet nose.
They that before so great a noise did keep,
Now slept, and in the rightest sense, fox sleep.

The Popinjay one fuddle had before,
But when these three were there, then it had four,
And while they slept secure, in came the wretch,
And does this pickel'd congregation catch.

AN ELEGY UPON REVEREND JOHN PORTER, D.D., AND PRE-BEND OF CHRIST CHURCH IN NORWICH.

A star has fal'n, an orb does disappear,
Was late the glory of our hemisphere ;
So vast his learning, this all-knowing man
Was lookt on as a living Vatican.
For piety, he was so all divine,
That Moses-like his very face did shine.
His loyalty I need not here maintain,
His sufferings show he lov'd his sovereign.
But maugre men and devils he laid down
His head in peace, and with a silver crown ;
Yet liv'd to see his Prince, and give God praise,
For ten illustrious Restauration dayes.
His sons all prosper, and his daughters are
Like polisht corners of the temple fair.
As if indulgent heaven intended he
Should have amends in his posteritie.
For his humility, this all men know,
Of parts so high, ne'er man had mind more low.

UPON A DOG NAMED FUDLE, TURNSPIT AT THE POPINJAY IN NORWICH.

Fudle, why so ? Some Fudle cap sure came
Into the room, and gave him his own name.
How should he catch a fox ? he'll turn his back
Upon tobacco, beer, French wine, or sack.
A bone his jewel is ; and he does scorn
With Æsop's cock. to wish a barley corn.

There's not a soberer dog, I know, in Norwich.
What......wou'd ye have him drunk with porridge ?
This, I confess, he goes a round, a round,
A hundred times, and never touches ground ;
And in the middle region of the aire,
He draws a circle like a conjuror.
With eagerness he still does forward tend,
Like Sicyphus, whose journey has no end.
He is the soul (if wood has such a thing)
And living posie of a wooden ring.
He is advanc'd above his fellowes yet,
He does not for it the least envy get.
He does above the Isle of Doggs commence,
And wheels th' inferiour spit by influence.
This though befalls his more laborious lot,
He is the Dog-star, and his days are hot.
Yet, with this comfort there's no fear of burning,
'Cause all this while th' industrious wretch is turning.
Then no more Fudle say, give him no spurns,
But wreck your tine on one that never turns,
And call him, if a proper name he lack,
A four-foot hustler, or a living Jack.

UPON THE REV. HERBERT ASHLEY, LL.B, ELECTED DEAN OF NORWICH FROM MANY RIVALS.

The racers mounted with day-breaking phosphor,
Hard did they ride, though not ride on and prosper.
Some to the place, suspicious of their right,
As if they meant to steal it, went by night.
Thus whipt and spur'd the rivals at those rates.
Their very horses lookt like candidates ;
Whilst Reverend Ashley with a sober face,
Went gravely on, and came off with a grace.
But the most Reverend, and Right Reverend too,
I might Right Honorable add too, where
Northampton carry'd it from Darby clear.

And happy was it for Christ-church, if I may say 't,
Has been too truly militant of late.
But now those animosities shall cease,
And Janus' temple give a sign of peace.
Joy to themselves, and us to see 'um so,
In order to the God of order go.
Heaven and his Majesty has in this choice,
Made your glad walls of Syon to rejoyce.
Well fare their holy fatherhoods, for you
Want but one step to be a father too.
Your name even prophecies of its own accord,
Herbert or Ashley, which you please, 'tis Lord.

AN ELEGY PERPETUATED TO THE MEMORY OF HENRY SERNE, ESQ., CAPTAIN OF THE TRIUMPH.

Thus fell he at hard fate's command,
Yet like himself with sword in hand:
What pitty 'twas he could not git,
So neer as to make use of it,
To try it out with manly strife
Of sword; he then had sold his life
So dear a bargain to the Dutch,
They ne'er had wisht another such.
He had so handy gripped his foe,
'But bullets no distinction know;
For canons are a like disease,
To Chineas and to Pyroéles.
Four Spanish ships at once he fought,
And from 'um all the garland brought;
But afterwards (pitty say I),
Where cowards live, the valiant dye,
This son of honour laid his head,
With honour, down on honour's bed.
And certainly he wants no room,
That has the ocean for his tomb,
Whom now in scorn of future harmes,
The seas embrace with out-stretcht armes.

The royal herring brings his crown,
And at his feet he layes it down ;
Ten thousand dolphins next resort,
And play about to make him sport,
A sea-horse was his horse of state,
For champion, he a sword-fish gate,
And Neptune, coming to the place,
Converts his trident to a mace.
Only the syrens from him swim,
Afraid to be out-charmed by him.
Thus, high or low, be where he will,
He's Captain of the Tryumph still.
But, having thus the ocean crost,
Let me now tell ye what we lost.
No plummet could his learning sound,
Alive and dead too, he's profound ;
So qualify'd he could prevail,
Alike with gown and coat of mail.
He had a hand would all things sute,
Either the sword, the pen, or lute ;
Thus we in one have lost all three,
Apollo, Mars, and Mercurie.
No more then on the question stand,
The sea's now richer than the land,
And we may well say loyalty
Lies in the bottom of the sea.

AN INSCRIPTION UPON A NEW BUILT HOUSE, IN A WOOD AT EASTON, NEAR NORWICH.

BY MRS. SARAH BUXTON.

Not vex'd by chilldren, and unawd by spouse,
To freedom Buxton builds this humble house :
A calm retreat which pining envy flies,
And vile detraction with 10,000 lies !
Here free to live by Nature's wholesome rules,
No slave to fashion, or to fashion's fools.

To friendship open and its sober joys,
Spinstress, no more lament, thus
    Fix your choice.
So fares it with this disapointed maid,
This hoary spinstress, of mankind affraid ;
To wit or beauty she had no pretence,
But pride she had misconstrued into sense.
" From vile detraction and 10,000 lies."
If you believe her angry tale, " she flies ;"
In vile detraction yet she bore her part,
With vile detraction wrung her sister's heart.
This queen of shreds and patches, and of shrubs,
M—rsh—m shall toast and quit his queen of clubs ;
Hither deform'd old maids in troops repair
Miss Ann shall nurse her spleen and vapours here,
And Jackey Buxton teize his infant heir ;
Ye R—ss—ls, S—ll—r's, Br—nthw—ts, hither come,
Hither ye blind and lame, and deaf and dumb ;
Here cards and scandal each sweet hour employs
For this is " friendship and its sober joys,"
Perpetual war with wedlock's fools engage,
All but the vile Canidia of the age.
That heart of bitterness, with soul of gall,
For her rank poison shall outvenom all.
But you ! to whom propitious Nature gave
That envied boon, bright beauty to enslave
Who hold true friendship with the man you love,
And Hymen's joys as not condemn'd above.
Avoid this seal of malice and despair,
This poetry, dear girls, is all an air.
    For say, old virgin, I'll appeal to you.
If e'er thy heart one tender passion knew ;
What were thy conquests, what thy triumphs ? say,
When youth was pleasant, and when thou wert gay :
What swain pour'd out his soul in ardent vows,
And press'd to be that happy man thy spouse ;
How many beaux, alas ! have sigh'd in vain !
What numbers those two fatal eyes have slain ?

Produce the record of your past amours.
And paint it, Buxton, over all your doors;
Then with the publick will I join my voice,
And say thou art that wretch thou art by choice;
Meanwhile let this inscription be display'd,
Then live or die or sleep a true old maid.

INSCRIPTION.

In frantick fury and in wild despair,
Neglected Buxton rears this mansion here;
From a gay world, from beaux and balls she flies,
And Bath and Tunbridge leaves to brighter eyes,
Tir'd of herself and tiring all mankind,
Her raving restless soul this cell design'd
Choked up with pride ill nature and ill blood,
And fix'd her BEDLAM in this little wood.

R. GARDNER.

THE COOK'S CATASTROPHE.

OCCASIONED BY A SOULDIER KILLING A COOK'S BOY CARRYING
A COVERED MESS THROUGH THE STREET.

Unhappy Boy, thus to be sent upon
Death's errand, with accursed Bellerophon!
Where God found meat (here the old proverb took),
The Devil and the Souldier found the Cook.
First mess was serving; but, ah, cruel force!
The cook himself became the second course;
For as the corps he carry'd to the womb,
The Bearer, by the way, met his own tomb.
But with this difference—as he lost his breath,
The stone, shou'd be above, was underneath.
And yet he could not without marble part,
Had there been none else, but the soldier's heart.
The boy might prate, alas! in such a case
Is not a cook allowed a little sauce?
A milk-white napkin o'er the mess was laid,
No ladies apron such temptations had!

Hunger, that breaks stone walls, at such a sight
Had pointed teeth, and made a coward fight.
The air was razor-keen, and might afford
A stomach that was sharper than his sword.
For Mars, his sons, and Neptunes too they say,
Do watch and fast far oftener than they pray :
But the boy moved with't fast as he was able,
For there his master kept no standing table.
With whom the hungry souldier pace would keep,
'Twould vex a dog to see a pudding creep :
The cloth was spread, but on it nothing lay,
The red-coat, therefore needs wou'd take away.
The both tug'd for't, neither could other brook
The hasty souldier, nor the teasty Cook.
At last it happened the unlucky cloth
Did prove, well-nigh, a winding-sheet to both.
The poor Cook's Boy, that little dreamt of it,
Ere he could take a turn, ah, a shrewd turn !
Has turned him now, alas ! into his urn.
And though for this, the souldier suffer'd not,
Know it, his hands are redder than his coat.

Norfolk Poets and Poetry.

THE REV. ROBERT SOUTHWELL.

[1560   1595.]

Robert Southwell was born at St. Faith's, Norfolk. He was educated at Douay, and at sixteen entered into the Society of Jesuits at Rome. In 1584 he came as a missionary to England, and became chaplain to Anne Countess of Arundel, in which situation he remained until 1592, when he was apprehended as a suspected conspirator against the Government and a Jesuit. He remained in prison three years, during which period he was cruelly racked many times with a view of extorting from him a disclosure of certain supposed conspiracies against the Government. At the close of the third year he sent an epistle to Cecil, Lord Treasurer, humbly entreating his lordship either to bring him to trial that he might answer for himself, or be permitted to have his friends come and see him. To this just request Cecil is said to have made the brutal remark that " if he was in so much haste to be hanged he should quickly have his desire." He was shortly after removed to Newgate, tried at Westminster for remaining in England contrary to the statute, found guilty, and executed at Tyburn, February 21st, 1595.

The prevailing tone of his poetry is religious resignation. Though composed under heavy persecutions, no trace of angry feeling against human being or any human institution occurs in his poems.

UPON THE IMAGE OF DEATH.

Before my face the picture hangs,
    That daily should put me in mind,
Of these cold names and bitter pangs
    That shortly I am like to find ;
But yet, alas ! full little I
Do think hereon, that I must die.

I often look upon a face
   Most ugly, grisly, bare, and thin ;
I often view the hollow place
   Where eyes and nose had sometimes been ;
I see the bones across that lie,
Yet little think that I must die.

I read the label underneath,
   That telleth me whereto I must ;
I see the sentence, too, that saith,
   Remember, man, thou art but dust ;
But yet, alas ! how seldom I
Do think indeed that I must die !

Continually at my bed's head
   A hearse doth hang which doth me tell,
That I ere morning may be dead,
   Though now I feel myself full well ;
But yet, alas ! for all this, I
Have little mind that I must die !

The gown which I am used to wear,
   The knife wherewith I cut my meat ;
And eke that old and antient chair,
   Which is my only usual seat ;
All these do tell me I must die,
And yet my life amend not I.

My ancestors are turned to clay,
   And many of my mates are gone ;
My youngers daily drop away,
   And can I think to 'scape alone ?
No, no, I know that I must die,
And yet my life amend not I.

Not Solomon, for all his wit,
   Nor Samson, though he was so strong,
No king nor power ever yet
   Could 'scape but death laid him along.

Wherefore I know that I must die,
And yet my life amend not I.

Though all the East did quake to hear
    Of Alexander's dreadful name ;
And all the West did likewise fear
    To hear of Julius Cæsar's fame ;
Yet both by death in dust now lie,
Who then can 'scape but he must die ?

If none can 'scape Death's dreadful dart,
    If rich and poor his beck obey ;
If strong, if wise, if all do smart,
    Then I to 'scape shall have no way :
Then grant me grace, O God ! that I
My life may mend, since I must die.

ROBERT GREENE.

[1560—1592.]

Robert Greene was born at Norwich. We learn upon his own authority
that his parents were persons well-known and respected among their
neighbours for "their gravity and honest life," and it may be presumed
that they were in good circumstances, as they not only placed their son
at Cambridge, where he took his degree of A.B. at St. John's College,
1578, but afterwards sent him to travel through Spain and Italy—a costly
undertaking in the sixteenth century. It has been supposed that he took
holy orders soon after his return from the continent, and was the same
Robert Greene who was presented to the living of Tollesbury in Essex,
June 19th, 1584; but of this there is no proof. It is unfortunately too true
that he was a boon companion with the dissipated wits of the day ; that he
deserted a lovely wife, lived a profligate life, occasionally chequered with
partial repentance; and died of a surfeit of pickled herrings and Rhenish
wine sometime in August, 1592. He appears to have been reduced at this
time to the lowest possible condition of distress and degradation, lodging
at the house of a struggling shoemaker, in Dowgate, London, and indebted
to his landlord, who could ill afford such bounty, for the bare necessaries
of life. His *Groat's Worth of Wit, bought with a Million of Repentance,*
is autobiographical, and is designed to depict some of his own personal ex-
periences, and point the moral of his own life. Notwithstanding his dis-

sipated life, Greene was a voluminous writer. Industry he certainly did
not lack, and the versatility of his powers is attested by the variety and
number of his works. Including novels, plays, and translations, no less
than forty-five independent publications are ascribed to him. The edition of his works, published in 2 vols. in 1831, was edited by the Rev.
Alexander Dyce.

THE SHEPHERD'S WIFE'S SONG.

Ah, what is love? It is a pretty thing,
As sweet unto a shepherd as a king,
  And sweeter too.
For kings have cares that wait upon a crown,
And cares can make the sweetest love to frown.
  Ah, then ! ah, then !
If country loves such sweet desires do gain,
What lady would not love a shepherd swain ?

His flocks are folded, he comes home at night,
As merry as a king in his delight,
  And merrier too.
For kings bethink them what the state require,
Where shepherds careless carol by the fire.
  Ah, then ! ah, then !
If country loves such sweet desires do gain,
What lady would not love a shepherd swain ?

He kisseth first, then sits as blithe to eat
His cream and curds, as doth the king his meat,
  And blither too,
For kings have often fears when they do sup,
Where shepherds dread no poison in their cup.
  Ah, then ! ah, then !
If country loves such sweet desires do gain,
What lady would not love a shepherd swain ?

To bed he goes, as happy then I ween,
As is a king in dalliance with a queen,
  And happier too.

For kings have many griefs affects to move,
Where shepherds have no greater grief than love.
Ah, then ! ah, then !
If country loves such sweet desires do gain,
What lady would not love a shepherd swain ?

Upon his couch of straw he sleeps as sound
As doth the king upon his beds of down,
More sounder too.
For cares cause kings full oft their sleep to spill,
Where weary shepherds lie and snort their fill.
Ah, then ! ah, then !
If country loves such sweet desires do gain,
What lady would not love a shepherd swain ?

Thus with his wife he spends the year, as blithe
As doth the king at every tide or sith,
And blither too.
For kings have wars and broils to take in hand,
When shepherds laugh and love upon the land.
Ah, then ! ah, then !
If country loves such sweet desires do gain,
What lady would not love a shepherd swain ?

THE REV. ROBERT POTTER.

[1721—1804.]

Robert Potter was educated at Emmanuel College, Cambridge, and
became B.A., 1741; M.A., 1788. His first preferment was the vicarage of
Scarning, Norfolk, and he was afterwards appointed vicar of Lowestoft
and Kessingland in Suffolk. In 1774 he published a volume of poems, and
three years afterwards appeared his translation of Eschylus. This at
once placed him in the highest rank as a translator, many parts of the
great Greek dramatist being rendered so exquisitely as to leave it in doubt
whether any other poet could have accomplished the task so well. He
afterwards published translations of Euripides and of Sophocles, *An
enquiry into some Passages of Dr. Johnson's Lives of the Poets ;* a translation of *The Oracle concerning Babylon,* and the *Song of Exultation*
from Isaiah xII. 14., and *A Sermon on the Thanksgiving for the Peace,*
1802. Potter had been a schoolfellow of Lord Thurlow's ; and had constantly

sent his publications to the Chancellor, though he never solicited a favour. On receiving a copy of Sophocles, however, his lordship wrote a short note, acknowledging the receipt of books from time to time, and the pleasure they had afforded him, and requesting Mr. Potter's acceptance of a prebendal stall in the Cathedral of Norwich, which with his vicarage rendered him comfortable for the remainder of his days. He was found dead in his bed on the morning of the 9th of August, 1804.

HOLKHAM.

O come, and range with me th' inspiring glades
Where Leicester spreads the lawns and forms the shades;
On Holkham's plains bids Grecian structures rise,
And the tall columns shoot into the skies;
Beneath whose proud survey, extended wide,
New scenes, new beauties charm on ev'ry side.
Here crowned with woods the shaded hills ascend,
In open light there the low vales extend;
Here in rich harvests waves the ripen'd grain,
And there fresh verdure cloathes the pastur'd plain,
Sweetly intermix'd, and lovely to behold,
As the green emerald enchased in gold.

* * * * *

Nor these alone : here virtue loves to dwell,
No cold recluse self-cavern'd in a cell;
Active and warm she breathes a noble part,
Glows in the breast, and opens all the heart;
To gen'rous deeds she fires the empassion'd mind,
The substitute of heav'n to bless mankind.
She thro' desponding misery's cheerless gloom
Pours joy, and gives neglected worth to bloom;
She in each bosom stills the rising sigh,
And wipes off ev'ry tear from ev'ry eye;
She to yon Alms-house, bosom'd in the grove,
From toil and care bids age and want remove;
There the tir'd eve of labour'd life to rest,
Fed by her hand, and by her bounty blest.

* * * * * *

Lo, Leicester comes ! before his mast'ring hand
Flies the rude genius of the savage land;

Therusset lawns a sudden verdure wear ;
Starts from the wond'ring fields the golden car ;
Up rise the waving woods, and haste to crown
The hill's bare brow, and shade the sultry down.
The shelter'd traveller sees, with glad surprise,
O'er trackless wilds th' extended rows arise ;
And, as their hospitable branches spread,
Blesses tho friendly hand that form'd the shade.
Joy blooms around, and cheers the peasant's toil,
As smiling plenty decks the cultivated soil ;
The bright'ning scenes a kinder genius own,
And nature finishes what art begun.

    *   *   *   *

" Gods, heroes, sages, an illustrious train,
Court you to Holkham's consecrated plain.
Haste then, ye sacred sisters ! haste, and bring
The laurel steep'd in the Castilian spring ;
On the choice bough a purer fragrance breathe,
And form for Leicester's brow th' unfading wreathe."
She ceas'd the raptured strain ; and dear to fame
Flows the proud verse inscrib'd with Leicester's name.

DR. ENFIELD.

[1749—1787.]

William Enfield was born of humble but respectable parents, at Sudbury in Suffolk, March 29th, 1741. In his seventeenth year he was sent to the Nonconformist Academy at Daventry, on leaving which he was chosen pastor of a congregation at Liverpool, where he remained seven years, and only took his leave in consequence of being invited to the office of tutor and resident conductor of the discipline at the Academy at Warrington. In 1785, two years after the dissolution of the Academy, he accepted an invitation, signed by the deacons and forty-six members of the Unitarian congregation at Norwich, to become co-pastor with Mr. Alderson. He first settled at the village of Thorpe, and received a few pupils, among whom were Lord Chief Justice Denman, and Dr. Maltby, Bishop of Durham. After a few years, however, he declined to receive any boarders, and removed to Norwich, devoting his leisure to literary pursuits. He was a frequent contributor to the periodical publications of the day, and the list of his numerous publications attests his unfailing industry. He was one of the founders of the Norwich Public Library, and became one of its earliest Presidents.

THE EXAMPLE OF CHRIST.

Behold, where, in a mortal form,
 Appears each grace divine ;
The virtues, all in Jesus met,
 With mildest radiance shine.

To spread the rays of heavenly light,
 To give the mourner joy,
To preach glad tidings to the poor,
 Was his divine employ.

'Midst keen reproach and cruel scorn,
 Patient and meek he stood ;
His foes, ungrateful, sought his life,
 He labored for their good.

To God he left his righteous cause,
 And still his task pursued ;
While humble prayer, and holy faith,
 His fainting strength renewed.

In the last hour of deep distress,
 Before his Father's throne,
With soul resigned he bowed and said,
 " Thy will, not mine, be done."

Be Christ our pattern and our guide,
 His image may we bear ;
O may we tread his sacred steps,
 And his bright glories share.

BISHOP HORNE.

[1730—1792.]

George Horne, D.D., Bishop of Norwich, 1789-1792, was an eminent divine of the Hutchinsonian school. He was born November 1st, 1730, at Otham, near Maidstone, in Kent. At the age of thirteen he was sent to school at Maidstone, and at fifteen was removed to University College, Oxford. He was elected a Fellow of Magdalen College, and appointed Principal in 1768. He afterwards became Vice-Chancellor of Oxford, and Dean of Canterbury, and in 1789 he was made Bishop of Norwich. He died January 17th, 1792, in his sixty-second year.

Dr. Horne paid particular attention to Hebrew and sacred literature, and published a number of controversial treatises in favour of Hutchinson, and against Sir Isaac Newton, Adam Smith, Law, Hume, Shuckford, Kennicott, and Priestley, but it is by his Commentary on the Psalms that he is most favourably known. A collective edition of his works, with a life, was published by his friend and chaplain, William Jones, of Nayland, in 1795-99.

A MORNING HYMN ON EASTER DAY.

Hark ! the shrill herald of the morn
Begins the sons of men to warn,
    And bids them all arise,
To celebrate his great renown, -
Who sends the light refulgent down,
    To bless our longing eyes.

At this the fainting shadows die,
The pow'rs of darkness swiftly fly
    Before the morning star ;
Pale trembling murder dares not stay,
And fiends, abash'd at sight of day,
    Back to their den repair.

'Tis this the weary sailor cheers,
Who now no more the tempest hears,
    Which morning bids to cease ;
O, come that day-spring from on high,
When discord shall with darkness fly,
    And all be light and peace !

'Twas this that drew repentant tears
From Peter, led by worldly fears
    His Master to disown ;
Warned by the monitor of day,
He cast the works of night away,
    And sought th' abjured sun.

Whene'er the bird of dawning crows,
He tells us all how Peter rose,
  And mark'd us out the road ;
That each disciple might begin,
Awake, like him, from sleep and sin,
  To think betimes on God.

Smote by the eye that looks on all,
Let us, obedient to the call,
  Arise to weep and pray ;
Till mournful, as on sin we muse,
Faith, like an angel, tells the news,
  " The Lord is ris'n to-day."

DR. AIKIN.

[1747—1822.]

John Aikin, M.D., born at Kibworth Harcourt, in Leicestershire, was
the only son of the Rev. J. Aikin, LL.D., and brother of Anne Letitia
Aikin, afterwards Mrs. Barbauld. As a surgeon he first settled at Chester,
and afterwards at Warrington, but finally took the degree of Doctor of
Medicine at Leyden, but in 1758 he removed from Warrington to Great
Yarmouth, where he entered upon the discharge of his professional duties.
In 1792 he left Yarmouth and settled in London, where he successfully
practised as a physician until failing health compelled him to abandon his
profession. He then retired to Stoke Newington, and devoted the remainder of his life to literature. His first publications were professional, and
were very favourably received, though he is now chiefly remembered as a
popular author, to whom in conjunction with his sister, Mrs. Barbauld,
we owe some of the first and best attempts to take science out of the narrow confines of the professionally learned, and to render it the means of
enlarging the understanding and increasing the pleasures of the general
body of readers. His *Evenings at Home*, and *The Natural History of
the Year*, have produced a host of imitators, but none have surpassed
these volumes in conciseness, accuracy, and usefulness. He was emphati-
cally a literary man. Dr. Watts gives a list of about fitty publications of
this industrious writer. From 1796—1807 he was literary editor of the
Monthly Magazine. In January, 1807, he started the *Athenæum*, which was
discontinued in 1809. He, with some coadjutors, commenced a General
Biography which extended to ten quarto volumes, and on this he was engaged nearly twenty years. From 1811 to 1815 he edited *Dodsley's Annual*

Register, and in 1820 his last publication, *The Select Works of the British Poets* (Johnson to Beattie) made its appearance. He died of apoplexy, December 7th, 1822.

ON THE DEATH OF JOHN HOWARD, ESQ.

Howard, thy task is done ! thy Master calls,
And summons thee from Cherson's distant walls,
" Come, well-approv'd ! my faithful servant, come :
" No more a wanderer, seek thy destined home.
" Long have I mark'd thee with o'er-ruling eye,
" And sent admiring angels from on high,
" To walk the paths of danger by thy side,
" From death to shield thee and thro' snares to guide.
" My *minister of good* I've sped thy way,
" And shot thro' dungeon glooms a leading ray,
" To cheer, by thee, with kind unhoped relief.
" My creatures lost and whelm'd in guilt and grief.
" I've led thee, ardent, on thro' wond'ring climes,
" To combat human woes and human crimes ;
" But, 'tis enough ; thy *great commission's* o'er ;
" I prove thy faith, thy love, thy zeal, no more.
" Nor droop, that far from country, kindred, friends,
" Thy life, to duty long devoted, ends.
" What boots it *where* the high reward is giv'n,
" Or *whence* the soul triumphant springs to heav'n ?"

THE EVILS OF WAR DEPRECATED.

While sounds of war are heard around,
And death and ruin strew the ground,
To Thee we look, on Thee we call,
The Parent and the Lord of all.

Thou who hast stamped on human kind,
The image of a heaven-born mind,
And in a father's wide embrace,
Hast cherished all the kindred race !

O see with that insatiate rage,
Thy sons their impious battles wage ;
How spreads destruction like a flood,
And brothers shed their brothers' blood.

See guilty passions spring to birth,
And deeds of hell deform the earth ;
While righteousness and justice mourn,
And love and pity droop forlorn. ·

Great God, whose powerful hand can bind
The raging waves, the furious wind !
O bid the human tempest cease,
And hush the maddening world to peace.

With reverence may each hostile land,
Hear and obey that high command,
Thy Son's blest errand from above,
" My creatures, live in mutual love."

SIR JAMES EDWARD SMITH.

[1759—1828.]

Sir James Edward Smith, the distinguished botanist, was born at Norwich on the 2nd December, 1759. His father was a man of cultivated mind, and from his mother he inherited his taste for flowers. The education of Mr. Smith was chiefly domestic, and his father intended him for some mercantile calling, but the love of science which he manifested induced his parents to consent to his going to Edinburgh to study medicine, where in 1782 he obtained Dr. Hope's gold medal for the best botanical collection. In 1784 he purchased the whole of the collection of manuscripts and natural history made by the celebrated Linnæus, which were brought to England in twenty-six cases, and cost £1088 5s. On the death of Sir James this celebrated collection was purchased by the Linnæan Society, and formed a part of their stores of natural history.

In 1788 he, with the assistance of Sir Joseph Banks and some others, founded the Linnæan Society, and Dr. Smith was elected its first President. He continued to reside in London until 1796, when he removed to Norwich. In 1814 Dr. Smith was knighted by the Prince Regent. The honour was conferred on him as institutor and President of the Linnæan Society. In 1818 Sir James became a candidate for the chair of botany at

Cambridge, but not being a member of the Church of England, he was not considered eligible by the authorities of the University. His death took place on the 17th March, 1828, after the illness of a single day. Lady Smith, his widow, at the time when this book goes to press (1872), resides at Lowestoft, having passed her hundredth year.

Sir James composed at different times several hymns, which have been incorporated into existing collections, but I give as a specimen of his poetical powers a song composed by him in 1803, and which was warmly commended by William Roscoe for poetry, feeling, and picturesque truth.

SONG.

The morning o'er the ocean breaks,
  The orient waves are liquid fire,
While William from the topmast seeks
  All that his fondest hopes desire.

You speck in night's retiring veil
  None but a lover's eye could spy—
" 'Tis land ! 'tis England ! messmates, hail !"
  " 'Tis land !" the joyful crew reply.

" Oh, Mary ! is thy tender breast
  Still to thy William fond and true,
As when we first our love confest ?
  As when with tears we bade adieu?"

Propitious gales and swelling waves
  To William faint and tardy seem—
But now the lab'ring ocean heaves,
  And thunders roll and lightnings gleam.

And now the shattered bark no more
  Resists the sweeping whirlwind's sway,
It shivers on its native shore,
  And death and horror close the day.

But love survives the wasting storm ;
  O'er William harmless thunders roll ;
His Mary clasps his clay-cold form,
  Her breath recalls his fleeting soul.

WILLIAM TAYLOR.

[1765—1836.]

William Taylor was born at Norwich in 1765. He was the only child of an eminent merchant of that city. He first studied under a Swiss refugee, and afterwards became a pupil of the Rev. Rochemont Barbauld of Palgrave, and in after life he gratefully acknowledged his obligations to Mrs. Barbauld, whom he styled the " mother of his mind." At the age of fourteen, he was removed from Palgrave, and placed in the counting-house of his father, who desired that he should succeed him in his business. Evincing considerable facility in acquiring languages, he was sent on the Continent under the care of one of the partners of the firm, for the purpose of perfecting himself in the French and Italian languages, which were cf importance for the proper conducting of his father's business. On his return to his native city he was encouraged in the prosecution of his studies, and two years afterwards, a second tour to the Continent was resolved upon, and he proceeded to Germany with the view of acquiring a familiar acquaintance with its language and literature. There he imbibed a taste, not only for the literature of Germany, but for the philosophy of that country, a taste which ever afterwards characterised his wiitings. On his second return to Norwich, he, with the consent of his parents, devoted himself to literature, instead of the mercantile profession, and when the French Revolution convulsed the continent of Europe he became an active politician. Literary distinction was still, however, his great aim, and a poetical translation of the *Lenore* of Bürger, was the first publication by which he became generally known. This was followed by several other translations from the German poets, which were afterwards collected together and published in three volumes under the title of *Survey of German Poetry*. In 1802 he accepted the editorship of a democratic weekly paper, *The Norwich Iris*, but its success was not equal to his anticipations, and it was given up after two years, and Magazines and Reviews became the principal vehicles by which his writings came before the public. A succession of severe pecuniary losses seriously diminished the comforts that had surrounded his parents, and his social position was in consequence, during the latter portion of his life, materially different from that of his youth and manhood. The kind sympathy of friends cheered him in his adversity, but the last years of his life were embittered by the loss of his aged parents and the decay of mental powers. He died in March 1836, and his remains were deposited beside those of his parents in the cemetery of the Octagon Chapel at Norwich.

HUDIBRAS MODERNIZED.

This Church doth wage perpetual wars
With dissidents, like cats and curs ;
People whose chief devotion lies
In odd perverse antipathies,

In falling out with that or this,
And finding somewhat still amiss ;
As if religion were intended
For nothing else but to be mended.
More peevish, cross, and splenetic,
Than dog distract or monkey sick,
That with more care keep holiday
By work than others do by play,
Compound for sins they are inclined to.
By damning those they have no mind to,
Still so perverse and opposite,
As if they worshipp'd God for spite ;
At jar with all and with each other,
They give the Raka to a brother.
Free-will one meeting disavows,
Another nothing else allows ;
Some the adult, some infants dip,
Some wet the noddle, some the hip.
Here the miraculous conception
Finds credit, there 'tis a deception ;
And yet the former party are not
Agreed who 'twas became incarnate,
But hesitate if to believe
The Logos or the Angel Yeve.
This makes the Testament his manual,
That fancies Swedenborg Immanuel.
These like St. Matthew's Gospel best,
With those Mark only stands the test ;
One pares St. Luke, another snips
Away the whole Apocalypse ;
A third betrays a disposition
To think St. John an imposition,
And may at last become so rude
As to uncanonize St. Jude.
Some hold imputed righteousness,
Th' atonement some, and others grace :
You thinks there are but few elect,
His brethren generously suspect

The universal restoration
Of all the damn'd of every nation.
And yet these differers from each other,
At any time unite their pother,
And join their various twigs of birch
To lash the back of Mother Church ;
As Scylla's dogs their yells forbear
Only their parent womb to tear.
Th' Apostles of this fierce religion, '
Our Knight delighted in besieging ;
To hate of whom by fast instinct
Of place and temper he was link'd,
As had he learn'd of Athanasius
To be to heretics ungracious.

HYMN.

God of the universe ! whose hand
  Has sown with suns the fields of space,
Round which, obeying Thy command,
  The peopled earths fulfil their race—

How vast the region where Thy will,
  Existence, form, and order gives,
Pleased the wide cup with joy to fill,
  For all that feels and breathes and lives !

Lord ! while we praise Thee, let us learn
  Beneficence to all below ;
Those praise Thee best whose bosoms burn
  To spread the gifts from Thee that flow.

So at the awful hour of change,
  Our souls the bands of death shall tear,
Through the whole starry vast to range,
  Thy goodness to admire and share.

MRS. OPIE.

[1769—1853.]

Amelia Opie, the only child of James Alderson, M.D., and of Amelia, his wife, was born on the 12th of November, 1769, in the parish of St. George's, Norwich. Her mother, a woman of considerable talent, died in 1784, and the daughter at the age of fifteen thus took the head of her father's table and the management of his domestic arrangements. Handsome and lively, possessing musical talents, her company was much sought, and she enjoyed society thoroughly, but she nevertheless contrived to devote some of her time to literature. In 1798 she married Mr. John Opie, an artist; and encouraged by her husband, she, in 1801, appeared before the world as the author of a simple moral tale that became extremely popular, entitled "Father and Daughter." In 1802 she published "Poems," from which my examples of her powers are selected. After her marriage she resided in London, and her anxiety to add something to the scanty income, induced her to apply herself diligently to literature, and several novels in consequence were written by her, which attracted at the time more than ordinary attention.

Mrs. Opie's father was a regular attendant at the Norwich Octagon or Unitarian Chapel. She was baptised there, and also regularly attended the same place of worship. Her uncle, Mr. Robert Alderson (the father of the late Baron Alderson), was for nearly ten years one of the ministers of the Chapel, and the congregation at that period embraced many of the men and women who had made society at Norwich conspicuous for its attraction to men of literary tastes and pursuits. On her return to Norwich after the death of her husband, she continued to attend the Unitarian Chapel until 1814, when she left the congregation, and from that period she attended the religious services of the "Friends."

In 1825 she formally joined the "Friends," wore the plain dress, used the plain language; and a few months later her father, to whom she had been so long and so lovingly attached, died. She continued to make Norwich her home, and breathed her last at midnight on the 2nd of December, 1853. Her remains were interred in the Friends' burial ground at the Gildencroft, Norwich.

The *Edinburgh Review* said of the following song that " it is scarcely surpassed by any in our language." And referring to it, Sir James Mackintosh, in a letter from India, says, " Tell the fair Opie that if she would address such pretty verses to me as she did to Ashburner, I think she might almost bring me back from Bombay, though she could not prevent his going thither."

A triple crown was awarded to this song, as it was selected by the Rev. Sydney Smith, in one of his lectures on Moral Philosophy, delivered at the Royal Institution in 1804-5, as possessing peculiar excellence in its style. He says, " If any man were to discover the true language of nature and feeling in this little poem of Mrs. Opie's, he would gain no credit for his metaphorical taste, because the beauties of it are TOO striking for a moment's hesitation."

Miss Brightwell, in her memoir, says, "The authoress was present at the time when Mr. Smith pronounced this eulogium upon her verses, and she used laughingly to tell how unexpectedly the compliment came upon her, and how she shrank down upon her seat in order to screen herself from the observation of those around her."

SONG.

Go, youth beloved, in distant lands,
   New friends, new hopes, new joys to find !
Yet sometimes deign, midst fairer maids,
   To think on her thou leav'st behind.
Thy love, thy fate, dear youth to share,
   Must never be my happy lot ;
But thou mayst grant this humble prayer—
   Forget me not, forget me not !

Yet should the thought of my distress,
   Too painful to thy feelings be,
Heed not the wish I now express,
   Nor ever deign to think on me ;
But, oh ! if grief thy steps attend,
   If want, if sickness be thy lot,
And thou require a soothing friend,
   Forget me not ! forget me not !

LINES FOR THE ALBUM AT COSSEY, THE SEAT OF SIR WILLIAM JERNINGHAM, BART.

Hail ! lovely scene with varied beauties graced,
Where Nature's form delights, adorned by taste !
Bleak rose yon hill, and its unsheltered head,
No waving trees with grateful gloom o'erspread,
From day's fierce beams to guard the dazzled sight,
And give in beauteous contrast shade and light.
Yon river wandered from its parent source,
But narrow, dark, ungraceful was its course ;

And no rich scenery on its bank's green side,
New beauties caught from the reflecting tide.
Say, then, what magic power's creative hand
Called forth such changes in the rugged land?
Round yonder hill's unsheltered barren head,
Who the bright wreaths of waving foliage spread,
That in rich masses deepening shadows throw,
And spot with quivering light each hill's green brow,
While Philomela keeps his vigils there,
And charms with plaintive song the wakeful ear?
Who midst yon flowery banks expanding wide,
Taught the bright stream to roll its deepened tide,
Woo to its clear expanse the beams of day,
And from its breast reflect the trembling ray,
While the clear wave each neighbouring object shows,
And softened beauty o'er those objects throws?
Who bade (soft shelter from day's garish power)
Here smile a cottage, and there frown a tower?
Who thus to Eden changed the untutored waste?
The wand, the magic wand, was thine, O Taste!
Waked by thy touch, thou bidst new beauties grow,
And those already there more brightly glow.
So when Pygmalion saw with fond surprise
Beneath his hand a beauteous form arise,
Still new attractions wantoned o'er the face,
When animation waked each latent grace;
The form, the features, both were there before,
But, when with life inspired, they charmed still more;
While the fair wonder to the sight improved,
And graceful too as beautiful she moved.
But though thy charms, O Cossey, I admire,
'Tis not to them I wake my trembling lyre;
'Tis not because such wonders round it rise,
I view this mansion with delighted eyes;
Ah, no! I pour the tributary lay,
Because these scenes not Taste alone obey;
Here true Beneficence delights to shine,
And proudly cries, " Here power supreme is mine!"

Yes, all around her smiling sway confess ;
Lo, peasants own it, and lo, nobles bless.
Here the lorn exile from his native land,
Still feels the pressure of affection's hand ;
Torn from the ties to his fond bosom dear,
Finds soothing friendship's voice console him here ;
And, while he seems in this luxuriant plain,
To view his native verdant vales again,
This friendly mansion and its owner's smile,
Can with more dear illusions still beguile ;
For looks of welcome to this social dome
Restore the vanished charms of love and home ;
O'er bleeding memory's wounds a veil they cast,
And make the present charm him like the past.
And she, the cloistered virgin, forced to fly
The fatal blaze of irreligious eye,
Forced, unprotected, amidst foes to roam,
Profaned her altars, and laid waste her home,
Here finds her weary wakeful wanderings o'er,
A sure asylum from destructive power,
To a still sacred altar here repairs,
Nor longer murmurs grief-impeded prayers ;
But, far away all thoughts of danger driven,
Unchecked she lifts her ardent soul to heaven.
Ye bounteous rulers of this fair domain,
Whom misery's fainting feet ne'er seek in vain,
Who, not content to bid pale want resign
The numerous slaves that in her fetters pine,
Try (harder task) a balsam to impart
To the deep wounds that rack the feeling heart,
Permit the muse who twines this votive wreath,
Warm from the soul a prayer for you to breathe.
But, oh ! what more can heaven on you bestow !
Still in your path increasing blessings flow ;
Lo ! these are riches rightly understood,
Distinctions, honours, all the world calls good ;
You boast an offspring to extend your line,
In whom your mingled charms and virtues shine.

But as so transient still is earthly joy,
Disease can banish it and death destroy,
Still I for you may heaven's high throne implore,
And bid its bounty grant one blessing more,
That *long* its sheltering wing may o'er you wave,
Its mercy guarding what its goodness gave.
But when death's tardy steps at length draw near,
And filial fondness sheds the tender tear,
Blest in that moment as in all the past,
Bright as your earliest days shall be your last.
Not round your dying couch such shapes shall rise,
As haunt the bed where selfish avarice lies,
But at that awful hour, when hope and fear
In long review hid actions past appear,
Which, as the life blood leaves the sinking heart,
By turns despair and confidence impart,
Then—as the Ixia's fragrance-breathing flowers,
The snowy pride of Afric's sultry shores,
Ne'er to the breeze their slender leaves inclose
While day's bright noon in all its lustre glows,
And wait till night's o'erhanging shades prevail,
And then expand their beauties to the gale.
So many a generous deed in life's high noon,
By you performed, and then forgotten soon
Shall softly soothing to your memory rise,
When the last lustre lingers in your eyes,
Shall in the night of death to cheer you bloom,
And gild the awful pathway of the tomb.

MISS AIKIN.

[1781—1864.]

Lucy Aikin was the daughter of John Aikin, M.D. She was born at
Warrington on November 6th, 1781 ; but when she was only three years
old, her father removed to Great Yarmouth to practise as a physician, and
this journey in a post-chaise of two hundred and forty miles, which took
six days to accomplish, was the earliest event that dwelt in her memory,

and she used to remark with great pleasure that her first view of the
ocean from Yarmouth jetty filled her little bosom with sentiments too big
for utterance. In 1792 her father settled with his family in London, and a
few years later failing health compelled him to abandon his professional
duties, when he removed to Stoke Newington, and his daughter remained
there with him until his decease in 1822. Her first efforts in writing were
in the way of translation, but she very soon contributed original articles
to the reviews, magazines, and to the *Annual Register.* In 1819 she produced *Memoirs of the Court of Queen Elizabeth.* Two similar works on the
reign of James I. and Charles I., followed. She also published a volume
of poetry, a work of fiction, *Lorimer*, and *Memoirs of Addison.* Miss
Aikin, after the death of her father, resided chiefly at Hampstead, and its
vicinity to the metropolis gave her that opportunity of intercourse with
men and women distinguished for their literary or political attainments,
which she thoroughly enjoyed. She died at Hampstead on the 29th of
January, 1864, in the eighty-third year of her age, retaining her memory
and her faculties to the last.

THE SWALLOW.

Swallow, that on rapid wing,
Sweep'st along in sportive ring,
Now here, now there, now low, now high,
Chasing keen the painted fly ;
Could I skim away with thee,
Over land and over sea,
What streams would flow, what cities rise,
What landscapes dance before mine eyes !
First from England's southern shore,
'Cross the channel we would soar,
And our vent'rous course advance
To the plains of sprightly France ;
On the verdant banks of Loire,
Sport among the feathered choir ;
Skim Garonne's majestic tide,
Where Bordeaux adorns his side ;
Cross the towering Pyrenees,
'Mid myrtle groves and orange trees ;
Enter then the wild domain,
Where wolves prowl round the flocks of Spain,
Where silk-worms spin and olives grow,
And mules plod surely on and slow.

Steering thus for many a day,
Far to the south our course away,
From Gibraltar's rocky steep,
Dashing o'er the foaming deep,
On sultry Afric's fruitful shore,
We'd rest at length, our journey o'er,
Till vernal gales should gently play,
To waft us on our homeward way.

MR. CORNELIUS WHUR.

[1782—1853.]

Cornelius Whur was a native of Pulham Market, and was born there in 1782. He followed the business of a gardener, and in early life became a Wesleyan Methodist, and for many years was a local preacher in connection with that body. In 1825 a so-called revival took place amongst the Pulham Wesleyans, and Whur published a poem thereon, called *The Triumph of Messiah's Arms, or The Reformed Village.* This excited a vast deal of interest, and was the beginning of a poetical controversy which lasted many weeks, the Church party being defended by the late Mr. Wm. Cole, of Ubbeston Hall, who then resided at Pulham Market. In 1837 our author published his *Village Musings,* and some years later another volume entitled *Gratitude's Offering.* Before his death he published a third volume, the title of which I have been unable to obtain. He was patronised by many clergymen, and Dr. Hall, rector of Fulborne, Cambridge, was a great friend to him. He died suddenly at Bungay, and was buried in the churchyard of Pulham Market on the 21st of March, 1853, aged 71.

The following is selected from his *Village Musings.*

THE QUAKER AND HIS ROBIN.

A most amiable man, residing at Tivetshall, a member of the "Society of Friends," has for several years nurtured and fed a redbreast, making it his daily companion. Bob, elated by such kind attentions, is become exceedingly consequential, ranging the premises as if lord and master, finding in all his movements "a goodly heritage." To Bob's fortunate and ever agreeable situation these lines apply.

Bad as the times are, rosy Bob,
 Thy song is heard each morning;
And sometimes ere the splendid orb
 Is seen—the sky adorning.

How is't thou singest ev'ry day,
    With such delighted piping,
While thousands to dull care a prey,
    Are wetted eyelids wiping?
Thou fliest here from tree to tree,
And often singest merrily.

Day after day thou flittest here,
    Enjoying ev'ry season;
And that thou droppest not a tear,
    Thou hast abundant reason. ˉ
From ev'ry plant, as if thine own,
    Thou takest fruit delicious;
And art by staying, bolder grown,
    Becoming most officious;
No sparrow, blackbird, wren, or thrush,
So boldly strips each bending bush.

And not contented with such scope,
    Some often see thee stopping
Hard by the doors, and if they ope,
    Thou goest therein hopping;
And master Bob, I have to say,
    And say it not in fable,
Thou mountest elbow chairs by day,
    Sometimes the quaker's table;
How 'tis thou darest make so free,
Is really wonderful to me.

Bob, hearing this as I suppos'd,
    Spoke thus, as if replying:—
"Not being rudely discompos'd,
    None see me frighten'd flying.
And when I first came hopping here,
    I'd not the least intention
To tarry thus year after year;
    But, O! what I could mention!
For 'twas a most auspicious day,
When I came here from spray to spray.

For I ne'er hear where'er I hop,
 Aught like a noisy bustle,
And yet I often heark'ning stop,
 And listen as leaves rustle,
And though I sometimes peep within,
 I never hear a riot,
No clamour or distracting din,
 The quakers are so quiet.
I seldom hear a social pray'r,
Yet find the calm of heaven there."

Bob, ere he finish'd, added this,
 By way of application:
" I've with the Quakers present bliss,
 And see no ostentation.
Since I've been here I've often had
 Some joys life's cup to sweeten,
And though unworthy, have been glad
 At many a ' silent meeting.'
For from beneath his ample brim,
I've many smiling looks from him.

And oftentimes with great delight,
 I see him fragments dropping,
And being spread within my sight,
 I pick them as I'm hopping.
And though his dialect is quaint,
 With manners unpretending,
I think my Quaker quite a saint,
 Requiring little mending."
When Bob had made this short comment,
He spread his wings and off he went.

ELIZABETH BENTLEY.

Elizabeth Bentley was born at Norwich in November, 1767, and was an
only child. Her father, Daniel Bentley, who, she said, had received a good
education, taught her to read and spell, but never gave her the least idea

of grammar. Being naturally fond of reading, she employed her leisure hours in perusing such books as were in the house, and such as she could borrow of her neighbours. When she was about ten years of age, her father was disabled from working at his trade by an attack of paralysis, but still retaining the use of his right hand, he taught her the art of writing. At this time he was compelled to go about selling vegetables for a living, but a few months before his death he obtained the place of book-keeper to the London coach, which then set out from the King's Head in the Market-place. He died in January, 1783, when his daughter was in her fifteenth year. About two years after her father's death, Elizabeth discovered in herself an inclination for writing verses, and her mother showing some of her prod1ctions to acquaintances, she was encouraged to proceed; and it was not till after this event that she obtained a small grammar, which she purchased second-hand to attain the art of express-ing herself correctly. In 1790 she published a small volume of poems for children, the Rev. John Walker, minister of St. Peter-per-Mountergate, Norwich, having kindly consented to revise the proof sheets for her. The profits arising from this publication were devoted to the purchase of a small annuity, and this, in conjunction with the income arising from a small school, enabled her to support with some comfort the declining age of her mother. After this, her verses on temporary subjects frequently contributed to fill the columns of the *Norfolk Chronicle,* but a period of thirty years elapsed before she again ventured to print another volume of poems. From the volume published in 1821, I have selected the examples here given.

ON THE DEATH OF DR. LUBBOCK.*

The voice of public sorrow bursting forth,
    Mixt with the widow's sighs, the orphan's tears,
Speaks the departure of a man of worth,
    In realms of bliss to live immortal years.

Ah ! were there aught in med'cine's balmy pow'r
    To mortals could prolong their fleeting breath,
When Heav'n decrees th' irrevocable hour,
    Or from its aim repel the shaft of death ;

Then had not he in practice skill'd to save,
    From joys domestic immaturely torn,
Thus droop'd a lingering victim to the grave,
    Nor left mankind a public loss to mourn.

* Richard Lubbock, M.D., an eminent physician of Norwich. He died September 2, 1808, in the 49th year of his age.

Lord ! how inscrutable thy ways to man !
Shall vain presumption thy decrees explore ?
'Tis *thine* in mercy each event to plan,
Ours to submit in silence and adore.

ON THE DEATH OF THE REV. MR. PEELE,*

NOVEMBER, 1804,

Let Fame her trophies to ambition raise,
Of monumental and historic praise ;
Truth shall forbid the memory of the just
To sink unnoticed in the silent dust,
Whose spirit summon'd by the Almighty Lord,
Now meets the faithful servant's bright reward.
His life was as his Christian doctrine pure,
Alike in virtue as in days mature;
His deeds, that spoke benevolence of mind,
Unceasing fiow'd to benefit mankind;
These to each heart his name shall still endear,
And long survive the sad funereal tear.

MRS. REBECCA GOOCH.

[1784—1841.]

The following verses are selected from a volume of Poems published in 1828 by Jarrold and Sons. Several of the Poems have attached to them the names of the places where they were composed, as Denton, Harleston, Bungay, Harston Hall, &c. The authoress was the daughter of a gentleman named Pashley, and was born at Denton about May, 1784. She married a Mr. Thomas Gooch, who was a bookseller, and resided for many years after her marriage in the village of Pulham. Her decease occurred in 1841.

MY NATIVE DALE.

Hail ! scenes of youth, when every hope was bright,
Sweet spot ! I love and venerate thee still ;
Each tree in memory wakes the past delight,
As oft I gamboll'd down the neighbouring hill.

* The Rev. John Peele was thirty-eight years minister of St. Peter's Mancroft, Norwich. He died October 26, 1804, in the 84th year of his age.

There is the spreading oak, beneath whose shade
  I've heard the murm'ring ring-dove's rural tale ;
Adown that mead in early spring I've strayed
  To pluck the primrose of my native dale.

Soon as that copse resum'd its vernal vest,
  How oft I've tript its lonely path along,
'Twas there the blackbird close concealed its nest,
  And thrushes charm'd me with their morning song.

Yon hanging wood adorns the prospect still,
  And just below the little babbling brook,
O'er pebbles rippling, skirts the woodland hill,
  And struggles on in many a pretty nook.

That distant park array'd in sober vest,
  A beauteous contrast to the livelier green ;
Those fine tall trees in richest foliage drest,
  Yon antique mansion* long has peeped between.

The pars'nage house that blush'd through evergreen,
  The broad-spread firs that swept the velvet lawn,
Hedges of beech and pretty walks between,
  With the good doctor, these have since withdrawn.

Yon gentle slope with daisies speckled o'er,
  And sunny bank where breath'd the violet blue,
Still smile so sweetly and invite the more,
  As I withdraw and bid a long adieu.

SAMUEL LANE.

Samuel Lane was born in the parish of St. Gregory, Norwich, in 1786, and was apprenticed to a tailor named Knights. He was sent to a boarding school at Brook, and proved himself an apt scholar, and in his reading showed an inclination for literature. When a boy, whilst visiting Norwich, he fell from the wall of St. Gregory's church-

* Flixton Hall, then the seat of Alexander Adair, Esq.

yard, and received so much injury that he was lamed for life. After serving his time, he commenced business for himself, but he did not prosper. He got into debt and into jail. He was very fond of the cup, and consequently, debt and misfortune followed. But the muse stuck to him. His ballads sold prodigiously, and unfortunately, the more drink he imbibed, the more freely came his rhymes; and the result may be easily guessed. When want had driven him on one occasion to seek an asylum in the Workhouse, the poet wrote verses on the walls so insulting to the governor, that he was turned out of the building. At length he went to London, and lived, where he died, in an obscure locality called Sheep's Head Court, Milton Square, the only furniture of his apartment being one chair and a bed of straw. His poetical effusions are confined to local circumstances, and many of his ballads sold in thousands. The one I republish was considered his best, but perhaps the most popular was one written on the decay of Guild-day at Norwich, and the removal of the old dragon Snap from the corporate processions.

DIALOGUE BETWEEN GILES JOLTERHEAD AND HIS DARTER DINAH ON THEIR VISIT TO THE NORWICH FESTIVAL.

Giles Jolterhead ! from Ashwellthorpe, a joskin raw was he,
To Norwich came on Tuesday last, our Festival to see ;
" Consarne my carcase," now says Giles, " I'll take my eldest
    darter,
And to the Festival we'll go, and see what they are arter.

Come Dinah, mor, put on your duds, and make yourself look tidy,
Who knows amongst these lords and dukes what good luck may
    betide ye ;
For dukes, and lords, and noblemen, in spite of all their bother,
Will sometimes fall in love, they say, with a red raw country
    mawther."

Then off to Norwich arm in arm, they smash'd along right well,
And when they got to town set up at the Barking Dicky Hotel,
On rolls and cheese, and decent swipes, so comfortably they baited,
Till Giles declared he felt himself more than half way "coxelated."

Giles paid his reckoning like a man, and off they both did toddle,
But where to find the Festival, put both of them in a muddle ;
They enquired of everybody they met " where the Festival was
    held ? "
Some said on " Heigham Cawnser " and some in " Chapel Field."

Some said 'twas held on the Ditches at the Holkham Arms or
  Checquers,
Whilst others swore right hard and fast 'twas held at the Nut
  Crackers.
At last they saw some carriages a smashing might and main,
So Giles and Dinah ran behind till they got to St. Andrew's
  Plain.

"Consarne it, Dinah, mor," says Giles, "here's a bustle and confu-
  sion,
Do they call this the Festival? Why 'tis more like a Revolution.
Here's the horse soldiers with their broad swords drawn up in
  battle array,
If the people do not mind their work, they'll surely kill and slay.

"By gums," says Giles, "now Dinah, mor, the safest way I think,
As we are no Revolutioners, is to climb St. Andrew's Bank."
"No, no," says Dinah, "that won't do, to the Festival we are
  come,
And to see it I am determined before I do go home."

Then away they crush'd through thick and thin, in spite of war's
  alarms;
Giles flourished high his crab stick with Dinah under his arm;
The gentry pouring in the Hall, Giles thought he needs must
  follow,
Till a consequential door keeper cry'd "Stop! you country fellow."

"What for," quoth Giles, "you saucy scamp, I'll get the King to
  fine ye,
My name it is Giles Jolterhead, and this is my mawther Dinah;
We are all the way from Ashwellthorpe, this Festival to see,
Besides my mawther have a mind a lady for to be."

Then up there came a great stout man, with a rare large three-
  cocked squiver,
With a great red nose on his fat face, like a lump of bullock's
  liver.

" Lawk ! who is he," says Dinah, " he look so full of wrath ?"
" Why that," says Giles, "'tis my belief, is his Majesty William
    the Fourth."

And with that Giles made a reverend bow, and sung God save the
    King,
The constable catch'd him a box on the ear, which made his thick
    head ring
"Come, dash my buttons though," says Giles, "if that is the way
    you treat me,
If ever I come to a Festival again, I'll give you leave to beat me."

Then next there comes the bellman, with his plate on his left
    breast,
Says Giles "that's the Duke of Sussex,* or else my mark I have
    missed ;
If I could but speak to his Grace I wouldn't mind laying a penny,
That if his Highness be not engaged, he would marry my mawther
    Dinah."

But his Highness pass'd with a lofty air, and took no notice of
    Giles,
Nor did he deign to cast one look on Dinah's amorous smiles.
"Consarne these dukes and lords," quoth Giles, " what a set of
    chaps they are,
They certainly don't like Dinah, because she have got sandy hair."

And then came a lady all in white with rings on her fingers
    three,
Says Giles, "Look, Dinah, that's the Queen, God save her
    Majesty ;
I have a good mind to step up to her Grace, and say that I waited
    upon her,
To ask if she can't give Dinah a place as one of her maids of
    honor."

* The only Festival at Norwich at which the Duke of Sussex attended
was that held in 1824, and it is that event, therefore, that the ballad commemorates.

But the lady she frowned, as well she might, at Giles's red-raw fist,
She took his nose betwixt her fingers, and gave it a lime-burner's
twist.
" Consarne it," says Giles, " leave go of my snout, or you'll spoil
my constitution ;
By George, if you treat your subjects so, no wonder at this revolution."

And now the fiddles began for to squeak, the trumpets, and the
bassoons ;
Says Giles, " The rebellion is broke out in the hall and these are
the dying groans ;
Run, Dinah ! run, mor !" now quoth Giles, "before their bayonets
prick ye."
Then off they quickly ran away to their quarters at the Barking
Dickey.

WILLIAM JOHNSON FOX.

[1786—1864.]

William Johnson Fox was born at Wrentham, in Suffolk, on the 1st of
March, 1786. After a few years his father removed to Norwich and commenced business as a small manufacturer, in which, as soon as his age permitted, William assisted him, and hence the well-known *nom de plume* of
the " Norwich Weaver Boy." Not liking the manufacturing business, he,
when about fourteen years of age, through the influence of an uncle, obtained a situation in tha Bank of Messrs. Kitt and Buck. At the age of
eighteen he felt a strong desire to become a Dissenting minister, and in
consequence he, in 1806, entered as a student at Homerton Academy. In 1809
he became minister of a small orthodox congregation at Fareham, Hants,
but having a few years later adopted wider theological views, he honestly
resigned his charge. His fame as a preacher having spread throughout the
country, he, in 1817, was invited to London as the minister of Parliament
Court Chapel, and many of the leading thinkers of the metropolis became
attendants on his ministry. In 1839 he delivered a lecture on "The Moral
View of the Corn Law Question," and he, a few years after, commenced
the Anti Corn Law Speeches at the first meeting held in Covent Garden
Theatre by the League. In 1847 he entered Parliament, having been returned, free of expense, at the head of the poll for Oldham, for which
borough he sat until 1863. Mr. Fox's first appearance as a journalist was
in 1821-2, when he wrote a series of articles for the *Norwich Mercury*, entitled the "Hyderabad Papers." He, from that time to his decease, was
a frequent contributor to several of the most influential and liberal

newspapers, magazines, and reviews. His letters to the *League*, under the title of the "Norwich Weaver Boy," and his contributions to the *Weekly Dispatch*, under the signature of "Publicola," being the best known of his productions. Mr. Fox died on June 3rd, 1864, and was buried at Brompton Cemetery.

MAN.

Not for false and fleeting joys,
Pleasure, that while tasted, cloys,
Nor for self-inflicted pain,
Borne to purchase heavenly gain,
    Did God make man ;

But for wisdom, happiness,
Blessed life and life to bless,
Love the soul of Deity,
And progress through eternity,
    Did God make man.

For cultured earth and conquered wave,
Fancy bright, and science grave,
Mind and heart with blending powers,
Building more than Eden's bowers,
    Did God make man.

And for mutual love and aid,
Never weary nor dismayed,
Strength renewing as we rise
Upward to unchanging skies,
    Did God make man.

PROPHETS.

Call them from the dead,
    For our eyes to see ;
Prophet bards whose awful words
Shook the earth, " Thus saith the Lord,"
    And made the idols flee—
    A glorious company !

Call them from the dead,
For our eyes to see ;
Sons of wisdom, song, and power,
Giving earth her richest dower,
    And making nations free—
    A glorious company !

Call them from the dead,
For our eyes to see ;
Forms of beauty, love, and grace,
" Sunshine in the shady place,"
    That made it life to be—
    A blessed company !

Call them from the dead,
Vain the call will be ;
But the hand of Death shall lay,
Like that of Christ, its healing clay,
    On eyes which then shall see
    That glorious company !

JOSEPH JOHN GURNEY.

[1788—1847.]

Joseph John Gurney was born August 2nd, 1788, at Earlham Hall. He was the youngest but one of eleven children left by Mrs. Gurney at her death, Elizabeth Gurney (Mrs. Fry) being the third. After passing through a course of preparatory study, Joseph Gurney resided some time at Oxford under the charge of a private tutor, and attended the lectures, without becoming a member of the University. He acquired the Hebrew and Syriac languages as well as Greek and Latin, mathematics, and a large amount of general knowledge. After the death of his brother John in 1814, he assumed his brother's Christian name in addition to his own. Upon the completion of his education, Mr. Gurney became a member of the Norwich banking firm, and devoted most of his time to secular business, but he was also actively engaged in many philanthropic researches, and in the zealous discharge of his duties as a minister (recognised 1818), of the religious society to which he was attached. In addition to missionary tours among the prisons of Scotland, Ireland, and England, Mr. Gurney paid three visits to the continent in 1841-3, and passed three years, 1837-40, in travelling in America. The journal of his travels was printed, but only for private circulation. He died January 4th, 1847, at Earlham Hall.

He was the author of several works that gained for him a good position in the Republic of Letters. His *Observations on the Distinguishing Views and Practices of the Society of Friends*, 1824, passed through seven editions in his lifetime, and was characterised by the Rev. E. Bickersteith as " the best defence of the Quakers." His essays on the *Evidences, Doctrines, and Practical Operations of Christianity*, 1827, have been several times reprinted, and in addition they have been translated into German and Spanish. *Biblical Notes to confirm the Deity of Christ*, 1830; *Brief Remarks on the History, Authority, and Use of the Sabbath*, 1831; *Sabbatical Verses*, 1837; and several other minor issues were among the numerous works that flowed from his pen.

Mr. Gurney was thrice married—first, to Jane Birkbeck, who died in 1822; secondly, to Mary Fowler, who died in 1836; and thirdly to Eliza P. Kirkbridge, who survived him.

ON SILENT WORSHIP.

Let deepest silence all around
　Its peaceful shelter spread ;
So shall that living word abound,
　The word that wakes the dead.

How sweet to wait upon the Lord
　In stillness and in prayer !
What though no preacher speak the word,
　A minister is there.

A minister of wondrous skill,
　True graces to impart ;
He teaches all the Father's will,
　And preaches to the heart.

He dissipates the coward's fears,
　And bids the coldest glow ;
He speaks, and lo ! the softest tears
　Of deep contrition flow.

He knows to bend the heart of steel,
　He bows the loftiest soul ;
O'er all we think and all we feel,
　How matchless his control.

And ah ! how precious is his love,
　In tenderest touches given :
It whispers of the bliss above,
　And stays the soul on heaven.

From mind to mind, in streams of joy,
　The holy influence spreads ;
'Tis peace, 'tis praise, without alloy,
　For God that influence sheds.

'Twas thus where God himself is known
　To shine without a cloud,
The angel myriads round his throne
　In solemn silence bowed.

And all were still and silent long,
　Nor dared one note to raise,
Till burst the vast extatic song,
　And heaven was fill'd with praise.

A MEMORIAL OF JOSEPH JOHN GURNEY.

BY BERNARD BARTON.

I append some verses written by Bernard Barton on the death of Joseph John Gurney, and touching the members of his family.

The poet writing (2mo.-15-1847) to his friend Jane B—— (Mrs. Biddell, of Playford) says of this poem : " I send thee a copy of my little tribute to the memory of Joseph John Gurney. It's a small matter, but I have taken no small pains to make it as worthy of its subject as my scant leisure and declining ability would permit. In fact, I have bestowed more pains on this sheet and a-half than on a volume in my better days—a sad proof how near I draw to my dotage. But I found this poor tiny effort was expected of me, both by those within and those without our pale, so I resolved not to shirk it, little as I felt equal to doing justice to such a theme. I have a notion it will be more kindly taken, as a general result, *out* than *in*, for some of our good Friends, who have no hearty liking to poetry or poets, will liken me to him of old who put forth an unbidden *ergo*, an unhallowed, hand on the ark of old. From thee, dear Jane, I hope for a more charitable verdict; but I look for it with some anxiety, as thou hast much of the better part of poetry and Quakerism too in thee, and none can judge better of any attempt to combine the two without wrong to either.—Thine affectionately,　　　　　　　　B. B."

Death and the grave one triumph more have gain'd !
    A prince hath fallen in our poor Israel !
And if, before, we mourned how few remain'd
    Of them whose names were cherished as a spell,
And in our heart of hearts were wont to dwell :
    One less is left to us of good and great,
Who, skilled to wield the sword invincible,
    Hath often " turn'd the battle to the gate ; "
Yet, when the fight was won, could meekly " STAND AND WAIT."

But not for this, although the Church must mourn,
    And Friends lament for one now gone before,
Beyond Death's dark inexorable bourne,
    Should we in selfish grief thy loss deplore,
As those who know not Hope : thy strife is o'er,
    Thy trial ended, and thy journey done ;
Sin, sorrow, suffering, cannot harm thee more ;
    Thy spotless robe, thy palm-branch thou hast won,
And more than conqueror art through God's redeeming Son.

Nor will thy course be profitless to us,
    If it instruct us, as it surely ought,
To follow in thy footsteps—knowing thus,
    And thus alone, the victory must be sought ;
That the world's warfare never can be fought
    By any worldly weapons of our own,
But by those arms of heavenly temper wrought
    In God's eternal armoury alone,
Whereby, arrayed in white, thou stand'st before the throne.

If unto thee peculiarly were given
    A work to do, a mission to fulfil ;
And thou in both hast well and nobly striven,
    Wielding thy weapons with no earth-born skill,
Simple obedience was thy safeguard still !
    Grant that to thee *ten* talents were assign'd,
Yet each to whom God's high and holy will
    Hath given but *one*, not less should bear in mind
Obedience in its use like recompense will find.

Thine was, in truth, no easy path to tread ;
 Eminence, affluence, all that worldlings deem
The end of life—full many a snare had spread,
 And might have lull'd thee in a fatal dream,
Hadst thou not known *things are not what they seem ;*
 And like a bird deliver'd from each snare,
Been shown by holy truth's unerring beam,
 There was a heavenly crown to win and wear,
With which no earthly gaud one moment could compare.

Thus wert thou made a follower of the Cross !
 And strengthened to thy task in heart and limb ;
Accounting all besides as dirt and dross
 To winning Christ, and being found in Him !
Joy's sensual cup may sparkle at the brim,
 And yet the dregs be bitterness below ;
False glory's wreath look bright, yet soon turn dim,
 Distain'd by blood and tears of human woe ;
Alas ! what seas of both have heroes made to flow !

True Soldier of the Cross ! God's Holy Word,
 His heavenly grace, thine inward eye unseal'd,
To choose the better part ; and both conferr'd
 On thee the Spirit's Sword, the Spirit's Shield !
Taught thee that sword right valiantly to wield,
 Till, through His power who was thy strength and stay,
Thou wast a victor in a glorious field,
 Whose bloodless triumphs shall endure for aye,
When earth, and sea, and sun shall all have pass'd away !

But in thy warfare thou hadst often need
 To blend with it soft judgment and true love ;
Thou hadst to advocate a simple creed !
 Taught, as we hold, by Wisdom from above.
" Wise as the serpent, guileless as the dove,"
 Might well thy motto and thy watchword be ;
For thou hadst much of error to disprove,
 And many a mind from prejudice to free,
Ere some thy aim could guess, or thy true mission see !

For our small section of the Christian fold
 Was most unjustly branded with the shame
Of dogmas we had been supposed to hold,
 Which hardly left to us a Christian name ;
Though such our early worthies would disclaim,
 And with an earnestness of truth sincere,
In terms as strong as they knew how to frame,
 Had striven to prove their Christian title clear,
To prize God's written word, its mysteries to revere.

But prejudice and ignorance on part
 Of others, or on ours a want of skill,
(Perchance in words) in many a brother's heart,
 The warmth of Christian fellowship would chill.
And one true mission given thee to fulfil
 Was to demonstrate that our spiritual creed,
Though lacking outward rites, *was Christian still,*
 Held by the Head ! and could in spirit feed
On TRUTHS whose *visible forms* it *little seem'd to heed.*

" Without were fightings and within were fears ;"
 While thou, in meekness, held'st thine onward way ;
But the seed sown by thee, perchance in tears,
 Hath borne some harvest in our later day,
Few of our Christian brethren now gainsay
 Our Christian faith, however some condemn
Our negligence of rites themselves obey ;
 Increasing charity hath taught to them
We may *the casket slight* yet *reverence* THE GEM.

To do this well and wisely was thy aim ;
 Evil and good report have been thy meed 1
But far beyond all perishable fame,
 And compensation by the world decreed,
Is his, who single-hearted strives to plead
 For Gospel Truth in Gospel Love sublime 1
The recompense laid up for those indeed,
 Who while on earth they journey heavenward climb,
Shall be awarded him who now hath done with time.

But not **by sect** or shore was limited
  A love so boundless, and so vast as thine,
Flowing from Christ, its copious fountain-head,
  It lived along the far extended line
Which links all human kind ; and could combine
  All people, and all lands in its embrace ;
Earth was to thee one universal shrine,
  For gospel love to consecrate, through grace,
By making human hearts Jehovah's dwelling place.

There was a breadth, a largeness in thy soul,
  A fulness, richness, amplitude of heart,
Which no sectarian limits could control,
  To set thee from thy fellow-men apart :
It comprehended Traffic's busy mart,
  The peasant's lowly cot, the noble's hall ;
Love unto God and man thy only chart,
  Poor, rich, learn'd, ignorant, the great, the small,
Thy sympathies could share, for God had made them all !

The kidnapp'd slave, the prisoner in his cell,
  The sceptred monarch in his regal dome ;
The giddy trifler, bound by Fashion's spell,
  The hardy sailor breasting Ocean's foam ;
ALL in that heart of thine could find a home
  Whence humble prayer up-rose for *all* and each ;
Yet though thy love thus far and wide could roam,
  It flowed no less to Want within its reach,
But there out-poured its balm in thought, and act, and speech !

And often on these errands, by thy side,
  A *kindred spirit*, who erst *bore thy name*,
Not less by virtue, than by blood allied ;
  With thee upheld the Cross, endured the shame :
The palace or the prison, to both the same,
  Provided deeds of mercy could be done ;
Here you might wretchedness or vice reclaim,
  There by your christian meekness might be won
Some votaries of the world a heavenly course to run.

Nor was it less your object and your care,
  By breaking up the mind's most barren soil,
The children of the poorest to prepare
  For *some* participation in that spoil
Which knowledge offers to the sons of toil !
  Your true philanthropy was not content
Into old wounds to pour your wine and oil,
  But in your progress, wheresoe'er ye went,
To *teach* and *train the young* your earnest aid was lent.

And well, I ween your recompense ye had ;
  Where'er ye trod, some flowers their sweets disclose,
The moral wilderness became more glad,
  The desert places blossom'd as the rose !
Something was done to soften Slavery's woes ;
  The prisoner's dungeon caught a transient ray
Of light, and life, from heaven ; and even those
  On whom the law's last mortal sentence lay,
Look'd up where crimes and tears shall all be wiped away !

If "*lovely in your lives*" you thus appear,
  And both are now from time and earth set free,
The grave could break no bonds that joined you here,
  Nor "*in your deaths can you divided be ;*"
Together now ye keep your jubilee
  In heaven's high courts, where the angelic choir,
On harps of gold hymning harmoniously,
  Surpassing far earth's faint and feeble lyre,
Sing praises to the Lamb and His Eternal Sire !

O, that some distant echo of that strain
  Could fall upon my wakeful, wistful ear :
That I might echo upon earth again
  The blissful music of that brighter sphere !
But deep humility and reverent fear,
  Bid me from that sweet aspiration turn
Once more to *Thee*, and from thy hallow'd bier,
  A humbler wish, a lowlier lesson learn,
As best belit on earth my lingering brief sojourn.

Is there who deems that this poor voice of mine
Would any trophy to THY MERIT raise?
Is there who thinks that round a name like thine
I seek to twine my tributary lays
That they may blossom on to after days?
He wrongs me much; this hasty wreath is thrown
To wither on thy grave, less in *thy* praise
(For thou wouldst rather praise of men disown),
Than in the praise of Him to whom be praise alone.

His love, His mercy, and His saving grace,
For thee thy every victory achieved;
And if with thee obedience still kept pace
With love of Him in whom thy heart believed,
Thou didst but give what thou hadst first received.
Not unto thee, then, would my muse accord
Praise which had only humbled thee or grieved,
Nay, might have been rejected and abhorr'd,
As giving unto thee the glory of thy Lord.

Then glory, honour, thanks to God on high!
Who made thee what thou wert: *the meed* was won,
Not by thy prowess or thy mastery,
But by thy truthful faith in His dear Son!
By this the fight was fought, the race was run,
Thy hope and charity kept pace with faith,
And earned for thee those welcome words, "Well done;"
And thou, set free from sorrow, sin, and scathe,
Hast conquered thy last Foe, and triumph'd over Death.

Farewell! I little thought that I, to whom
Time had allotted some few winters more,
Should live to strew these verses o'er thy tomb;
Would I could offer better from my store!
But humble gifts best suit with givers poor;
And, poor as are my own, these lines may tell
How deeply I thy friendship's loss deplore,
How fondly on thy memory love to dwell.
Farewell! once more; a long, on earth a last, Farewell!

TO ELIZA P. GURNEY.

BY BERNARD BARTON.

Think not, dear Friend, because my verse
Hath rather led me to rehearse
  The loss our Church has known,
That while I seek to pay her debt.
I for one moment could forget
  Bereavement like thine own.

But sorrow is a holy thing !
And such a sanctity must cling
  Around a grief like thine,
That I respect it far too much,
Lightly on such a theme to touch.
  In these brief lines of mine.

Yet while thy husband's public worth
Gives to this feeble tribute birth,
  As justly can I prize
Virtues as priceless, pure, and true,
Which their own peaceful halo threw
  Round home's dear sanctities.

The genial smile, the gentle tone,
The Christian kindness ever shown.
  By him to each and all,
At home, to inmate or to guest,
Put on their brightest and their best
  Affection to enthral.

If there the spell of each seem o'er,
If there they can delight no more,
  So potent was their sway :
Cherish'd in memory still they live,
Nor can the soothing joy they give
  With death itself decay.

For the dark grave but holds " in trust "
The relics of the good and just ;
  The graces these enshrined

Share not the frame's mortality ;
Too heavenly and too pure *to die,*
They leave in living memory
Their monument behind !

SONNET IN MEMORIAL OF ELIZABETH FRY.

BY BERNARD BARTON.

Thy name, now writ in heaven, will live on earth,
So long as human hearts are left to prize
That sterling virtue whose deep source supplies
Each Christian grace, a woman's highest worth !
And heaven forbid we e'er should dread a dearth
. Of these in England ; where the good and wise
Have, by their reverence of such sanctities
Honour'd the country which had given them birth.
True gospel preacher of that law of love
By Jesus taught, not for thyself would I
Indite this simple, brief obituary !
May thy example kindred spirits move
To follow thee ; and thus themselves approve
Numbered with those whose record on is high !

SARAH MARTIN.
[1791—1843.]

Sarah Martin, the self-denying workhouse and gaol missionary, was born in June, 1791, at the village of Caister, near Great Yarmouth. She lost her parents by death when she was very young, and the little orphan became the charge of her grandmother, a widow of limited means, but of a kind and religious disposition. Of her education little is known. She was not more than fourteen years of age when she was apprenticed to a dressmaker, and she afterwards followed the occupation as a means of a living, working by the day in the families that employed her. Her subsequent self-sacrificing labours to instruct the poor and the guilty of the workhouse and the gaol in the ways of righteousness and peace, which extended over a period of thirty years, are, I hope, too well known to need repetition here. Her poems, few in number, and chiefly homely attempts at sacred poetry, were published after her decease, which took place on the 14th of October, 1843. A splendid stained glass window has been erected to her memory in the parish church at Great Yarmouth.

RECOLLECTIONS OF MY BELOVED GRANDMOTHER

WHO DEPARTED THIS LIFE ON JUNE 26TH, 1826.

Thy memory is so dear, that every thought
Of thee is with the richest profit fraught,
Whether I contemplate thy life below,
Or the high glory which surrounds thee now :
I think on all thou wert on earth to me,
And mourn my loss, while I rejoice for thee.
Thy sweet affection watch'd my helpless years
Of early infancy, thy faithful cares
Still blest my youth, I was the charge when here
In sickness and in health to thee most dear,
And when affliction pointed to the skies,
Thou at that moment didst desire to rise ;
But for one earthly wish and 'twas exprest,
For my sake didst thou linger to be blest.
The kind desire was granted : life was given
A few years longer, then, full ripe for heaven
Thrice favour'd saint, no long affliction stayed
Thy gentle spirit in its trembling shade,
But mercy favoured thee, soon burst thy prison,
'Twas but a few brief hours and thou wert risen :
Speech was denied, thy fading eyes were closed,
Thy spirit on thy Saviour's name reposed :
Yet did one precious, memorable sign
Refresh this sad and sorrowing heart of mine,
When as I read of Him whose blood was shed,
To be " the Resurrection of the dead,"
Thy gentle hand sought mine, and while it prest,
Love, joy, and peace, my grateful soul possest ;
And though my inmost spirit felt the wound ;
When left below without thee, yet I found,
E'en then, unnerved and sinking, that the hand
Which beckoned thee away, was still my friend :
Thy swift departure to the world of day,
Was like a fair translation, one bright ray
Of bursting glory caught thy lifted eye,

By heaven supported, as I watched thy bed,
And saw thee till the last, last breath had fled,
Then, though I wept, the wish did not prevail
That thou again shouldst breathe earth's tainted gale,
That thou shouldst still forego the immortal bliss
To see thy God, thy Saviour, " as He is ! "
I wept because I love thee, for my heart
So close united, found it hard to part.
There may be some who love me now : a tear
From a kind friend may yet fall on my bier,
But none can love me with regard like thine :
Yet was I called the treasure to resign,
Hush'd be the deep complaint : I will rejoice
And praise the mercy with my heart and voice
Which formed thy life by faith, then bade thee rise
To glory not unveiled below the skies.
Thy prayer for me ascended ere I knew
Or joy or hope beyond earth's bounded view,
To see me rescued from the iron reign
Of ignorance of God, and burst its chain.
To see me in the golden day of youth
Devoted to the cause of blessed truth !
Thy prayer is heard, and in this world of tears,
Of anxious labours, and prolific fears,
Where for ourselves or others, all will find
Much to afflict and bow the labouring mind,
Divine religion strews my way with flowers,
Celestial pleasures gild my peaceful hours.
E'en here a chalice meets my favoured lip,
'Tis hope transporting, 'tis delight to sip.
Oft to my elevated thought 'tis given
To rise with rapture e'en on this side heaven :
The high desire that others may be blest,
When it expands a mortal's glowing breast,
Savours of heaven, so pure and so serene,
In it our cares revolve, unfelt, unseen :
Like a bright orb, before whose sacred fire
A million meteors fraught with death expire.

Such happiness didst thou for me implore,
And thy example taught my soul with power.
Thine was a life of prayer and kindest love,
I dwell upon it now thou'rt far above ;
And love to trace, if conquest I obtain
O'er many an evil which attempts to reign,
A lesson learned of thee, by words or deeds,
And praise that God from whom all good proceeds.
Ah ! if ascended spirits see or know
Aught of the lives of those they loved below,
My deep contrition thou hast seen—still see,
For my offences 'gainst thy God and Thee,
When counsel was rejected, and my heart,
Cold, faithless, and ungrateful, could depart
From truth, though spoken by a mortal tongue,
As pure as guardian angels could have sung :
But malice does not mar the bliss of heaven,
Hope whispers those offences are forgiven.
And my heart glows with rapture to arise
To meet thee in the joys of paradise.
To burst these mortal bands, whose slight control
But for a moment bow the impatient soul !
To shorten that brief moment may I be,
Almighty God, employed in serving thee !
Thus if one rayless heart illum'd I see,
Or one offender from his crimes set free,
I will not murmur, let me live, e'en here
Thy presence to my heart the gloom shall cheer,
Shall chasten every mortal joy, and reign
Supreme o'er human bliss or human pain,
And gild with bright magnificence the way
From earthly scenes, to heaven's eternal day.

THE EPITAPH.

Thy loss, sweet spirit still is mourned by me,
E'en while I bless the hand that removed thee,
From this dark world's afflictions, conflicts, woes,
To heaven's eternal glory and repose.

THE REV. PERRY NURSEY.

The Rev. Perry Nursey was born at the Grove, Little Bealings, Suffolk and was educated at Dr. Clarke's of East Berghelt, and other schools, after which he was entered at Corpus Christi College, Cambridge, and passed a very good degree. He was curate at East Dereham for several years, also at Tittleshall, and after that he went to Burlingham St. Andrew and St. Peter, as curate to the Rev. J. Burroughes, where he remained more than twenty years, and was, during that curacy, elected chaplain to the Blofield Union. In October, 1863, Dr. Pelham, Bishop of Norwich, unsolicited presented him to the living of Crostwick, near Norwich, for the faithful discharge of his duties as curate. He died at Crostwick rectory in April, 1867, in the 68th year of his age, and in the burial ground of that little parish his remains were interned.

The Rev. Perry Nursey married first Miss Smith, sister to Colonel Smith, and daughter of the Rev. W. Smith, rector of Palling and Waxham, near Great Yarmouth, by whom he had three sons ; and secondly, Miss Boult, of Beccles, by whom he had five children. He published, 1829, a volume of poems, called, *Evening and Other Poems*, which was dedicated to his father, Perry Nursey, Esq.

STANZAS.

Flow on, gentle stream, through this far-winding vale,
    Still through these green banks let thy bright waters roll ;
And oh ! let thy murmurs float light on the gale,
    While the bright dreams of childhood now steal o'er my soul.

How oft when the morning sun peep'd o'er the hill,
    And the dew drop of summer look'd bright on the mead,
How oft have my infant steps, lonely and still,
    Paused near thee to listen the shepherd's loved reed !

In the hot noon of summer, how oft have I found
    Beneath thy green willows a peaceful retreat !
Lull'd to rest by the wild hum of bees, and the sound
    Of thy waters that temptingly danced at my feet.

How oft 'mid the stillness of eve have I loved
    Along thy cool margin unheeded to stray,
While the nightingale's song every care hath removed,
    And stole with its sweetness my charm'd soul away !

Flow on then, fair stream, through this far-winding vale,
  Still through these green banks let thy bright waters roll :
Oh ! still let thy murmurs float light on the gale,
  While the bright dreams of childhood thus steal o'er my soul.

DR. HINDS.

The Right Rev. Samuel Hinds, D.D , some time Bishop of Norwich, son
of the late Abel Hinds, Esq., of Barbadoes, was born in that island in 1793,
and educated at Queen's College, Oxford, where he graduated in 1815, and
obtained the Chancellor's prize for the Latin essay.   He became Vice-
Principal of Alban Hall, Oxford; Principal of Codrington College, Barbadoes; was vicar of Yardley, Herts, 1834-43; and in the last-mentioned year
went to Ireland and became rector and prebendary of Castleknock, Dub-
lin, and chaplain to Archbishop Whately. He was afterwards successively
chaplain to the Earl of Bessborough and Earl of Clarendon, Dean of Car-
lisle, and in 1849 succeeded Dr. Stanley in the see of Norwich, which he resigned in 1857.   Dr. Hinds died at his residence, Notting-hill, on February
7th, 1872, in his 79th year.

THE OFT-FORGIVEN.

Yes, I'll believe thee though thou art
  A dream for ever fading ;
I'll take thee to my ruined heart,
  Without one weak upbraiding.

More oft have I to God returned.
  And he still turned to me ;
He never yet my sorrow spurned—
  Oh ! how could I spurn thee?

MARTHA AND MARY.

Blame not a sister, if her way
  Of seeking God's not thine ;
Chide not if she at home will stay,
  Nor in thy good work join.

O'er heath and hill, from door to door,
  Go thou and seek and find
His praise who yet may praise her more
  Whom thou dost leave behind.

III.

Anecdotes of Norfolk Worthies.

Anecdotes of Norfolk Worthies.

REPUTED INSOLENCE OF QUEEN ELIZABETH.

Archbishop Parker, who was born at Norwich, was noted for the splendour of his hospitality when called upon to entertain, as he frequently was, either foreign ambassadors or ecclesiastics, English peers, or even Queen Elizabeth herself. It is said by Sir John Harrington that on one of these occasional visits, after having expressed her thanks to the Archbishop, the Queen turned round to his wife and said, "And you—madam I may not call you, and mistress I am ashamed to call you—but yet I do thank you."

A VERDICT GETTER.

Sir James Scarlett* was renowned as a verdict getter. A country attorney once paid him a very high compliment when he thought he was undervaluing his qualifications, by saying, "Really there is nothing in a man getting so many verdicts who always has the luck to be on the right side of the cause." His weight with the Court and jury was not unhappily expressed by another person when asked at what he rated Mr. Scarlett's value. "A thirteenth juryman," was the answer. A remarkable instance is remembered in Westminster Hall of his acting in the face of the jury at the critical moment of their beginning to consider their ver-

* Sir James Scarlett was elected M.P. for Norwich in 1832, and two years later, on Sir Robert Peel coming into power, he was made Chief Baron, and raised to the peerage as Baron Abinger of the City of Norwich.

dict. He had defended a gentleman of rank and fortune against a charge of an odious description. He had performed his part with even more than his accustomed zeal and skill. As soon as the judge had summed up, he tied up his papers deliberately, and with a face smiling and easy, but carefully turned towards the jury, he rose and said loud enough to be generally heard that he was engaged to dinner, and in so clear a case there was no occasion for him to wait what must be the certain event. He then retired, deliberately bowing to the Court. The prosecuting counsel were astonished at this excess of confidence or of effrontery, nor was it lost upon the jury, who began their deliberation. But one of the junior counsel having occasion to leave the Court found that all this confidence and fearlessness had never crossed the threshold, for behind the door stood Sir James Scarlett, trembling with anxiety, his face the colour of his brief, awaiting the result of the "clearest case in the world" in breathless suspense.

AN UNDERGRADUATE'S WAGER LOST.

When the Rev. Robert Robinson* first occupied the pulpit at Cambridge, he was exposed to annoyance from the younger gownsmen. They incurred no danger of rustication, or even suffering an imposition for irregularities of that kind. It was soon after his settlement there that a wager was made among a party of undergraduates. One of them wagered that he would take his station on the steps of Robinson's pulpit, with a large ear trumpet in his hand, and

---

* The Rev. Robert Robinson was born at Swaffham in January 1735, and having commenced preaching among the Methodists, he accepted an invitation from the congregation at the Tabernacle, Norwich. But it was not long before he became a Baptist, and in 1759 he went to Cambridge, preceding Robert Hall as the minister of the congregation in St. Andrew's-street, and there he remained during the rest of his life. He was considered the richest colloquial preacher of his day, and in all Dissenting circles his *bon mots* formed a staple of after-dinner conversation, as much as those of Sidney Smith did at a later period of history in all companies.

remain there till the end of the service. Accordingly, he mounted the steps, put the trumpet to his ear, and played the part of a deaf man with all possible gravity. His friends were in the aisle below tittering at the hoax, the congregation were scandalised, but the preacher alone seemed insensible to what was going on. The sermon was on God's mercy ; or, whatever the subject might have been at first in due time it turned to that, and the preacher proceeded to this effect :—

"Not only, my Christian friends, does the mercy of God extend to the most enormous of criminals, so that none, however guilty, may not, if duly penitent, be partakers of the Divine grace; but there are none so low, so mean, so worthless, as not to be the objects of God's fatherly solicitude and care. Indeed I do hope that it may one day be extended to "—and then leaning over the pulpit he stretched out his arm to its utmost length, and placing it on the head of the gownsman finished his sentence—" to this silly boy."

The wager was lost, for the trumpet fell, and the discomfited stripling bolted.

BOTTLES AND CORKS.

An elderly officer, once travelling in the old Cambridge coach to London with an eminent lawyer, made many enquiries concerning the Rev. Robert Robinson. "I met him," said he, " in this very coach when I was a young man, and when my tone of conversation was that universal among young officers, and talked in a very free tone with this Mr. R. I did not take him for a clergyman, though he was dressed in black, for he was by no means solemn ; on the contrary, he told several droll stories. But there was one very odd thing about him, that he continually interlarded his stories with the exclamation, '*Bottles and corks !*' This seemed so strange, that I could not help at last asking him why he did so, saying they did not seem to improve his stories at all. 'Don't they ?' said Mr. R., 'I'm glad to

know, for I merely used these words by way of experiment.'
'Experiment,' said I, 'how do you mean that?'   'Why, I
will tell you. I rather pride myself on story-telling, and
wish to make my stories as good as they can be. Now I
observed that you told several very pleasant stories, and
that you continually made use of such exclamations as 'G—d
d—n it!' 'B—t me!' Now I can't use such words, for they
are irreverent towards the Almighty, and I believe actually
sinful; therefore I wanted to try whether I could not find
words that would answer the purpose as well, and be quite
innocent at the same time.' All this," said the officer,
" was said in so good-humoured a tone, that I could not
possibly take offence, though apt enough to do so. The reproof had an effect upon me, and very much contributed to
my breaking myself of the habit of profane swearing."

A COLD COMPLIMENT.

A coxcomb teasing Dr. Parr, Master of the Free Grammar School, Norwich, from 1778 to 1792, with an account
of his petty ailments, complained that he could never go
out without catching cold in his head. "No wonder,"
returned the doctor, "you always go out without *anything*
in it."

OPERATION FOR A BARONETCY.

Sir Astley Cooper's* success as an operator consisted
chiefly in his knowing how and when to operate; yet on an
important occasion his courage had nearly forsaken him. In
1821, George the Fourth having a small tumour in the
scalp, an operation for its removal was resolved upon, and
Cooper was selected to perform it. On the day appointed
he waited upon his Majesty. Lord Liverpool and other
Cabinet ministers occupied a room adjoining that in which

---

* Sir Astley Cooper was born in the village of Brooke, near Norwich,
where his father was curate.

the King was. A short time before the operation was com-menced, Cooper was observed to be pale and nervous, when Lord Liverpool, taking hold of his hand, said, "You ought to recollect that this operation either makes or ruins you; courage, Cooper." And he was so impressed by this timely rebuke, that every appearance of anxiety vanished from his countenance, and he performed the operation with his usual coolness and dexterity. A few months after this the King conferred a baronetcy upon him.

THE FORCE OF HABIT.

Old Peter Le Neve, the herald, who thought ridicule con-sisted in not being of an old family, made this epitaph—and it was a good one—for young Craggs, whose father had been a footman :—"Here lies the last, who died before the first of his family!" This old Craggs, who was angry with Arthur Moore, who had worn a livery too, and who was get-ting into a coach with him, turned about and said, "Why, Arthur, I am always going to get up behind; are not you?"

TALKING POLITICS.

As politics spoil conversation, Horace Walpole proposed that everybody should forfeit half-a-crown who said any-thing tending to introduce the idea either of Ministers or Opposition. Upon this, Hannah More, who was present, added that whoever mentioned *pit* coal, or a *fox* skin muff, should be considered as guilty, and it was accordingly voted.

COSTLY EPICURISM.

One day, an epicure, entering the Bedford Coffee House in Covent Garden, inquired, "What have you for dinner, John?" "Anything you please, sir," replied the waiter. "Oh, but what vegetables?" The *legumes* in season were named, when the customer having ordered two lamb chops, said, "John, have you cucumbers?" "No, sir, we have none yet, 'tis so very early in the season, but if you please I will step into the market and enquire if there are any." The waiter did so and returned, " Why, sir, there are a few, but they are half a guinea a piece." " Half a guinea a piece ! Are they small or large ? " " Why, sir, they are rather small." " Then buy two." The epicure who thus ordered the costly cucumbers was Charles, Duke of Norfolk, who died in 1815.

THE LETTER H.

Sir James Scarlett, when at the bar, had to cross-examine a witness whose evidence, it was thought, would be very damaging unless he could be bothered a little, and his only vulnerable point was said to be his self-esteem. The witness presented himself in the box—a portly over-dressed person—and Scarlett took him in hand.

Q.—Mr. John Tomkins, I believe ?

A.—Yes.

Q.—You are a stock broker ?

A.—I *ham !*

Scarlett regarded him attentively for a few moments, and then said, " And a very fine, well-dressed *ham,* you are, sir." The shout of laughter which followed completely disconcerted the witness, and the counsel's point was gained.

BALLAD-SINGING DIVINE.

Dr. Richard Corbet*, Bishop of Norwich, was a great humourist, both in his words and actions. " After he was D.D.," says Aubrey, " he sang ballads at the Cross at Abingdon. On a market day he and some of his companions were at the tavern by the Cross (which, by the way, was then the finest in England.) A ballad singer came in and

---

* Richard Corbet, D.D., student of Christ Church, Oxford, then Dean and next Bishop of that place, from thence translated to Norwich, and died July 28th, 1635.

complained that he had no custom, he could not sell his ballads. The jolly doctor, on hearing this, pulled off his gown, and put on a ballad singer's leather jacket; and being a handsome man, with a voice of great power and compass, he soon sold a great many ballads, and drew around him a large audience."

YAWNING'S CATCHING.

One evening at the commerce table at the Princess Amelia's, Horace Walpole was seen to gape—a great sin on any Palatine Hill. A few days after, the Princess calling at Strawberry Hill, and spying the shield with Medusas on the staircase, she said to Walpole, " Oh ! now I see where you learnt to yawn."

A GENTLEMAN'S FASHION.

In the reign of Henry VII., Sir Philip Calthrope, a Norfolk knight, sent to a tailor in Norwich as much cloth of fine French tanney as would make him a gown. It happened one John Drake, a shoemaker, coming into the shop, liked it so well that he went and bought of the same material as much for himself, enjoining the tailor to make it of the same fashion. The knight being informed of this, commanded the tailor to cut his gown as full of holes as his shears could make it. John Drake's was made " of the same fashion," but he vowed he never would be of the gentleman's fashion again.

CLAW AND CLAW.

Lord Erskine and Dr. Parr, who were both remarkably conceited, were in the habit of conversing together and complimenting each other on their respective abilities. On one of these occasions Parr promised that he would write Erskine's epitaph, to which the other replied " that such an intention on the doctor's part was almost a temptation to commit suicide."

GETTING THE WORST OF IT.

Porson, born at East Ruston, near North Walsham, where his father was parish clerk, was once disputing with an acquaintance, who, getting the worst of it, said, " Professor, *my opinion* of you is most contemptible." " Sir," returned the great Grecian, " I never knew an *opinion* of yours that was not contemptible."

A VALUABLE PAIL OF WATER.

Dr. Messenger Monsey* was for years the victim of that incredulity which makes the capitalist imagine a great and prosperous country to be the most insecure of all debtors. He preferred investing his money in any wild speculation to confiding it to the safe custody of the Funds. Even his ready cash he for a long time could not bring himself to trust in the hands of a banker. When he left home for any length of time he had recourse to the most absurd schemes for the protection of his money. Before setting out on one occasion for a journey to Norfolk, incredulous with regard to cashboxes and bureaus, he hid a considerable quantity of gold and silver and bank notes in the fire-place of his study, covering them up artistically with cinders and shavings. A month afterwards, returning, luckily, a few days before he was expected, he found his old house-maid preparing to entertain a few friends at tea in her master's room. The hospitable domestic was on the point of lighting the fire, and had just applied a candle to the doctor's notes when he entered the room, seized on a pail of water that chanced to be standing near, and throwing its contents over the fuel and the old woman,

---

* Dr. Messenger Monsey was the son of a Norfolk clergyman. He studied physic under Sir Benjamin Wrinch at Norwich, and after some years private practice he, through the interest of Lord Godolphin, was elected physician to the Royal Hospital at Chelsea. He was also well known as Sir Robert Walpole's Norfolk doctor.

extinguished the fire and her presence of mind at the same time. Some of the notes, as it was, were injured, and the Bank of England made objections to cashing them.

PORSONIANA.

When Porson was told that Dr. Pretyman, then Bishop of Lincoln, had been left a large estate by a person who had seen him only once, he said, " It would not have happened if the person had seen him twice."

He used to call Bishop Porteus, Bishop *Proteus* for having as he considered changed his opinions from liberal to illiberal.

He was sometimes very uncourteous in society. Dining one day at Horne Tooke's at Wimbledon, some differences occurred between the host and himself, and on Porson being subsequently asked for a toast, he replied, " I will give you the man who is in all respects the very reverse of John Horne Tooke."

GO SOBER.

That Duke of Norfolk who was intimate with Foote the comedian was much addicted to the bottle. On a masquerade night he asked Foote what new character he should go in ? "Go sober," said Foote.

WALPOLE'S NORFOLK DOCTOR.

The eccentric Messenger Monsey was a great favourite with Sir Robert Walpole, who always extolled the merits of his Norfolk doctor, but never advanced his interests. Instead of covering the great minister with adulation, Monsey treated him like an ordinary individual, telling him when his jokes were poor, and not hesitating to worst him in argument. " How happens it," asked Sir Robert over his wine, " that nobody will beat me at billiards, or contradict me, but Dr. Monsey?" "Other people," put in the doctor, " get places— I get a dinner and praise."

THE FEARLESS BOY.

Horatio Nelson, when about ten years old, was sent with his brother William to a large school at North Walsham, where the following incident occurred. There were some fine pears gròwing in the schoolmaster's garden which the boys regarded as lawful booty, and in the highest degree tempting, but the boldest among them was afraid to venture for the fruit. Horatio volunteered upon the service. He was lowered down at night from his bed room window by some sheets, he plundered the tree, and was drawn up with the pears, which he distributed among his schoolfellows without receiving any for himself. "I only took them," he said, "because every other boy was afraid."

BARON ALDERSON'S HUMOUR.

Amongst the grimly humourous addresses attributed to judges speaking from the bench to prisoners at the bar, Baron Alderson's* rejoinder to a man convicted of swindling is memorable. In reply to the final enquiry why sentence should not be passed upon him, the prisoner, with blasphemous obstinacy, persisted in asserting his innocence. The miserable fellow concluded his address by saying deliberately, and in a singularly solemn tone, " May God strike me dead, now at this moment, and here where I stand, if I am not innocent." As the speaker's guilt had been clearly ascertained, every hearer was painfully moved by this abominable self-imprecation. A thrill of horror ran through the Court. A minute of painful silence ensued, and then the judge substituted another emotion in the minds of all present by saying, in a cold matter-of-fact voice, " Prisoner at the bar, as Providence has not interposed in the behalf of society,

* Born at Great Yarmouth; son of Mr. Robert Alderson, who for many years held the combined offices of Recorder at Norwich, Yarmouth, and Ipswich.

the sentence of the Court is that you be transported for twenty years."

Another very humourous story is told of the same judge, that in passing sentence on a wretched bigamist, whose crime was attended by many palliating circumstances, he roused the laughter of his auditors and created a general sympathy for the criminal. Eyeing the prisoner—an honest artizan, whose wife had been a thief, virago, and habitual drunkard, and who had not taken a second woman to church until he had good reason to believe as well as hope that his wife was dead—the judge is reported to have said: " Prisoner at the bar, I find it difficult to express my sense of the crime which is charged against you, and which you have not ventured to deny. Your crime belongs to a class of offences which, if they were not promptly punished, would cause an unspeakable amount of human misery, and would ere long bring about the utter demoralization of our species. Your sin is not merely an infringement of a human enactment, it is a violation of divine law. The sentence of this Court is that you be imprisoned for one day, without hard labour."

THE TWENTY-FIFTH CHILD A BISHOP.

Benjamin Bathurst, Esq., the father of the late Bishop of Norwich, having married, first Miss Poole an heiress, he had issue by her twenty-two children; by his second wife, Miss Brodrick, daughter of Dr. Brodrick, a brother of Lord Middleton's, Mr. Bathurst had a second family of fourteen children of whom the late bishop was third child and second son. He was a seven-months' child, and his daughter, Mrs. Thistlethwaite, says that she had heard that he was so extremely small an infant that he could not be dressed like other children for some time after his birth, but was obliged to be wrapped in cotton. The bishop used to say in a joke that he was wrapped in cotton and put into a quart mug.

ASK HIM IN TO LUNCHEON.

John Gurney, Esq., of Earlham Hall (the father of Mrs. Fry), was a member of the Society of Friends, but he did not strictly regard its peculiarities. He was a strict preserver of his game, and had an intense repugnance to everything bordering on poaching. Upon one occasion when walking in his park he heard a shot fired in a neighbouring wood. He hurried to the spot and his naturally placid temper was considerably ruffled on seeing a young officer, with a pheasant at his feet, deliberately re-loading his gun. As the young man, however, replied to his rather warm expressions by a polite apology, Mr. Gurney's wrath was somewhat allayed, but he could not refrain from asking the intruder what *he* would do if he caught a man trespassing on his premises. " I would ask him in to luncheon," was the reply. The serenity of this impudence was not to be resisted. Mr. Gurney not only invited him to luncheon, but supplied him with dogs and a gamekeeper, and secured him excellent sport for the remainder of the day.

SIR ROBERT WALPOLE'S TEMPER.

Walpole's good temper was equal to his hospitality, if there is any truth in the following. " General Sutton, the narrator, was one day sitting by my father," says Horace Walpole (his son), " at his dressing. Sir Robert Walpole says to John, who was shaving him, ' John, you cut me ;' presently afterwards, ' John, you cut me ;' and again with the same patience, ' John, you cut me.' Whereupon Sutton started up and cried, ' By Heaven, if he can bear it I can't, and if you cut him once more I'll knock you down.' "

CHARLES DUKE OF NORFOLK.

In cleanliness the duke was negligent to so great a degree that he rarely made use of water for purposes of bodily refreshment and comfort. Nor did he change his linen more frequently than he washed himself. Complaining one day to Dudley North that he was a martyr to rheumatism, and had ineffectually tried every remedy for its relief, " Pray, my Lord," said he, " did you ever try a clean shirt."

PARTNERSHIP DISSOLVED.

Dr. Parr had a high opinion of his own skill at whist, and could not even patiently tolerate the want of it in his partner. Being engaged with a party in which he was un-equally matched, he was asked by a lady how the fortune of the game turned, when he replied, " Pretty well, madam, considering that I have three adversaries."

AN ODD BIRD.

A late Duke of Norfolk had a fancy for owls, of which he kept several. He called one, from the resemblance to the Chancellor, Lord Thurlow. The duke's solicitor was once in conversation with his grace, when to his surprise the owl-keeper came up and said, " Please you, my lord, Lord Thurlow's laid an egg."

PORSON AND THE PORTERS.

Travelling by coach to Norwich, Porson, when the coach arrived there, found himself beset by several porters, one offering to carry his portmanteau to his lodging for eighteen-pence, another for a shilling, another for ninepence, upon which Porson shouldered the portmanteau, and marching off with it, said very gravely to the porters, " Gentlemen, I leave you to settle this dispute among yourselves." When, however, he went to stay with a friend for only a couple of days or so, he did not encumber himself with a portmanteau, he would merely take a shirt in his pocket, saying, " *Omnia mea mecum porto.*"

A SHORT CREED.

A sceptical man conversing with Dr. Parr, observed that

he would believe nothing that he did not understand. Dr. Parr replied, "Then, young man, your creed will be the shortest of any man's I know."

DR. PARR AND SIR JAMES MACKINTOSH.

Dr. Parr had a great deal of sensibility, and when Rogers the poet read to him in Lincoln's Inn Fields the account of O'Coigley's death (he was hung for high treason in 1798) the tears rolled down his cheeks. Sir James Mackintosh trying to vex Parr one day, called O'Coigley a rascal. Parr immediately rejoined, " Yes, James, he was a bad man, but he might have been worse; he was an Irishman, but he might have been a Scotchman; he was a priest but he might have been a lawyer; he was a republican but he might have been an apostate."

Parr said of Mackintosh that he came up from Scotland with a metaphysical head, a cold heart, and open hands.

ARRANGING PRECEDENCE.

The lady of Sir Robert Walpole enchanted with the strains and popularity of the most celebrated Italian singers of the day, Cuzzoni and Faustini, invited them to assist at a concert at her house. The nobility who were present gave their hostess little trouble about precedence, but to prevail on either of the opera singers to relinquish the *pas* was found impossible. In this dilemma Lady Walpole very ingenuously invited Faustini to accompany her to a remote part of the house, under pretence of showing him some beautiful china, and during their absence the company obtained a song from Cuzzoni, who supposed that her rival had quitted the field. A similar expedient was used with equal success to obtain the happiness of a song from Faustini.

TRYING TO BRIBE A JUDGE.

On one occasion when Baron Alderson went the Welsh

circuit as judge, the defendant in an action which stood for trial in Cardigan, sent to him on his arrival in that town a statement of his case, with a two-pound note enclosed !

BISHOP STANLEY AND HIS ROOKS.

Bishop Stanley, whilst residing at Norwich, was sometimes spoken of as " Jackdaw Stanley," by those rev. gentlemen whose ease he incommoded. This unepiscopal epithet was thus derived. The bishop was very anxious to establish a rookery in the palace grounds, and for this purpose he had conveyed from the Cathedral Close a quantity of nests. He thus established a cawing colony in his own trees by depopulating those of others. Soon after, and while some of the citizens were yet annoyed at losing their favourite rooks, a few mischievous boys broke into the bishop's grounds and robbed the nests. One of the culprits was taken before the magistrates and charged with the theft, his lordship being present in the court to urge the suit. When the young urchin was asked what reason he could assign why he should not be sent to gaol for the robbery, he boldly confronted the bishop, and said that he did not take his rooks. " They warn't yours," said he : " you stole them from the Dean and Chapter : I took them from you." A peal of laughter followed this defence, and the duty-enforcing bishop was after this often spoken of in the diocese as " Jackdaw Stanley."

SIR EDWARD COKE A RIOTER.

Sir Edward Coke felt very acutely the loss of the Lord Chief Justiceship, and after his deprivation he tried to regain the favour of Buckingham the king's favourite, by marrying his daughter, Lady Frances, only fourteen years old, who was a very rich heiress, to Buckingham's elder brother, Sir William Villiers, who was nearly thrice her age, and exceedingly poor. Sir Edward's wife, however, Lady Hatton, became frantic with rage when she heard of the proposed match, not so much at her disapproval of Sir John Villiers, as on account of such an important family arrangement having been made without consulting her. When the first burst of her resentment had passed over, she appeared more calm, but this arose from her having secretly formed a resolution to carry off her daughter, and marry her to another. The same night, Sir Edward still keeping up his habit of going to bed at nine o'clock, soon after ten o'clock she sallied forth with the Lady Frances, from Hatton house, Holborn. They entered a coach which was waiting for them at a little distance, and travelling by unfrequented roads they arrived next morning at a house of the Earl of Argyle's at Oatland, then rented by Sir Edward Withipole, their cousin. There they were shut up in the hope that there could be no trace of the place of their concealment. While they lay hid Lady Hatton, not only did everything possible to prejudice her daughter against Sir John Villiers, but offered her in marriage to the young Earl of Oxford, and actually showed her a forged letter purporting to come from that nobleman, which asserted that he was deeply attached to her, and that he aspired to her hand.

Meanwhile, Sir Edward Coke, having ascertained the retreat of the fugitives, applied to the Privy Council for a warrant to search for his daughter, and as there was some difficulty in obtaining it, he resolved to take the law into his own hands. Accordingly, the ex-Chief Justice of England mustered a band of armed men, consisting of his sons, his dependents, and his servants, and himself putting on a breastplate with a sword at his side, and pistols at his saddle bow, he marched at their head upon Oatland. When they arrived there they found the gate leading to the house bolted and barricaded. This they forced open without difficulty, but the outer door of the house was so secured as long to defy all their efforts to gain admission. The ex-Chief Justice repeatedly demanded his child in the king's name, and laid down for law, that, "if death should ensue it would be justifiable homicide in him, but murder in those who opposed him." One of the party, gaining entrance by a window, let in all the rest, but still there were several doors to be broken open. At last Sir Edward found the object of his pursuit secreted in a small closet, and without stopping to parley, lest there should be a rescue, he seized his daughter, tore her from her mother, and placing her behind her brother, rode off with her to his house at Stoke Pogis, in Buckinghamshire. There he secured her in an upper chamber, of which he himself kept the key.

GREY HORSES FOR THE JUDGE.

Baron Alderson, on one occasion was met at Lancaster by the sheriff, on horseback, with a cortege of eighty persons all mounted on grey horses. The judge was placed in a coach drawn by six greys, and seven outriders were mounted on greys also.

NAT LEE AND SIR ROGER L'ESTRANGE.

Sir Roger L'Estrange once visited Nat Lee, the author of *Alexander the Great*, whilst he was confined in a mad-house. Sir Roger was at that time censurer of the press, and Lee did not entertain a high opinion of his abilities. Upon the knight enquiring whether the poet knew him, Lee answered:

> Custom may alter men, and manners change,
> But I am still strange Lee, and you L'Estrange;
> I'm poor in purse, as you are poor in brains.

COKE OF NORFOLK.

The venerable proprietor of Holkham, so well known as "Coke of Norfolk," was for many years a leading man among the Whigs, when Whiggism meant opposition to everything that the Tories proposed. He was the Father of the House of Commons, as well as the most successful agriculturist in England, and becoming very wealthy, was con-

sidered the first commoner in England. It is said that
George IV., knowing that he valued his position as a commoner more than any title that monarchy could confer, swore
that he would knight him on one occasion when Mr. Coke
was the bearer to his Majesty of a violent petition from the
Whigs. Mr. Coke, having heard of his Majesty's expressed
intention, declared that if the King attempted it he would
knock off the sword.

ENCOURAGING TO YOUNG PHYSICIANS.

The success of Sir Astley Cooper was beyond that of any
medical practitioner of modern times, but it came very
gradually. His earnings for the first nine years of his professional career progressed thus :—In the first year he netted
five guineas; in the second, twenty-six pounds; in the
third, sixty-four pounds; in the fourth, ninety-six pounds;
in the fifth, a hundred pounds; in the sixth, two hundred
pounds; in the seventh, four hundred pounds; in the eighth,
six hundred and ten pounds; and in the ninth, the year in
which he secured his hospital appointment, eleven hundred
pounds. But the time came when patients stood for hours in
his ante-rooms waiting to have an interview with the great
surgeon, and after all their patience, were dismissed without
being admitted to the consulting room. Sir Astley's man,
Charles, with all the dignity that became so eminent a man's
servant, used to say to these disappointed applicants, in a
tone of magnificent patronage, when they re-appeared the
next morning, after their effectless visit, "I am not at all·
sure that *we* shall be able to attend to you to-day gentlemen,
for *we* are excessively busy, and our list is perfectly full for
the day ; but if you'll wait I will see what can be done for
you!"

SIR ROBERT WALPOLE'S BRIBERY.

During Sir Robert Walpole's Administration he wanted
to carry a question in the House of Commons to which he

knew there would be great opposition, and which was disliked by some of his own dependents. As he was passing through the Court of Requests, he met a member of the Opposition whose avarice, he imagined, would not reject a large bribe. He took him aside and said, " Such a question comes on this day, give me your vote, and here is a bank bill for £2000," which he put into his hands. The member made him this answer : " Sir Robert, you have lately served some of my particular friends, and when my wife was last at Court the King was very gracious to her, which must have happened at your instance. I should therefore think myself very ungrateful," putting the bank bill into his pocket, " if I were to refuse the favour you are now pleased to ask me."

HENRY CRABB ROBINSON AND JOSEPH JOHN GURNEY.

Henry Crabb Robinson, in his diary, dated January, 1826, says, "My ride to Norwich to-day was diversified by an agreeable incident. On the road a few miles out of London we took up a very gentlemanly Quaker. He and I did not at once get into conversation, and when it became light I amused myself by reading till the coach stopped for breakfast. Then our conversation began, and permitted very little reading afterwards. He told me his name on my making an inquiry concerning Hudson Gurney. I was speaking to J. J. Gurney. We soon entered on controversial subjects. I praised a work of *Quaker Autobiography* without naming it. He said, ' Thou meanest John Woolman,' and added, ' Let me not take credit for a sagacity I do not possess, Amelia Opie has told me of thy admiration of the book.' We now knew each other, and talked like old acquaintances. He is kind in his feelings, if not liberal in his opinions. He read to me some letters from Southey. In one Southey thus expressed himself, ' I cannot believe in an eternity of hell. I hope God will forgive me if I err, but in this matter I cannot say, Lord, help thou mine unbelief.' J. J.

c c

Gurney spoke of Mrs. Opie very kindly, and of the recent death of her father, Dr. Alderson, as edifying. He was purged from unbelief."

PORSON AND GIBBON.

Soon after the *Letters to Travis* were published, Gibbon wrote a note to Porson requesting the pleasure of his acquaintance. Porson accordingly called upon the great historian, who received him with all kindness and respect. In the course of conversation, Gibbon said, "Mr. Porson, I feel truly indebted to you for the *Letters to Travis,* though I must think that occasionally while praising me you have mingled a little acid with the sweet. If ever you should take the trouble to read my history over again, I shall be much obliged and honoured by any remarks on it which might suggest themselves to you." Porson was highly flattered by Gibbon's having requested this interview, and loved to talk of it. He thought the *Decline and Fall* beyond all comparison the greatest literary production of the eighteenth century, and was in the habit of repeating long passages from it, yet he used to say that there could not be a better exercise for a schoolboy than to turn a page of it into English.

DR. PARR'S EGOTISM.

At a party at Charles Burney's, Dr. Parr was called on to name a toast, and gave " The *third* Greek scholar in Europe." Being called on to explain who this might be, he said, " Our excellent host. The first Greek scholar is my friend here (indicating Porson). Don't blush Dicky. The second, modesty does not permit me to name." Now and then Parr's egotism was checked. Having asked a lady what she thought of his spital sermon, she answered, " My opinion is expressed in the first five words of the sermon itself, ' Enough, and more than enough.' " He was out of humour for the rest of the evening.

USELESS WARNINGS.

Horace Walpole said it was of no use warning a man of his folly, if you do not cure him of being foolish.

DR. PARR'S PURGATORY.

Dr. Parr thought the Unitarians might be saved, but they must be *scorched* first; and he delighted in drinking hob-a-nob with a man who was sure to be scorched before he could be fit company for him.

THE TAYLORS OF NORWICH.

It was of this celebrated family that Sydney Smith said they reversed the ordinary saying, that it takes nine tailors to make a man.

BISHOP STANLEY'S COURTESY.

In the summer of 1828, Henry Crabb Robinson, who was travelling with a friend in the Pyrenees, arrived, after a long walk, at Arreau, and thus records in his diary an agreeable adventure with Dr. Stanley. He says : " Shutt and I had reconciled ourselves to dining in a neat kitchen with the people of the house, when a lively-looking man in black, a sort of Yorick in countenance, having first surveyed us, stepped up and very civilly offered us the use of the parlour in which were himself and his family. ' We have finished our dinner,' he said, ' and shall be happy to have your company.' The lady was a most agreeable person, and the family altogether very amiable. We had a very pleasant evening. The gentleman was a good Liberal Whig, and we agreed so well that on parting next day, he gave us his card. ' I am a Cheshire clergyman,' he said, ' and I shall be glad to see you at my living, if you ever are in my neighborhood.' " H. C. R. says, " When I next saw him, he was become Bishop of Norwich. This kindness to us strangers in this little adventure in the Pyrenees, was quite in harmony with his

character. The best of Christian bishops, he was the least
of a prelate imaginable."

ILLITERATE PREACHING.

The Rev. R. Robinson was desirous of repressing the conceit
which so often leads the illiterate to become instructors of
their brethren ; yet, on one occasion, in opposition to what
seemed to him a disposition to undue interference, he said, "I
have in my pig-stye ten white pigs and one black one. The
other morning, as I passed by, I heard the black pig squeak-
ing away lustily, and I thought to myself, That's pig
language ; I don't understand it, but perhaps it pleases the
white ones, they are quiet enough."

SIR ASTLEY COOPER'S FEES.

The highest amount that Sir Astley Cooper received as
fees in any one year was £21,000. This splendid income
was an exceptional one. For many years, however, he
achieved more than £15,000 per annum. As long as he
lived in the city after becoming celebrated he had an enormous but fluctuating revenue, the state of the money
market having an almost laughable effect on the size of the
fees paid him. The capitalists who visited the surgeon in
Broad Street, in three cases out of four paid in cheques, and
felt it beneath their dignity to put pen to paper for a smaller
sum than five guineas. After Sir Astley moved to the West
End, he had a more numerous and at the same time more
aristocratic practice ; but his receipts were never so much
as they were when he dwelt within the Lord Mayor's jurisdiction. His more distinguished patients invariably paid
him their guineas in cash, and many of them did not
consider it inconsistent with their patrician position to give
single fees. The citizens were the fellows to pay. Mr.
William Coles, of Mincing Lane, for a long period paid Sir
Astley £600 a year, the visits of the latter being principally
made to Mr. Cole's seat near Croydon. Another city man

who consulted the surgeon in Broad Street, and departed
without putting down any honorarium whatever, sent a
cheque for £63 10s. The largest fee Sir Astley Cooper
ever received was paid him by a West Indian millionaire
named Hyatt. This gentleman having occasion to undergo
a perilous and painful operation, was attended by Drs. Lett-
son and Nelson as physicians, and Sir Astley as chirurgeon.
The wealthy patient, his treatment having resulted most
successfully, was so delighted that he feed his physicians
with 300 guineas each. "But you, Sir," cried the grateful
old man, sitting up in his bed and speaking to his surgeon,
" shall have something better. There, Sir, take *that*." The
that was the convalescent's nightcap, which he flung at the
dexterous operator. " Sir," replied Sir Astley, picking up
the cap, " I'll pocket the affront." It was well he did so,
for on reaching home he found in the cap a draft for 1000
guineas.

PORSON'S EXTRAORDINARY MEMORY.

Porson was remarkable for the extraordinary retentive-
ness of his memory—a memory that had been cultivated
without the aid of pens and paper, or even pencils and slates,
and his powers in this respect seem to have been almost
incredible. When at school he used frequently to repeat a
lesson without making a blunder which he had learned
twelve months previously, and had not seen the book in the
interim. At Eton he would construe Horace from memory
when his book had been abstracted and an Ovid put in its
place. Still later in life he declared that he could repeat
Smollett's *Roderick Random* from beginning to end, and he
used to recite *verbatim* whole pages of the Edgeworth's
Essay on Irish Bulls. He once entertained a company at a
friend's house by giving a translation from memory of an
Italian novel which he had set up all night to read, and
although there were above forty names introduced in the
story he only forgot one. He also repeated the whole of the

Rape of the Lock, and noted the various readings, and made observations as he went on. He seemed to be capable of repeating a hundred authors, grave or comical, learned or frivolous, by heart, and was as much at home in setting a child right in his twopenny fable book as in recounting how often a certain word occurred in Thucydides and in what passages. It was indeed a treat to hear him pour out his stores of anecdotes, his racy remarks on passing events, and his marvellous, almost incredible, abundance of literary illustration of antiquity and past times drawn as it seemed from every channel into which the mind of man could dive. It appeared as if he had read thousands of volumes and not forgotten a single line, in many cases a single word, and the way in which he was ever bringing quotations to bear into juxtaposition, or to bear upon any subject that happened to arise for discussion, was hardly to be credited without personal experience.

SECRET OF SUCCESS.

Sir Thomas Buxton relates that he once asked Sir James Scarlett what was the secret of his pre-eminent success as an advocate. He replied that he took care to press home the one principal point of the case without paying much attention to the others. He also said that he knew the secret of being short. "I find," said he, "that when I exceed half-an-hour I am always doing mischief to my client, if I drive into the jury important matter, I drive out matter more important that I had previously lodged there."

BELIEF IN THE DEVIL.

In the days when Robinson flourished, an imputation of scepticism as to the existence of a personal Devil influencing the actions of men was nearly as fatal to character, as now that of being inclined to "Atheism." It was at a meeting of ministers that Robinson once overheard one of them whisper to another that on that essential point of faith he was not sound. " Brother ! brother ! " he cried out, "don't misrepresent me. How do you think I can dare to look you in the face and at the same time deny the existence of a Devil? Is he not described in Holy Writ as the accuser of the brethren ? "

On another occasion, a good but not very wise man asking him in a tone of simplicity and surprise," Don't you believe in the Devil?" Robinson answered him in like tone, " O dear no ! *I* believe in God, don't you?"

DRAWING A TOOTH.

Amongst the eccentricities of Dr. Monsey may be mentioned the way in which he extracted his own teeth. Round the tooth sentenced to be drawn he fastened securely a strong piece of catgut, to the opposite end of which he affixed a bullet. With this bullet and a full measure of powder a pistol was charged. On the trigger being pulled, the operation was performed effectually and speedily. The doctor could only rarely prevail on his friends to permit him to remove their teeth by this original process. Once a gentlemen who had agreed to try the novelty, and had even allowed the apparatus to be adjusted, at the last moment exclaimed, " Stop, stop, I've changed my mind !" " But I haven't, and you're a fool and a coward for your pains," answered the doctor, pulling the trigger. In another instant the tooth was extracted, much to the timid patient's delight and astonishment.

MAKING FREE OF THE CELLAR.

Dr. Corbet, Bishop of Norwich, was well known for his convivial habits, professed wit, and conversational qualities, which made him acceptable to the best of companies. An anecdote of him and his chaplain, Dr. Lushington, a learned and ingenious man, to whom the bishop was much attached, is thus related by Aubrey : The bishop, he says, would take the key of the wine-cellar, and he and his chaplain would go and lock themselves in and be merry. First he put off his episcopal hood, saying, "There lays the doctor;" then he puts off his gown, "There lays the bishop." Then it was, "Here's to thee Corbet; here's to thee Lushington."

PRINCIPLE IN HIGH LIFE.

On one occasion, James II. gave the Duke of Norfolk the sword of the State to carry before him to the Catholic Chapel. When they arrived at the chapel door, the duke halting there, stepped aside to allow the King to pass. "My Lord," said his Majesty, "your father would have gone further." The duke, with great readiness of wit, answered, "Your Majesty's father was the better man, and he would not have gone so far."

A FOOL CONFIRMED.

Dr. Parr, who was neither very choice nor delicate in his epithets, once called a clergyman *a fool*, and there was probably some truth in his application of the word. The clergyman, however, being of a different opinion, declared he would complain to the bishop of the usage. "Do so," added the learned Grecian, "and my Lord Bishop will *confirm* you."

NELSON'S NIGHT CAP.

Dr. Burney visited Lord Nelson at his beautiful villa at Merton, and having neglected to put a night cap into his portmanteau, borrowed one of his lordship. Before retiring to rest he sat down to study, as was his common practice, having first put on his cap, and was shortly after alarmed by finding it in flames. He immediately collected the burnt remains, and returned them with the following lines:

> Take your night cap again, my good lord, I desire,
> I would not retain it a minute;
> What belongs to a Nelson, wherever there's *fire*,
> Is sure to be instantly *in it*.

JOHN WILSON CROKER AND SIR ROBERT PEEL.

Mr. John Wilson Croker, M.P. for Yarmouth, and Sir Robert Peel, although professedly public friends, entertained as statesmen a deadly enmity towards each other, and neither ever missed an opportunity of throwing in a piece of bitter sarcasm. They were, in fact, political rivals, and Croker had not the generosity of Canning. Sir Thomas Lawrence painted the portraits of this illustrious trio about the same time; as they progressed, the one came under the observation of the other, and Canning remarked to Peel that Sir Thomas had caught the very quiver of Croker's lip. "He has, truly," said Peel, "and it is well for him to have missed the venom of his arrow."

ONLY A LIQUID.

Whilst conversing with a party of congenial friends, Porson, on one occasion, seemed at a loss for something to cheer the inward man, and drawing his glass mechanically towards him, he took up one bottle, then another, without finding wherewithal to replenish. A friend observing this, he inquired what the professor was in search of. "*Only a liquid!*" answered Porson.

NELSON'S GENEROSITY.

Nelson's triumph at the Nile and subsequent ones in Italy were acknowledged by the King of Naples in the most liberal manner. Ferdinand dined with Nelson, and when the King drank the admiral's health a royal salute was fired from all his ships and batteries. In addition, Ferdinand gave him a magnificent sword, and also the dukedom of Bronti in Sicily, with a domain valued at £3000 a-year. The sword, as an honorary present, Nelson gladly accepted, but he could hardly be persuaded to enrich himself by the King's munificent grant, till Ferdinand claimed of him that he should not cause his royal name to be handed down to posterity under the stigma of ingratitude. The very first use which Nelson made of his newly-acquired wealth was to place a sixth of it at the yearly disposal of his father, who, by the singular goodness of Providence, was permitted to live to see his son attain to the topmost pinnacle of human glory, with a heart as tender and affectionate, as pure and true, as when on his first boyish entrance into his profession he perilled his life to take home a bear skin as a present.

AURICULAR CONFESSION.

A cunning juryman, addressing the clerk of the court when administering the oath, said, "Speak up; I cannot hear what you say," "Stop, are you deaf?" asked Baron Alderson. "Yes, of one ear." "Then you may leave the box, for it is necessary that jurymen should hear both sides."

GENTLY, JEMMY.

Sir James Mackintosh invited Dr. Parr to take a drive in his gig. The horse became restive. "Gently, Jemmy," says the doctor; "don't irritate him : always soothe your horse, Jemmy. You'll do better without me. Let me get down, Jemmy." Once on *terra firma*, the doctor's view of the case was changed. "Now, Jemmy, touch him up. Never let a horse get the better of you. Touch him up! Conquer him, don't spare him; and now I'll leave you to manage him. *I'll walk back.*"

ACCOMMODATING PRINCIPLES.

In one of Sir Robert Walpole's letters he gives a very instructive picture of a skilful minister and a condescending Parliament. "My dear friend," writes Sir Robert, "there is scarcely a member whose purse I do not know to a six-dence, and whose very soul almost I could not purchase at the offer. The reason former ministers have been deceived in this matter is evident—they never considered the temper of the people they had to deal with. I have known a minister so weak as to offer an avaricious old rascal a star and garter, and attempt to bribe a young rogue who set no value upon money with a lucrative employment. I pursue methods as opposite as the poles, and therefore my administration has been attended with a different effect."

PORSON'S FAVOURITE BEVERAGE.

Porson's favourite beverage for breakfast was porter. One Sunday morning meeting Dr. Goodall (Provost of Eton) he said, " Where are you going ? " " To church." " Where is Mrs. Goodall ? " "At breakfast." " Very well, I'll go and breakfast with her." Porson accordingly presented himself before Mrs. Goodall and being asked what he chose to take, he said " Porter." It was sent for pot after pot, and the sixth pot was just being carried into the house when Dr. Goodall returned from church.

BRIEF LET IT BE.

When Baron Martin was at the bar and addressing the Court of Exchequer in an insurance case he was interrupted by Mr. Baron Alderson observing, " Mr. Martin, do you think any office would insure your life ? Remember yours is a very brief existence."

DR. PARR'S DIRECTIONS FOR HIS FUNERAL.

Dr. Parr left in his own handwriting minute directions for his funeral. He described the hour and the place of interment, the order of the procession, the manner of preparing the church for the occasion, the mode of conducting the service, he enumerated the clerical friends to be invited, the persons to be engaged as bearers, and described the very ornaments of the coffin. But the most extraordinary part of these directions was the following: " I lay particular stress upon the following directions—My hands must be bound by the crape hatband which I wore at the burial of my daughter Catherine, upon my breast must be placed a piece of flannel which Catherine wore at her dying moments at Teignmouth. There must be a lock of Madelaine's hair, enclosed in silk and wrapped in paper bearing her name, there must be a lock of my late wife's hair preserved in the same way, there must be a lock of Sarah Wynne's hair preserved in the same way. All these locks of hair must be laid on my bosom as carefully as possible, covered and fastened with a piece of black silk to keep them together."

THE DUKE OF NORFOLK'S LOSS BY GAMBLING.

" The late Duke of Norfolk," says the author of *Rouge et Noir* writing in 1823, " in one evening lost the sum of £70,000 in a gaming house on the right side of St. James's Street. Suspecting foul play, he put the dice in his pocket, and, as was his custom when up late, took a bed in the house. The blacklegs were all dismayed, till one of the worthies, who is believed to have been a principal in poisoning the horses at Newmarket, for which Dan Dawson was hanged, offered for £5000 to go to the duke's room with a brace of pistols and a pair of dice, and if the duke was awake to shoot him ; if asleep, to change the dice ! Fortunately for the gang, the duke ' snored,' as the agent stated, ' like a pig ;' and the dice were changed. His Grace had them broken in the morning, when finding them good, he paid the money, and left off gambling."

CRITICISMS ON DR. PARR.

The distinguished scholar, Dr. Parr, who, to the massy erudition of a former age, joined all the free and enlightened intelligence of the present.—*Thomas Moore.*

That model of pedants.—*Sir W. Scott.*

There is a lovingness of heart about Parr, a susceptibility of the affections, which would endear him, even without his Greek.—*William Taylor.*

Having spent an evening at Mr. Langton's with the Rev. Dr. Parr, Johnson was much pleased with the conversation of that learned gentleman, and after he was gone said to Mr. Langton, " Sir, I am obliged to you for having asked me this evening ; Parr is a fair man ; I do not know when I have had an occasion for such free controversy. It is remarkable how much of a man's life may pass without meeting with any instance of this kind of open discussion.— *Langton's Johnsonia.*

Porson had no very high opinion of Parr, and could not endure his metaphysics. One evening Parr was beginning a regular harangue on the origin of evil, when Porson stopped him short by asking, " What was the use of it ?" Porson, who shrank on all occasions from praise of himself, was only annoyed by the eulogies which Parr lavished on him in print when Parr published the *Remarks on Combe's Statement,* in which Porson is termed a " giant in literature," &c. Porson said, " How should Dr. Parr be able to take the measure of a giant?"—*Porsoniana.*

A great scholar, as rude and violent as most Greek scholars are, unless they happen to be bishops. He has left nothing behind him worth leaving, he was rather fitted for the law than the church, and would have been a more considerable man if he had been more knocked about among his equals. He lived with country gentlemen and clergymen who flattered and feared him.--*Sydney Smith.*

Of Bentley's feuds—of Porson's—Parr's
Most savage Greek and Latin wars

few remains are left, and mankind would have been nothing the worse if their battles had never been waged at all. Dr. Parr was renowned for his smoking, even more than Dr. Isaac Barrow. He would empty twenty pipes of an evening in his own house, and when he was on his good behaviour in fashionable circles, it is said he pined after the weed.--*Dr. Madden.*

To half of Bushby's skill in mode and tense,
Add Bentley's pedantry without his sense ;
From Warburton take all his spleen you find,
But leave his genius and his wit behind;
Squeeze Churchill's rancour from the verse it flows in,
And knead it stiff with Johnson's turgid prosing ;
And all the piety of Saint Voltaire,
Mix the gross compounds—Trial—Dr. Parr.—*Epigram.*

BISHOP JEGON.

Dr. John Jegon, Dean and Bishop of Norwich, was the last of the Elizabethan bishops. He was previously Master of Corpus Christi College, and was known as a strict disciplinarian. Whilst he was there, he was made the subject of the following pasquinade :—

Doctor John Jegon, Bene't College Master,
Broke the scholars' heads, gave the walls a plaister.

To which the Master replied :

Knew I but the wag that writ this in his bravery,
I'd praise him for his wit, but flog him for his knavery.

CRITICISMS ON HORACE WALPOLE.

He was, unless we have formed a very erroneous judgment of his character, the most eccentric, the most artificial, the most fastidious, the most capricious of men. His mind was a bundle of inconsistent whims and affectations. His features were covered by mask within mask. When the outer disguise of obvious affectation was removed, you were still as far as ever from seeing the real man. He played innumerable parts, and over-acted them all. When he talked misanthropy he out-Timoned Timon, when he talked philanthropy he left Howard at an immeasurable distance.— *Macaulay.*

Mr. Walpole is spirits of hartshorn.—*Lady Townshend.*

Horace Walpole was an agreeable, lively man, very

affected, always aiming at wit, in which he fell very short of his old friend George Selwyn.—*Lord Ossory.*

He united the good sense of Fontenelle with the Attic salt and graces of Count Anthony Hamilton.— *Walpoliana.*

I must do him the justice to say that except the delight he has in teazing me for what he calls over-strictness, I have never heard a sentence from him which savoured of infidelity. —*Hannah More.*

I am sorry to say that he omits no opportunity of burlesquing Scripture, religion, and the clergy.—*Bishop Porteus.*

His birth was premature, and he was all his life a very slight, feeble, and unmanly figure. He died in 1797. The late publication of his *Memoirs* has lowered his reputation for candour, disinterestedness, and truth; and they have by their undisguised and undeniable falsehood and malice excited a strong impression against the accuracy of his other anecdotical works. His *Letters* too, which are charming in their style and topics, are unhappily tinctured with the same readiness to sacrifice truth to either prejudice or pleasantry.—*Lady Suffolk's Correspondence.*

MRS. OPIE'S OPINION OF LORD BYRON.

His voice was such a voice as the Devil tempted Eve with : you feared its fascination the moment you heard it.

FINIS.

PRINTED AT THE "NORFOLK NEWS" OFFICE, EXCHANGE STREET, NORWICH.

INDEX.

BV - #0041 - 091222 - C0 - 229/152/22 - PB - 9781331681519 - Gloss Lamination